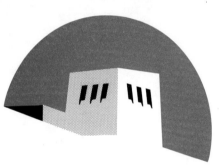

The Complete Guide to

Conflict Resolution in the Workplace

The Complete Guide to
Conflict Resolution in the Workplace

Marick F. Masters and Robert R. Albright

AMACOM
American Management Association

New York • Atlanta • Brussels • Buenos Aires • Chicago • London • Mexico City
San Francisco • Shanghai • Tokyo • Toronto • Washington, D.C.

This publication is designed to provide accurate and authoritative
information in regard to the subject matter covered. It is sold with the
understanding that the publisher is not engaged in rendering legal,
accounting, or other professional service. If legal advice or other expert
assistance is required, the services of a competent professional person
should be sought.

Library of Congress Cataloging-in-Publication Data

Masters, Marick Francis, 1954–
    The complete guide to conflict resolution in the workplace / by Marick F. Masters and
Robert R. Albright.
        p.   cm.
    "September 2001."
    Includes bibliographical references and index.
    ISBN 0-8144-0629-7
    1. Conflict management.   2. Dispute resolution (Law)   I. Albright, Robert R.   II. Title.

HD42 .M38   2001
658.4'053—dc21

2001055987

Printing number

10   9   8   7   6   5   4   3

Contents

Acknowledgments   *vii*

Introduction   1

Part 1: Getting a Handle on Workplace Conflict   **9**

    Chapter 1:   Understanding Workplace Conflict   11

    Chapter 2:   Diagnosing Conflict   29

    Chapter 3:   Dealing with Conflict   69

Part 2: Alternative Means of Resolving Conflict: From Negotiation to Alternative Dispute Resolution with Third Parties   **97**

    Chapter 4:   Negotiation   99

    Chapter 5:   Facilitation   121

    Chapter 6:   Mediation   141

    Chapter 7:   Arbitration   163

    Chapter 8:   Potpourri   185

Part 3: Special Topics   **203**

    Chapter 9:   Confronting Workplace Violence   205

    Chapter 10: Resolving EEO Disputes   221

    Chapter 11: Dealing with the Unions   235

    Chapter 12: International Perspectives on Workplace Conflict   249

Part 4: Design, Implementation, and Development   **267**

    Chapter 13   Establishing an Integrated Conflict
                 Resolution System   269

    Chapter 14: Education and Training   289

Part 5: Conclusion   **297**

    Chapter 15: Workplace Conflict Resolution Map and
                 Guideposts   299

Appendix A: Solutions to Exercises   303

Appendix B: EEO Mediation Simulation   313

Sources   323

Index   335

Acknowledgments

We want to acknowledge support from several quarters in our collaborative effort to write this book. First, we are indebted to our respective institutions—the University of Pittsburgh, the U.S. Coast Guard Academy, and Rensselaer Polytechnic Institute—for their supportive environments. Second, we thank our colleagues who, over the years, have given us rich ideas and feedback. Third, we are grateful to the many organizations in the private, public, and not-for-profit sectors—with which we have worked on many projects—for providing us with a vast reservoir of experiences to relate and stories to tell. (We have scrupulously avoided mentioning names of individuals and companies with whom we have worked, in order to protect both the innocent and the not-so-innocent.)

Fourth, we would like to thank our research assistants, David Eplion and Feng Ju, who worked on this project and diligently searched background material. Fifth, we are extremely grateful to Ms. Pat Koroly, who worked tirelessly to type numerous drafts of this lengthy manuscript.

Finally, we thank our families who have been patient with our long absences during the writing process.

Introduction

On Tuesday, December 26, 2000, Michael McDermott, a software tester who was employed by Edgewater Technology Inc., a computer consulting firm, at its Wakefield, Massachusetts office, walked into work and shot and killed seven co-workers. He was reportedly upset with the company's accounting department over the prospect of the Internal Revenue Service's plan to garnish his wages to pay back taxes.

On September 2, 2001, an ex-employee of an IKEA site in the Pittsburgh area was arrested for setting fires at the Robinson Town Centre IKEA. He had been fired in March 2001, and in May he made a threatening phone call to the manager who fired him.

When you are asked about conflict in the workplace, these kinds of tragic incidents are often the first to come to mind. Such tragedies leave indelible psychological marks. They are the events that the media cover microscopically while they are unfolding in real time. But they are extreme, and relatively rare, manifestations of workplace conflict. You should not allow these brutalities to prevent you from managing more ordinary conflict effectively, rationally, and creatively.

In reality, conflict at work involves an array of attitudes and behaviors that directly and indirectly touch the lives of those of us with any connection with the production of a good or delivery of a service. Although we may shun conflict or wish to banish it forever from our conscious thoughts, it is, strictly speaking, neither inherently good or bad.

To put this thought into perspective, consider that we, as individuals and a society, tolerate conflict in many aspects of our lives as part of the normal course of affairs. In fact, we pay to see conflict. We buy tickets to football, baseball, hockey, and basketball games. We participate in political campaigns that involve conflicts in the vast realm of ideas. We challenge property tax reassessments when we believe they mistakenly overvalue our property. Our entire judicial system is set up on an adversarial

1

model: We demand defense attorneys who will fight prosecutors to the bitter end. Johnny Cochran and F. Lee Bailey are media stars. And the advertising media are infested with competing claims and counter-claims. We use this kind of conflict as a means of getting at the truth: Which is the better team? Which political philosophy should prevail? Has the prosecution proven its claim beyond a reasonable doubt? Which health-care insurance plan provides superior coverage at a lower cost? If we did not have disagreements—the essence of conflict—these questions could not be answered.

Why, then, the negative lens through which we often view conflict at work? The answer is both simple and complicated. First, we lack a reasonable understanding of conflict and how it occurs at work. Second, in the workplace, we are often expected to agree, to be agreeable, and, in some cases, to be subservient. No one likes a squeaky wheel, especially in the next cubicle. What supervisors want employees who question their authority or judgment? Third, and this is the complicated part, we generally are ill-equipped to manage conflict effectively. We know it exists. In fact, we may be conscious of its presence even when it goes unexpressed. Furthermore, we know it is often legitimate. We may believe that a person does have a legitimate complaint or genuine grievance. But our management tool kit of responses is often woefully lacking. How do we handle conflict constructively, particularly when interests, rights, and powers clash? How do we deal with conflict when emotions become involved or when one or more of the involved parties appears emotionally or psychologically imbalanced or disturbed?

Coping with conflict is something that we are rarely taught in any formal sense, although this is beginning to change as the field of conflict management gains a bigger foothold in all tiers of our educational system. It is generally something we pick up, to the extent that we do, from experience. In the workplace, we learn how to manage conflict on-the-job. Unsurprisingly, a lot of trial-and-error goes into our education. The result: We make too many errors.

We know that managers spend a lot of their time on conflict. It is estimated that managers, on average, spend close to 20 percent of their working time dealing with personality clashes among employees—just one of the "57 varieties" of conflict. You would think that companies would have effective systems in place to help you handle this important part of your job. Unfortunately, such is not the case, often because of the stigmatized view we have of conflict.

Consider, however, the costs of not performing this job function well. If the other 80 percent of a manager's time is devoted to "real" work—e.g., setting schedules, allocating resources, dealing with customers, preparing technical reports, or checking on compliance with ever-rising quality standards—what would an organization's tolerance for mistakes be? We guarantee you that, on average, it would be much less than it is for how well managers handle conflict. Yet, we know that errors occur in this 80 percent, not all of which is conflict-free. In short, if we cannot manage conflict effectively, we are probably making a lot of mistakes in an important area of our work. These mistakes need not be fatal or particularly injurious. Nor need they be, on an isolated basis, anything beyond the minor. But, cumulatively, these mistakes can be very costly to an organization. Moreover, conflict that is not effectively managed can escalate to unacceptable levels or at least enormously costly levels: a major strike, high levels of voluntary turnover, systematic under-performance, or a massive lawsuit.

Therefore, it is important to build the tool kits of conflict resolution at work. That is the objective of this book: to guide you, the manager or human resources (HR) professional, on how to deal with conflict effectively and constructively.

More specifically, our goals are to:

- Give you a better understanding of conflict at work
- Provide you with the means to diagnose and measure conflict—to develop an early warning system to signal when conflict may be expected to rise to levels that, if improperly managed, pose a threat
- Equip you with a variety of tools and techniques to resolve conflicts of various kinds and degrees of severity
- Inform you on how to design and implement effective and adaptable systems of conflict management

With this information and the tool kits, you will be able to develop conflict management as a distinctive organizational capability. To be blunt, we hope to take the mystery out of effective conflict management. And, to begin to unravel the mystery, we stress that eliminating conflict at work is not the goal we seek nor is it one to which you should aim.

In the chapters that follow, we will try to guide you through the increasingly murky terrain of conflict management and resolution. As the literature in this area mushrooms and as advocates of different approaches multiply, it becomes easier to get lost in the forest. Serious mistakes, for managers individually and organizations collectively, can result as one wanders about the forest. This book offers practical guidance for answering the following questions:

- What is workplace conflict?
- What approaches exist to deal with conflict?
- What are the different techniques (e.g., negotiation, mediation, arbitration) available to resolve conflict?
- When should these techniques be used?
- How can they be used?
- What are their relative advantages and disadvantages?
- What are the ethical and legal concerns associated with alternative means of addressing conflict?

The book is divided into five major parts. Part 1, "Getting a Handle on Workplace Conflict," presents three chapters. In Chapter 1, "Understanding Workplace Conflict" we define workplace conflict and present a classification of the types of conflict managers confront at work. The chapter examines the array of parties who may become involved, the effects of conflict, and the range of approaches organizations may choose to use to address conflict at work. Chapter 2, "Diagnosing Conflict," guides you through the web of possible causes and also shows how you can measure conflict, in terms of its frequency and cost. In Chapter 3, we provide practical steps on how to deal with conflict. What can you do, on a day-to-day basis, to cope with conflict? How can you handle difficult situations? What options can you offer to your organization to resolve workplace conflict without resort to litigation?

The five chapters in Part 2 elevate the guide to developing organizational responses to conflict that individual employees and managers can use within a dispute resolution system. Chapter 4 covers the essentials of negotiating collaboratively, including the principles of win-win negotiating and practical tips on how to negotiate effectively in a wide variety of workplace situations. These, by the way, are tips not only for managers but also for everyone in the world of work, and they are transferable to a host of contexts other than workplace conflicts.

Chapter 5 provides guidance on how to use facilitation techniques to deal with disagreements at work. You may use these techniques yourself or retain third-party facilitators. In both situations, facilitation is occurring, but the latter genuinely offers the advantage of perceived neutrality and impartiality. Chapter 6 deals with mediation as a means of resolving conflicts. Traditional mediation, which emphasizes settlement, is covered. In addition, a comparatively new type of mediation— called transformative mediation—is discussed. Unlike its traditional counterpart, the transformative model stresses empowerment and recognition, not settlement. This is strikingly—and, to some, alarmingly—counterintuitive. We show how to use and when to use mediation. We also show you how to select a mediator.

The topic of arbitration is reviewed in Chapter 7, where we discuss when and how to use arbitration, its different formats, and how to select an arbitrator. Chapter 8, labeled "Potpourri," covers a host of other forms of third-party dispute resolution techniques. These methods vary in operation, sophistication, and practicality. Included among them are factfinding, ombuds, peer reviews, early neutral evaluation, and minitrials. Again, we offer guidance on when and how to use the approaches, based on real company illustrations.

The four chapters in Part 3 cover several special topics that are important in the domain of workplace conflict. Specifically, Chapter 9 provides you with information on confronting workplace violence. It walks you through the process of developing a comprehensive program to deal with this troublesome reality, and it provides tips on how to be on the look out for potential offenders. Furthermore, it outlines a series of steps to implement to secure and indemnify your organization.

Chapter 10 explores how to resolve EEO disputes, which are conflicts that arise over questions involving the rights of employees. Not infrequently, conflicts over interests and powers may involve overt and underlying EEO issues. We review the application of conflict management techniques in this swelling area of workplace disputes. Among the topics addressed are how to use third-party techniques to avoid litigation, and how to use relatively new procedures that have been instituted by the Equal Employment Opportunity Commission (EEOC) to expedite the resolution of formal complaints through mediation before a formal EEOC investigation is launched. The chapter also provides a guide on establishing an effective program for handling incidents of sexual harassment.

Chapter 11 provides you with information on dealing with unions. We show you how important effective conflict resolution is in keeping unions at bay. The chapter also offers guidance on how to remain union-free and how to negotiate with unions more effectively where they are a workplace presence.

In Chapter 12 we show how workplace conflicts are resolved in other countries. The chapter addresses the prevalence of ADR cross-nationally and alerts managers to various international labor conditions and standards that may impact the level of conflict they experience across the globe.

Part 4 is devoted to designing and implementing a conflict resolution system. Chapter 13 presents a step-by-step guide to establishing and integrating a comprehensive system. It offers a practical example of what such a system might look like. Chapter 14 addresses the steps managers need to take to educate and train their employees—including other managers—and their organizations to operate in an effective conflict resolution mode. The best-designed system will fail in practice if people do not know how to use it. We also consider issues associated with developing a pool of qualified third-party neutrals so that companies can avail themselves of the array of conflict resolution techniques in existence.

Part 5 contains the concluding chapter, which presents a practical map on how to understand workplace conflict resolution. The chapter provides ten guideposts to follow in developing an organization-wide approach to effective conflict resolution.

At the end of most chapters, there are a few practical exercises to stimulate your thinking on how to apply various conflict-resolution techniques and to deal with relevant situations. Suggested "solutions" to the exercises are presented in Appendix A at the back of the book.

Appendix B contains an "EEO Mediation Simulation" case for you to practice at work with colleagues you want to educate and train. Finally, the "Sources" section lists useful books, government reports, journals, and Web sites that can guide you and give additional information about specific topics in this expansive area of conflict resolution, especially as it pertains to the workplace.

PART 1

GETTING A HANDLE ON
WORKPLACE CONFLICT

The three chapters in this Part lay the foundation for introducing procedures and systems to deal with workplace conflict. Chapter 1, "Understanding Workplace Conflict," gives you a comprehensive picture of the subject, what it means, and why it is important. In Chapter 2, "Diagnosing Conflict," you are given the tools to assess the scope and impact of workplace conflict in your organization. Chapter 3, "Dealing with Conflict," gives you, the manager and professional, the tools to handle conflict yourself. It will make your job a lot easier and more enjoyable.

Chapter 1

Understanding Workplace Conflict

"Wal-Mart slapped with massive sex-bias suit on behalf of 700,000."

"87,000 Verizon employees strike for fifteen to eighteen days over disputes about forced overtime, job security, work-induced stress, employee monitoring, wages, benefits, and union-organizing rights."

"126,000 employee grievances and arbitrations pending at U.S. Postal Service."

"Unionized pilots' slowdowns cost United Airlines customer loyalty and money."

"EEOC sues American Airlines for discriminating against the mentally disabled in violation of the American with Disabilities Act."

"Worker sues company for sex harassment; feared to be vengeful."

"Ex-employee kills four and self at Navistar plant."

You hear and read about such newsworthy headlines every day. As managers, however, you know that these incidents represent only the tip of the iceberg. Conflicts abound at work. They exist in many forms, some of which are more recognizable than others. Based on your own experiences in the workplace, you know firsthand the toll that conflicts can take—personally, professionally, and organizationally. Most of us have experienced some degree of anxiety, grief, pain, and suffering because of conflict at work—with a colleague, superior, subordinate, or client/customer.

Memorandum

To: General Managers

From: Company President

Re: Conflicts at Work

Date: July 10, 2001

It has recently been brought to my attention that our company's managers, on average, are spending about 20 to 25 percent of their valuable time coping with personality clashes at work. I, too, have found myself devoting a lot of time to such matters. With growing frequency, conflicts between individuals, units, departments, and divisions are taking my time. Disagreements cannot seem to get resolved at the level close to where they arise.

Also, our company has recently been charged with sex discrimination and harassment in a highly embarrassing lawsuit. We have a backlog of these and other EEO-related claims.

We need to get a handle on this problem of conflict at work. It is sapping the time, energy, and resources that we need to devote to other more productive and profitable pursuits in our highly competitive business. Therefore, I am convening a meeting of general managers tomorrow morning at 10:00 A.M. to discuss how we can respond to this problem. I invite your creative participation.

How we handle conflict affects not only the quality of work life but also our personal lives. The physiological and psychological ramifications of conflict extend beyond the formal time and space limitations of the workplace.

As the hypothetical memorandum from the company president to the general managers suggests, conflict at work can be costly. Can you afford to mismanage it? The answer is probably not for long. Therefore, you do not want to leave effective conflict management to chance.

Success in business and in life depends in significant measure on how we handle conflict. To deal effectively with conflict at work, you need to respond at three distinctive levels.

First, you must be able to cope with the conflicts that you personally encounter at work, whether they arise with peers, superiors, subordinates, or external parties with whom you do business.

Second, you must be able to develop others in your organization to cope effectively with conflicts that arise among them. It is decidedly in your self-interest to do so, for conflicts that are not resolved may reach your desk and thereupon consume your precious time.

Third, you need to be able to guide your company toward an effective approach to dealing with workplace conflicts. Just as organizations rely upon systems to operate from a production or service-delivery standpoint, they must use systems to address conflict. Each conflict may be somewhat different, but conflicts at work are usually not random occurrences. They reflect systemic processes and patterns in how work gets done. You can benefit from identifying patterns in the causes of conflict and successful approaches on how to deal with those issues before they fester into problems. Your best approach is not to suppress conflict but rather to create an organizational environment that understands conflict, knows how to address it, and can resolve it, where necessary, to the mutual satisfaction of the parties without damaging broader organization interests.

CHAPTER OBJECTIVES

In this chapter, we address several specific questions to provide a basic understanding of workplace conflict:

- What is workplace conflict?
- What types of conflict pervade the workplace?
- Who gets involved in workplace conflict?
- What are the possible effects of workplace conflict, especially when it is mishandled?
- What is on the menu of tools, or techniques, that managers can use to deal with conflict?

WHAT IS WORKPLACE CONFLICT?

We need to break that question into two parts. First, what is conflict? Second, in light of today's rapidly changing work systems and arrangements, what defines the workplace?

Conflict

Simply put, conflict exists when two or more parties disagree about something. These parties are interdependent, meaning that the resolution of the conflict to mutual satisfaction cannot occur without some mutual effort. The disagreement may be real or merely perceived, but it is psychologically felt by at least one of the parties. Also, conflict may or may not result in an observable response. The absence of overtly conflictual behaviors is not indicative of the absence of conflict.

Basically, conflict exists when there is *a disagreement between two or more parties who are interdependent*. As such, conflict may recede or evolve into formal challenges, contests, or disputes. It may result in harm or good. It may involve many or a very few. It may be amenable to mutual resolution or require intervention to solve. Conflict may be legitimate or seem highly petty, misguided, and irrational. Wherever disagreement occurs, you have conflict.

The Workplace

A simple definition of the workplace is the setting in which work is performed. You may interpret that as the physical location at which people interact in the process of producing goods or services for an organizational purpose. Such a boundary-based definition, however, is too restrictive. Today's workplace is increasingly seamless. For many of you, it is more a psychological space of activity than a physical site. Technology makes it possible to work with others who are separated from any common physical setting. Therefore, the term workplace is something of a misnomer. A more apt description is the various arrangements and mechanisms—including physical location—through which work flows. The nexus is work—its flow and result—be it a good or service. From this, we define workplace conflict as *disagreements between two or more parties interdependent in the workplace, be it a common physical site or another medium through which work is performed.*

In this vein, the disagreement may arise over a variety of matters and for even more reasons, not all of which need be connected with work or the work site. In addition, conflicts may be exhibited at the emotional, attitudinal, and behavioral levels. Behavioral manifestations become particularly disturbing when they threaten a person's well-being.

WHAT TYPES OF WORKPLACE CONFLICT OCCUR?

Scenario
You are a hospital administrator. You have a broad range of responsibilities, ranging from staffing, evaluating, and terminating employees to budgeting and public relations. It is a typical workday. There are no crises, but you are both stretched and stressed. You are under increasing pressure from the hospital board to control costs. At the same time, you face retention and recruitment problems because the pay and benefits you can offer to a wide array of staff (technicians, nurses, clerical, and custodial) are not competitive. Staff morale is low, and patient care is consequently suffering. The level of significant complaints from patients and their families is on the rise. On top of this, you are not happy with the performance of some of your direct reports, and your administrative assistant just quit because you would not promote her to a higher grade.

These are the day-to-day realities of managing. The relationships and situations within this administrator's orbit create the potential for all sorts of conflicts, even when there is no purposeful intent to create them. In fact, these conflicts may be quite legitimate. Staff may have a well-founded beef about pay and other working conditions. The board may be concerned that the administrator is a poor steward of the hospital's resources. The administrator may, in turn, deem the board penny-wise and pound-foolish. In the midst of this, a former administrative assistant may have felt to be a victim of gender discrimination, and nurses may feel deliberately undervalued because of a gender bias. To relate to this situation and how you might handle it, conduct the following exercise. You should think concretely about the conflict you face at work.

Exercise 1.1: Conflicts at Work

You have finished a long day. It is time to take stock of what has transpired. List the disagreements or conflicts you had or felt this week, the parties involved, and the status or outcome of these disagreements.

Conflicts (What?)	Party (Who?)	Status
1. _____	_____	_____
2. _____	_____	_____
3. _____	_____	_____
4. _____	_____	_____
5. _____	_____	_____
6. _____	_____	_____
7. _____	_____	_____
8. _____	_____	_____
9. _____	_____	_____
10. _____	_____	_____

You may be surprised by how long your list is. You may also be surprised by the variety of people or parties involved. And, you may be surprised by the sheer number of conflicts that are unresolved. Take the exercise a step farther, and ask yourself when and how these conflicts are likely to be resolved (if at all). Then compare those outcomes to what should be. The exercise is analogous to benchmarking your conflict status at work.

On any given day, you may be able to generate a long list of disagreements—latent, active, or red-hot—over numerous issues. Regardless of their status or intensity, most conflicts at work fall into one or more of three overlapping categories: *interests, rights, and power.*

The distinctions, although not conceptually or practically pure, are nonetheless useful, because the conflict resolution technologies that should be available will vary depending upon the nature of the disagreement. When rights are involved, you may want to consider using a third-party neutral (e.g., a mediator or arbitrator) to ensure that the process is unbiased.

Interests. Conflicts over interests concern disagreements that affect what people want or need to receive as a result of their association with work. These matters run the gamut, from general treatment in the workplace to more specific concerns such as assignment, evaluation, scheduling, promotion, and compensation. Conflicts over interests occur among and between employees at various levels across an organization. You may be not directly or indirectly involved, but nonetheless materially impacted by them because of your managerial role. These types of conflicts may or may not involve underlying rights. They may or may not be associated with power relationships. You need to appreciate, however, the fact that making decisions that adversely affect interests can give rise to rights-based disputes, which are magnified by power imbalances.

Rights. Today, workers enjoy a host of legally protected rights. These rights emanate from a variety of sources: statutes, regulations, and court decrees. In addition, there are many unwritten common laws, such as those that may impact the area of just or unjust dismissal. Furthermore, organizations often establish their own systems of internal rights, through standard practice, contractual agreement, or policy statements. For example, an organization might establish a policy with respect to the right to privacy regarding personnel records. It could also establish policies regarding dismissal, with respect to the situations that warrant discipline, the application of progressive discipline, and the procedural protections afforded employees who are being disciplined.

The popular press is filled with stories about the violations of employee rights. The rights asserted by employees under federal law arise from labor relations protections (e.g., the National Labor Relations Act), antidiscrimination protections (e.g., the Civil Rights Act, the Age Discrimination in Employment Act, the Americans with Disabilities Act), and requirements regarding workplace standards (e.g., the Fair Labor Standards Act, the Occupational Safety and Health Act, and the Employee Polygraph Protection Act). If conflicts arise over the rights of employees, organizations may enter an entirely different realm of dispute resolution *expectations*, in which employees have the right to seek external redress. A key prevention strategy is for organizations to address interest disputes with a likelihood of raising legal questions in an effective way that recognizes the protections afforded the parties.

Power

There are numerous occasions in which conflicts involve a test of power. In this regard, power is the ability to thwart someone else's efforts or to attempt to impose a settlement by raising the costs of disagreement to prohibitive levels. For example, when firms merge with or acquire another, there is often a power struggle. Which management team is to enjoy the upper hand? Whose personnel system is to survive? Which business strategy will prevail? Or, closer to home, who will have to relocate, lose or gain responsibilities, or adjust behaviors as a result of the merger or acquisition? In this context, the sheer exercise of power—Who has it? When should it be used? How should it be used?—can provoke controversy.

WHO GETS INVOLVED IN WORKPLACE CONFLICT?

In the past, this might have been an easy question to answer: employees. Conflicts occurred between employees across and within various levels of the organization. And they tended to be concentrated in the same physical space. Today, however, as authority and responsibility are pushed downward and outward, as companies flatten their organizational ranks, as employment relationships become more varied and contingent, and as businesses form alliances and joint ventures, the answer is not so straightforward. Your own span of interactions is growing in size, complexity, and variety.

New work arrangements involving cross-functional projects and matrix structures expand your range of interactions on a daily basis. To promote effective and efficient service, you are expected to deal more regularly and intently with the customer. To respond to shifting market demands, you need to work more closely with suppliers and vendors. In addition, to perform in turbulent product markets, you rely upon an increasingly tenuous and transient labor force.

Conflict at work, therefore, becomes more diverse in terms of the variety of parties who may get involved. You may have more conflicts with those over whom you do not exercise direct control or with whom you do not have a formal, legal employment relationship.

- Conflicts may arise between managers and employees across units or divisions with no direct lines of authority.
- Conflicts may arise between managers and employees within a firm and those whose work is contracted or leased temporarily.
- Conflicts may arise between managers and employees, on the one hand, and suppliers and customers, on the other hand.
- Conflicts may arise among and between managers and employees in more traditional reporting or employment relationships.

The vital point is that conflicts will arise among the many parties with interests, rights, and powers associated with the work. We will focus on conflicts that arise among and between managers and employees, but the technologies of conflict resolution can be applied to a multitude of conceivable working relationships. Your company should not overlook this point because the skills and techniques of effective conflict management and resolution are highly portable.

Figure 1.1 summarizes the three dimensions of workplace conflict. Such conflicts represent disagreements that occur in conjunction with the flow of work and among parties that are often interdependent. As the workplace becomes both more virtual and seamless in nature, the parties that are potentially involved in conflict expand in scope and variety. As a result, the practical utility of the technologies of conflict resolution widen.

WHAT ARE THE EFFECTS OF CONFLICT AT WORK?

Scenario

The ambitious project manager in a high-growth pharmaceutical company is assigned a massive construction project, requiring the coordinated efforts of a large, multifunctional group. The manager must be able to manage relationships well at three levels: with those who are superior and have the resources needed to get the job done; with those who are peers; and with those who are subordinate. From the get-go, problems are encoun-

Figure 1.1 Workplace Conflict

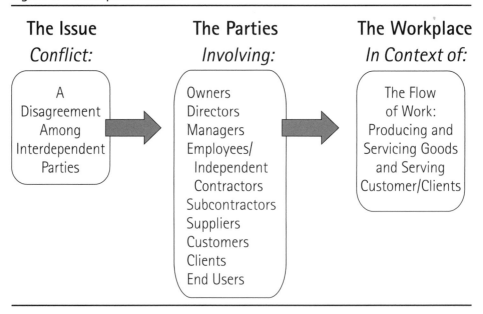

The Issue *Conflict:*	The Parties *Involving:*	The Workplace *In Context of:*
A Disagreement Among Interdependent Parties	Owners Directors Managers Employees/ Independent Contractors Subcontractors Suppliers Customers Clients End Users	The Flow of Work: Producing and Servicing Goods and Serving Customer/Clients

tered. Promised resources are not forthcoming in a timely manner. Managerial peers procrastinate, withholding efforts that they choose to expend on their own projects. Subordinates withdraw because they do not like the stressed-out demeanor of their boss. Disagreements multiply, tensions mount, and unproductive behaviors result.

What are the effects of this conflict-prone situation? You may relate to them at three levels. First, the conflicts will affect the parties, including the project manager, personally. These effects can be psychologically, emotionally, and physiologically debilitating, even though they may not be verbalized or shown outwardly.

Second, the conflicts will impact the parties professionally. The project manager's prospects for advancement depend on how well things get done. In terms of leadership potential, he or she will be judged by the quality of interactions with the many others involved in the project. Are conflicts allowed to impair performance? Are subordinates resentful of mistreatment? Are peers distrustful, envious, or doubtful? Do superiors resent having conflicts filter to their desks, knowing that they could and should have been dealt with at the lower ranks? The manager's future promotions will hinge in part on the answers given to these questions. And in this era of 360° reviews, it is likely that many will be asked for their opinions.

And third, there is the organizational impact. Is the project done on time, on budget? Have conflicts turned into formal disputes that need to be litigated? Have relationships been damaged to the point where future interactions are avoided or unwanted? Ultimately, the quality and quantity of time we devote to productive versus nonproductive activities is what affects the bottom line.

Exercise 1.2: Effects of Conflict

Think of a conflictual situation in which you have recently been involved. (Use an example that is more than a minor, fleeting disagreement.) Describe the conflict briefly. Then list the effects that it had on you personally and professionally. Finally, think of what effects the conflict may have had on the organization.

Describe the conflictual situation:

_____

_____

_____

_____

_____

_____

List the personal, professional, organizational effects:

Personal	Professional	Organizational
1. _____	1. _____	1. _____
2. _____	2. _____	2. _____
3. _____	3. _____	3. _____
4. _____	4. _____	4. _____
5. _____	5. _____	5. _____

You may look more systematically at the effects of workplace conflict along personal, professional, and organizational effects. You know that these areas are not separated by firewalls. What affects you personally may well affect you professionally. And the personal and professional effects have organizational consequences. You may look at this another way: how well you handle the personal effects of workplace conflict has professional and organizational implications. Most of you probably know of a situation where someone allowed his or her personal frustration and anger to erupt into an outburst which was professionally and organizationally harmful.

More specifically, conflicts at work may affect you personally in three ways. First, they affect how we feel (our emotions). Confrontations or disputes may anger us, scare us, intimidate us, or cause us sorrow. On the other hand, disagreements can also be exhilarating, energizing, and illuminating.

Second, conflicts affect how and what we think (the psychological effect). If we are in conflict with someone, we often interpret everything that person does or says in the light of the conflict. When we dislike the conflict, we translate that into disliking the person. Such thinking can carry on for quite some time, long after the conflict occurred.

Third, conflicts affect how we behave—the actions we take. We may sometimes react angrily when disagreeing with someone. We may vent or verbalize the anger. We may internalize it and avoid contact with the person or situation with which the disagreement is associated. If the conflict becomes intolerable, we may leave the organization, exercising the powerful "exit" voice at work.

Professionally, the effects occur in the areas of advancement, opportunity, and networking, all of which are interconnected. How we manage conflict will affect our chances for advancement. If we cannot cope effectively, we may be judged unqualified for certain positions. If we are viewed as provoking conflict for needless reasons, we may suffer the same fate. Creating conflicts, allowing conflicts to escalate, and resolving disputes ineffectually can cause problems that will haunt us throughout our professional careers.

In a similar vein, conflicts can affect the range of opportunities we are given. If your boss thinks that you cannot handle a situation without provoking a conflict, then she or he may give the project to someone else. Likewise, if your boss thinks that you cannot handle the conflicts that inevitably will arise in a complex, expensive, multiparty project, he or she may simply eliminate you from consideration. You are not demoted, nor are you always aware that you have been removed from the list of candidates under consideration. But the effects are nonetheless occurring, to your professional detriment.

Last, conflicts will affect your networking. If you are prone to avoid conflicts, you will necessarily attempt to escape many working situations, thereby missing valuable opportunities to network. Conversely, if you are prone to provoke disagreement, especially if you do it in a disagreeable fashion, others may avoid you. You thereby acquire an unfavorable reputation that will always precede you.

At the organizational level, you see the effects of conflict in at least three ways.

• *First, conflicts can drive up the costs of doing business*: delays, litigation, waste, and re-works. You should be mindful, however, that the failure to disagree can sometimes be costly. How many of us have failed to stop decision makers from making a mistake, which eventually proved costly, because we did not want to rock the boat. The net result is that organizational performance is affected on the bottom-line.

• *Second, conflicts can also affect productivity*. While conflict may stimulate effort and engagement, it may also encourage avoidance, procrastination, or hesitation. We are capable of engaging in all kinds of unproductive behaviors because of conflicts. We refuse to cooperate. We withhold information. We avoid doing the work. We pass assignments on to others who are less capable. The organizational implications of conflict follow a certain logic. Conflict will affect the two or more parties immediately involved (a supervisor and employee, for example) and those who interact with the supervisor and employee if they cannot handle or cope with the situation.

• *Third, conflicts expose organizations to risks and opportunities*—sides of the same coin. As an example, a conflict between a manager and a subordinate can elevate to litigation over a rights-based dispute. Conflicts expose organizations to litigation, and that is one of the principal reasons why they are feared. However, there is an upside: Conflicts may expose organizations to new opportunities. If an employee has a conflict and chooses to leave, the organization can look for replacements who may be of superior quality.

In summary, conflicts produce effects at the personal, professional, and organizational levels. Effects at one level reverberate to the others. Although we may tend to look at these effects as costs, we need to acknowledge that there are benefits to conflict. One must disagree to challenge the status quo. Complacency and silence are powerful enemies of progress. The key is to disagree without being disagreeable and to offer ways of resolving disagreements constructively.

EXPLORING YOUR OPTIONS

Scenario

A manager of a department of sales representatives, who happens to be a women, has been denied a promotion to the next highest management position by the vice president of sales, who happens to be a man. The reason offered for her denial was lack of experience. She believes the real reason is a gender bias: the vice president does not think a woman could perform well in that higher-level position. She has a legal right under the Civil Rights Act to file a complaint alleging sex discrimination with the Equal Employment Opportunity Commission (EEOC). As the HR professional, how do you resolve this conflict before it gets out of control and thrust into the courts?

It is in these very types of situations that you want to be able to look into your conflict resolution tool kit and not find it empty. What are your options? What techniques might be used to resolve the conflict? How would you approach the situation? You could simply hold tight and hope the situation just goes away, and sometimes it does. In some instances, avoiding the situation or giving it time to cool down is a wise approach. In other circumstances, however, that may not be desirable, especially when there is a high risk of losing any control of the outcome and exposing the organization and individuals involved to costly embarrassment.

Fortunately, the techniques available to resolve conflict are plentiful. In the scenario presented above, the HR professional might consider the options on the menu below:

Option 1: Negotiation. Have the principals sit down and discuss their concerns and try to work out a mutually satisfactory solution.

Option 2: Facilitation. Attempt to facilitate a solution as a third party convening a meeting between the principals. You may be able to facilitate the meaningful exchange of information to promote mutual understanding.

Option 3: Mediation. Arrange for an outside third-party mediator to attempt to mediate a solution between the principals. If the parties agree through a mediated session, their settlement can be made binding.

Option 4: Ombuds. Turn the case over to a company ombuds who will conduct an investigation and attempt to get the parties to agree to a solution.

Option 5: Advisory Arbitration. Turn the case over to an outside arbitrator who will conduct a hearing at which both sides, represented by counsel, will present their respective cases. The arbitrator will then render a decision, which will be advisory, not binding. The intent, however, is that the advice will carry some weight.

Option 6: Binding Arbitration. Turn the case over to an outside arbitrator who will conduct a hearing and render a binding decision.

In this simple scenario, you have been given six options: negotiation, facilitation, mediation, ombuds-investigation, advisory arbitration, and binding arbitration. These options can be structured so that they can be used sequentially with limited backward or forward movement. This gives greater versatility to the menu, making it somewhat a la carte.

Manager's Checklist: Assessing Workplace Conflict

You are beginning the task of assessing how your organization handles workplace conflict, as well as the general understanding of the phenomenon. Ask yourself these questions, remembering that you will ultimately be tasked with designing a comprehensive conflict resolution system.

Question	Yes	No	Don't Know
1. My company has an explicit or implicit view of workplace conflict?	☐	☐	☐
2. My company views workplace conflict as inherently bad?	☐	☐	☐
3. My company is generally aware of the types and frequencies of workplace conflicts?	☐	☐	☐
4. My company is generally aware of how much workplace conflicts cost the organization's bottom line?	☐	☐	☐
5. My company has worked on developing a capacity to resolve conflict effectively?	☐	☐	☐
6. My company is generally poor at identifying the causes of workplace conflict?	☐	☐	☐
7. My company attempts to suppress workplace conflict?	☐	☐	☐
8. In my company, people feel comfortable voicing their concerns about work?	☐	☐	☐
9. I have a problem in my company with undue competitiveness and hostility?	☐	☐	☐
10. Workplace violence is a noticeable problem or fear in my organization?	☐	☐	☐
11. My company has a partial conflict resolution system already in place?	☐	☐	☐

Chapter 2

Diagnosing Conflict

"Ford's CEO (Jacques Nasser) ousted after rift with company chair-
man (William Clay Ford, Jr.)."
"Forty-two Ford managers file class-action suits alleging age and race
discrimination."
"Motorola's CEO (Christopher Galvin) criticized for indecisiveness,
detachment."

Conflict at work is on the rise. You know that from your own personal
experiences. Employees across all ranks are increasingly willing to challenge, dispute, and litigate. We spend a lot of time trying to calm the
waters in the turbulent workplace where uncertainty, change, and speed
reign supreme.

You also know—because of statistics compiled by various sources—
that workplace conflict is a growing concern. Lawsuits over work-related
actions have mushroomed. Studies show an increasing level of workplace
incivility. And workplace violence has affected a large percentage of us.

In addition, your daily experiences with workplace conflict tell us that
much of it is unhealthy. A lot of it seems to result from personality
clashes. Personal conflicts at work may be well camouflaged as disagreements over legitimate interests, workplace rights, or the appropriate distribution and use of power. But the false mask is easily peeled.

To deal with conflict, personally and organizationally, you need to
know what causes it. The sources of conflict have a lot to do with whether
it is going to have beneficial or poisonous effects. They also have a decisive

bearing on how the conflict should be handled, or what methodologies should be used to resolve it.

You also need to know how conflict is manifested or how it is shielded from public view. Sometimes the manifestation of a conflict becomes the problem, or at least another problem laid on top of the underlying cause. Take the situation where a supervisor withdraws from a work situation because a disgruntled employee may be encountered. You now have to deal with two issues: the disgruntled employee and the withdrawn supervisor.

Finally, to understand workplace conflict, you need to know how to measure it and to assess how much it costs. There are several reasons why this is necessary.

• First, measurement helps you assess whether or not the sheer scope of conflict is a problem. For example, turnover in and of itself may not be a bad thing. It is often welcome because it gives an organization a chance to bring in new life and energy—fresh ideas. However, a high level of turnover among top performers, concentrated in a single unit or under one set of managers, is indicative of a serious problem.

• Second, because conflict affects individual and organizational performance, you should be aware of how you compare to others in your realm of competition. It could well be that conflict is diminishing your competitiveness. A company plagued by strikes may have difficulty competing against a competitor that is not so bothered. A company that has created an atmosphere where new ideas and risk-taking are encouraged may gain the edge in innovation. Fear and stagnation can result from unhealthy conflict or concerns about how disagreement or dissension might be received by higher-ups.

• Third, measuring the costs of conflict is important to making the case for conflict resolution program development and skill-based training within an organization. Building a conflict resolution capability within your organization is not inexpensive. It should not be done on the cheap. Nor should it be sold as an inexpensive proposition. Advocates of conflict resolution programs and skill-based training should couch their arguments in terms of the sizable net benefits to gain. Conflicts can cost a lot when they are problems. Needless personal feuds in a project can delay progress, force the need to hire additional personnel, lead to low productivity and morale, and provoke disputes that result in costly litigation. You must be willing to sum up these costs and compare them to the cost of assigning a facilitator to facilitate multiparty partnering and thereby avoid these problems. Such a comparison would often reveal that the investment in a facilitator and facilitation yields a high rate of return.

CHAPTER OBJECTIVES

In this chapter, you are given the tools you need to diagnose conflict in your organization. We first present an overall picture of the causes, indicators, and costs of conflict at work. With this picture as a guide, we then review the various types of factors that may give rise to conflict. From this point, we proceed to look at the indicators of conflict, which are the signs you need to watch for to determine whether or not you have a problem or a crisis in the making. Finally, we explore the costs of conflict. At the end, we offer a set of checklists to guide your thinking.

CONFLICT DIAGNOSIS AND MEASUREMENT MODEL

Figure 2.1 presents a model to guide you through the process of diagnosing and measuring conflict in your workplace. We intend for the framework to be encompassing. The potential causes of conflict are vast, as are the indicators and costs, yet they can be categorized to lend order to the diagnostic process.

We encourage you to use this model as a practical guide to assessing the degree to which conflict stressors are present in your own workplace. Formulate in your own mind a picture of which indicators of conflict are present in your organization. And do some rough mental calculations as to how much conflict is costing you and your company. When you draw

Figure 2.1 A Model on Diagnosing and Measuring Conflict

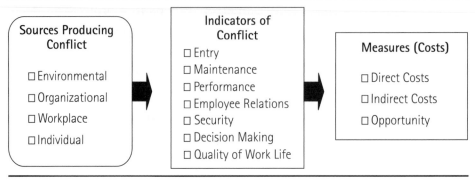

such a picture, you are much more able to deal with conflict constructively and competently, from both a personal and organizational perspective.

SOURCES OR CAUSES OF CONFLICT

Many factors may cause conflict at work. We look at four areas—environment, organization, workplace, and individuals—as possible sources of where conflicts arise. Obviously, interplay occurs across these areas because we, as individuals, do not work in vacuums. We work at various sites within an organizational context that is affected by the broader environment. However, we need to be able to distinguish among the sources of conflict because the appropriate resolution must address the real cause.

Figure 2.2 identifies several of the possible sources of workplace conflict. These conditions may be viewed as potential stressors or causes of conflict. As will become obvious, some of these stressors or causes are largely beyond the control of any company or manager. A pivotal variable, however, is the individual. Some individuals are better suited to deal with conflict than others.

Scenario
You are a plant manager in a major manufacturing company. Your company operates in a very competitive market, confronted

Figure 2.2 Sources of Workplace Conflict

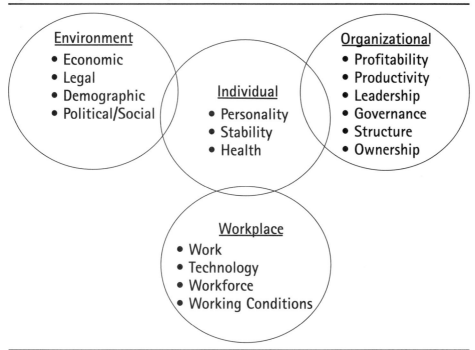

with aggressive domestic and international competitors. Its market share has shrunk, layoffs have been announced, and profits are lagging. On top of these realities, your plant is in the process of reconfiguring its technology, redesigning work, and exploring new models of business—outsourcing, leasing, contracting, and joint ventures. Furthermore, while it is downsizing, it faces a class-action age-discrimination lawsuit. Your company has also been recently acquired by another in a mega-merger, which has brought about changes in corporate management and personnel policies. In this context, your increasingly diverse workforce is more assertive than the ones you remember from the past. Employees want to be empowered, and they expect their interests to be given serious consideration and their rights to be fully protected. Within the workforce, there is evidence of drug abuse and violent behaviors.

Exercise 2.1: Possible Sources of Conflict

Considering the scenario above, list the possible sources of conflict in this kind of working situation. What is going on at the individual, workplace, organizational, and environmental levels that might lead to conflict—or disagreement—of any sort? Do not attempt an exhaustive list, but jot down six to ten of the major sources you might expect to see.

1. _____

2. _____

3. _____

4. _____

5. _____

6. _____

7. _____

8. _____

9. _____

10. _____

We will now pepper you with illustrations of the possible sources and causes of workplace conflict. You should relate readily to the litany. We use examples spread widely across organizations. The task we ask you to perform is to determine the extent to which these factors are present in your organizations and in your working lives. Then think about how your companies and you personally would operate in such situations. Are you prepared to deal with the conflicts and tensions that will inevitably arise? Or, conversely, are you likely to ignore them, to deny them, or to do things—inadvertently or not—that exacerbate them? Many conflicts are inherently difficult—that is why they are conflicts. But you and your company have a chance to manage them well or make the situations worse and the effects more costly. We cannot control everything around us, but we can control how we respond to events and circumstances. Exercising such control is the key to effective conflict management and resolution.

Environmental Sources

Your environment will affect the nature and scope of conflict you may generally encounter at work. You can dissect the environment into several distinguishable contexts that will exert independent effects on the potential for conflict. They include the labor and product markets, the legal context, labor force demography, and the political and social contexts surrounding the working environment. Separately and together, these environmental contexts can have a profound impact on the propensity for conflict at work.

The illustrations below present situations likely to produce greater levels of conflict in terms of frequency, significance, difficulty, and cost.

The Labor Market. The economy teeters on recession. The company's profits have fallen sharply. Layoffs have occurred. More are in the offing. Employees fear job loss. And their workloads have increased as their ranks have shrunk. An environment ripe for tension and conflict prevails.

The Product Market. A company faces an extraordinarily competitive product market. Competition stems not only in the typical form of quality and price but also in the threat of obsolescence. Technological advancements threaten to render its products obsolete. Thus, the resulting pressure to create, innovate, and get to market is enormous. In such a pressure cooker, conflicts are bound to grow and intensify, as people vie for survival.

The Legal Context. A plethora of laws and regulations give employees rights in the workplace. A company with a workforce that is not representative of the surrounding demography invites charges that its staffing policies are discriminatory. A company that implements layoffs in a way that adversely affects older workers invites age-discrimination charges. A company that terminates a manager for unclear reasons invites a wrongful discharge suit. A company undergoing lawsuits may have conflicts over who is at fault, whether to plea-bargain, or how it should change in response to the underlying issues. Legal actions occasion their own tensions and conflicts.

Remember, *the law does not create the conflict*. It establishes a mechanism through which employees may challenge company actions. It facilitates the voice of conflict. In addition, to comply with the law, companies may be forced to make changes, which in turn generate their own set of conflicts.

Demographics. A company's aging workforce is confronted with an influx of Generation X workers. As you know, Generation X workers bring a different set of skills and expectations to work. They are more likely, for instance, to be technologically savvy and motivated, less "devoted" to the company on a long-term basis, and more interested in the balance between work, leisure, and family. This can create tensions in the workplace over how work is done, working hours, workplace amenities and services, and general management philosophy. Simply put, the old guard may clash with the new turks. The potential for all kinds of conflict exists, from what is acceptable dress at work to who will make the fundamental business decisions.

Political Situation. A company is opening a new facility in one of the former Soviet bloc countries. The political situation lies between uncertain and turbulent. The judicial system is essentially undeveloped. Fiscal and economic policy cannot be anticipated with any reasonable degree of certainty.

The company faces the possibility of numerous workplace-related controversies over such matters as workers' rights, employment practices (e.g., compensation), expatriation, and ownership rights, with a variety of affected constituencies: unions, governmental agencies, local suppliers, other businesses, and social-religious organizations. For instance, conflicts could arise between a U.S. management team sent to the local site to run the operations and the locally hired managers over various interests (e.g., career opportunities), rights (employment security), and powers (decision-making authority).

Social Context. A privately owned manufacturing company located in a rural area proximate to a major city has a very restrictive and paternalistic style of managing its employees. Its working hours are long and rigidly enforced. Breaks and lunch periods are of the absolute minimum in terms of allotted time, and again are rigidly enforced. A conforming dress style and physical appearance is rigidly enforced. Pay and benefits are good, but the work itself and the working schedule are both demanding.

This style of management, although socially acceptable in the late 1940s and early 1950s when the company was founded, runs counter to prevailing social expectations today. Balancing work and family falls by the wayside. Leisure is something almost unthinkable. Bleeding the company colors is taken as a given. Unsurprisingly, tensions exist. New hires question the old way of doing things. Senior managers look askance at such youthful skepticism. Women and minorities have reservations about their genuine acceptability in the company, particularly at the higher levels.

New and future entrants into the workforce bring a set of social expectations and values, which differ significantly from those of their predecessors. Resulting clashes occur over a variety of organizational policies and practices. Demands for change or dissatisfaction with the status quo accelerate, affecting a host of workplace relationships and activities. Organizations need some way of adapting to these pressures—preserving the best of the old while introducing the best of the new—in order to continue to succeed. Failure to do so can be expected to result in performance problems, informal and formal complaints, and even more overt challenges.

Organizational Sources

As porous entities operating in these various environmental contexts, with the constant influx, processing, and exit of resources (e.g., human resources), organizations cannot help but be affected, with direct and indirect implications for conflict. On the one hand, the pressures may directly affect the bottom-line, which, in turn, creates conflicts over the allocation of resources. On the other hand, organizations' responses to real or anticipated environmental opportunities and threats will yield their own set of difficulties, both expected and unintended consequences.

Consider a company with an aging workforce covered by a health-care system whose costs are rising at a fast pace. It may respond by attempting to shift a portion of the employer-paid part of its health-benefits program to employees. This attempt will inevitably provoke consternation and conflict. Indeed, company efforts to raise the employee share of the health-care burden have been one of the major triggers of the labor strikes that have occurred in the eighties and nineties.

Financial. For example, Ford Motor Company lost money in the second quarter of 2001. Its cash reserves had shrunk because of acquisitions and the recall of Firestone tires, and it announced layoffs of 4,000 to 5,000 white-collar employees. In such financial difficulties, anxiety rises and morale dips.

In these types of situations, disagreements and conflicts will arise over who is at fault (the blame game), who should suffer, and how they should suffer. Labor contracts will need to be renegotiated, layoffs and early retirements will proliferate, managers will be chopped, and suppliers' contracts and relationships will be critically challenged. It is a recipe for profuse tensions and hostilities.

Restructuring. A company is under enormous pressure to gain operating efficiencies and improve customer satisfaction and service. It has recently completed a top-to-bottom strategic and operational review and decided upon a massive "modernization," restructuring the company into four distinctive product lines. Its new organizational structure is functionally designed, with accounting, finance, human resources, information technology, and marketing serving each of the product lines. Massive relocations, consolidations, and other changes are necessitated by this reorganization. To gain operational efficiencies, this plan is coupled with an effort to eliminate employment redundancies and shift employees to more profitable product lines.

Needless to say, such restructuring, no matter how well intended, well planned, and logically required, produces controversies. Whose interests, rights, and powers are going to be affected? Who are the winners and losers? Will there be opportunities to influence how specific personnel decisions are made and implemented? Were the interests and rights of the affected parties appropriately aired in the development of the plan? Will there be breaches of existing labor and employment contracts? Will the rights of minorities and women be protected? Is there "political" favoritism in the design and implementation process? Who in management will change? How will management change? These issues feed conflict.

Mergers and Acquisitions. A French-owned, U.S.-operated steel manufacturing company acquired two smaller Canadian steel companies. As the dominant partner in this acquisition, it sought to take some control over the Canadian companies. Management positions, titles, and responsibilities changed. Human resource systems had to be integrated. A new company culture prevailed at the Canadian sites. You get the picture. Vested interests, rights, and powers were upset. Pressures to conform grew. Inevitably, resistance was encountered.

For eighteen months, the French-owned, U.S.-operated company enjoyed being the dominant partner. When its management team faced conflicts, it usually decided the matters in ways that preserved its interests, rights, and powers. After all, it did not make the acquisition to become like those it acquired. Just the opposite was intended.

But eighteen months later the tables turned, when the French-owned and U.S.–Canadian-operated company was acquired by a much larger U.S. steel company. In this case, the dominant partner essentially took the reins of power and began changing things to conform to *its* interests and needs. The flow of resources—people, money, and raw material—changed. The same set of frictions that existed in the first acquisition was now repeated in the second.

Mergers and acquisitions, although sounding antiseptic, can be terrifying for those managers and employees caught in the middle. Intense political competition to survive, and to survive mostly intact, will ensue. The harsh realities of adverse change will occur, or, often more hauntingly, be feared for a seemingly interminable time.

Strategy. A pharmaceuticals company decides to reduce dramatically its drug-discovery cycle time—i.e., the time that elapses between conceptualizing, testing, approving, producing, and marketing a new drug. Each phase of this process is subjected to intense work-process and value-added analysis. As a result, the company decides to reduce cycle time by 50 percent, which becomes the strategic goal set forth in the planning process. Implementing requires eliminating unnecessary, non–value-adding steps, reorganizing jobs and teams, imposing strict management controls, and so on and so forth. Adjusting to these changes upsets the status quo. Some whose interests and needs have been relatively suppressed in the past receive increased power and responsibility because of the value—especially speed—they add. Others' pre-existing fiefdoms have crumbled.

A strategic decision, particularly if it is really strategic in nature, has important consequences. Not only does reducing cycle time upset the applecart, it also consumes time and energy that could be devoted elsewhere. To make the goal achievable, old conflicts have to be put to rest and new ones solved in productive ways. Those with interests and perceived rights and powers associated with the old way will suffer under the new way. And those that benefit from the strategic change will have their fair share of conflicts in moving forward. The same is true not only in the case of dramatically reducing cycle time but in opening new markets or developing new lines of business.

Philosophy. A well-known bricks-and-mortar company has had a long-standing paternalistic approach to managing employees. For the most part, it has been a "better standards" employer, offering higher wages and more benefits than other employers in the areas where it competes. It has done so in part because of market realities. Its business is neither "pretty," nor is the work particularly exciting.

As a paternalistic company, it has attempted to meet the basic needs of its employees, whom it treats literally like children. Therein lies the paternalism. Its children are to be fed and seen and are expected to do their chores. But they are not to be listened to or heard. Along the same lines, they can and should be told what to do and corrected when they are doing wrong.

As might be expected, as these children grow up they may begin to have questions and concerns. They may rebel. And, moreover, as the operating technologies they are expected to use with great ease become ever more sophisticated, these employees must be expected to think and act more like adults than like subservient kids. An intrinsic contradiction is created in the organization. The paternalistic philosophy prevails, where managers manage, but it clashes with advancing production technologies that demand an increasingly sophisticated and self-motivated worker. The culture cannot forever exist comfortably with either the expectations of the workforce or the needs of the organization. But, as always, there are strong defenders of the status quo.

The organization perforce will move to a more egalitarian style of management, or it will find its future very short-lived. The changes will come not only in stylistic terms but also in management itself. As one CEO commented, "the train is leaving the station, and those who are not on it will be left behind. Furthermore, those who cannot ride comfortably in it will be kicked off." To take effect, this change requires new methods of hiring, orienting, training, and rewarding employees and their managers. Square pegs will not fit into round holes.

Leadership. A struggling company's long-term CEO retires and is replaced, after an extensive executive search, with an external CEO. The new CEO comes on board, and quickly sees the need for radical change. Not known for his interpersonal charm, the new CEO pushes hard for these changes. The old management, wanting to give the new CEO a fair chance to succeed, assents to most of them, albeit not without lingering resentment. When a quick turnaround in corporate performance is not evident, the detractors begin to form a cabal. Senior management is soon divided between those who support the new CEO and those who want him ousted. Not so subtle executive-room warfare breaks out, and there are some casualties.

The tensions are felt through the managerial ranks and percolate down to the rank-and-file. Uncertain about which side to take and fearful of offending either one, many postpone decisions. Others update their resumes. A few leave. Organizational performance suffers even more. Prospects of a hostile takeover loom.

Policy. A company is keenly interested in motivating its workforce at all levels to performing at higher standards. Toward this end, it is revamping its pay-reward policy from one that is individually based to one that is more group- and organization-based. The company has recently revised its operations to conform to a team-based model of servicing clients. An individually based merit system of pay rewards seems incongruent with the new operational form. Therefore, the pay-reward policy has been changed. Part of the reward, in the form of annual incentive pay increases, will be based on individual meritorious performance. But the lion's share will be based on rewarding group and organizational performance, the latter operationalized as profit sharing.

In concept, this new policy approach has considerable face validity and appeal. The greater one's stake in the organization's success, the higher one's motivation to perform for the betterment of the whole. Like everything else, however, the devil is in the detail. Are group members working equally hard? Are groups evenly organized in terms of abilities and potential for success? Should individuals suffer financially because of organizational mismanagement beyond their control?

Organizations too often approach policy changes as intellectual pursuits. People should work in groups, and be rewarded accordingly. It is that simple. But human nature is not. This kind of policy adjustment can have powerful implications for how people are treated. Dissension may be encountered. Groups may struggle to perform and have to overcome numerous conflicts in the process—between individuals who have competing views on how to achieve the best results. The essential point is that policies have intended and unintended consequences. In this example, one of the unintended consequences could be intense inter-group competition at the expense of the whole. The compensation change has unintentionally elevated unhealthy individual competition and conflict to the group level.

Workplace Sources

The workplace context itself may trigger conflict. Possible causes include the nature of work, the technology used, the relationships among co-workers and others, the degree of safety and health risks associated with the work, the contingency nature of work, and the intensity and style of supervision. The immediacy and proximity of these conditions are almost inescapable. Employees may try, particularly in the short run, to distance themselves from wider organizational and environmental factors. But as long as the work is being done, these workplace factors will exist as either real or potential sources of conflict. In fact, even when one is not engaged in the act of working, these potential stressors may be felt, because the challenges, risks, and worries of work are not confined to the workplace but are akin to psychological (in some cases physiological) states that an individual carries at all times.

Workload and Design. A CEO of a company, in an executive training session with her direct reports, is asked about the company's human resource strategy for the 21st century. She replies matter-of-factly that workers, including managers, will work harder, smarter, and for more variable pay. That strategy may well be the unavoidable reality. But it is a recipe for conflict. What is harder? How much further effort can be demanded? What is smarter? Who is going to pay for the education and training? And more variable pay opens up all sorts of potential disagreements about the ratio of variable to fixed pay, the measurement of performance, and the methodology of determining how variable pay is actually awarded. These issues directly, immediately, and significantly affect the interests of those involved in work and the workplace.

The nature of work itself can yield stressors in two principal ways, although the direction of the effects is not always clear. Although it is well established that giving people more challenge through work—in the form of more task variety, task significance, and autonomy—increases the motivating potential of a job, it may also produce stress or tension if individuals are not properly equipped to handle the new challenges. Also, conflicts may arise over whether such job enrichment or work embellishments are going to be properly rewarded through pay, promotion, or recognition.

At the same time, highly mundane, repetitive, and dead-end work can generate tensions. People may resent the nature of their work and the lack of opportunity associated with it. This could lead to conflicts among coworkers and between management and labor, especially if the former pushes the latter to do more while management is perceived as having the better jobs.

The same kind of argument can be made with respect to the amount of work required. Piling on work can result in strong disagreements over whether people are being treated fairly. Is work being distributed evenly or are the shirkers and free-riders just ignored and given minimal assignments while those more demonstrably amenable or compliant are loaded up with more work? Conversely, when individuals who are capable and willing are not given sufficient work to demonstrate their true value, they may feel intentionally marginalized and underutilized. Purposeful and not-so-benign neglect or indifference can leave employees highly frustrated and eager to contest a situation that devalues them.

Technology. A company, which has operated on a traditional assembly-line production basis, is introducing an entirely new technology. The technology renders many of the old jobs obsolete, requires greater operational knowledge and sophistication, organizes work around teams, and reduces the need for direct supervision. The technology provides the feedback necessary to avoid and correct mistakes, which can be done on a real-time basis.

The engineering and scientific marvels of technological advancements are often the bane of workplace life. Jobs are threatened. Implicit and explicit contractual relationships about how work is done are destroyed. The proverbial old dog must be taught new tricks. First-line supervisors are squeezed in a thick vise of technological change. New and differently skilled workers are needed and often can only be gotten at higher than traditional levels of compensation. Cross-functional teams, whose members speak a different professional language or work idiom, must now communicate and operate as a unit, not as a set of silos.

Workforce Composition. A German-owned company buys a U.S. company located in the South. It exports a team of managers to run the U.S. facilities. The existing management is diverse in terms of gender, race, ethnicity, and national origin, whereas the German team is not. The U.S. clerical, manual, and professional workforce is also diverse.

In this situation, you have intercultural differences compounded by demographic diversity. Although diversity is a laudable goal with enormous potential to make businesses better on many dimensions, it also poses its own set of potential tensions. Cultures may differ in terms of how they conduct business and manage. These differences can create conflicts in managerial styles, performance expectations, and behavioral norms. Mere miscommunications due to language differences may also lead to conflict.

Safety/Health Risks. A hospital has recently reported having three incidents of HIV-positive tests among its nurses who perform phlebotomies. The nurses, who are unionized, have had serious reservations as to whether or not the hospital was taking sufficient precautions to prevent such incidents. These concerns extend beyond those nurses performing phlebotomies to all nursing staff who come into contact with blood. Others in the hospital—including lab technicians and custodians, who each belong to different unions—are also of the opinion that inadequate preventive measures are being taken. Each of the unions plans to bring this very important issue to the attention of the hospital administration. The initial vehicle for doing so is the existing labor-management partnership. In addition, they will seek language in the upcoming contract negotiations to develop a sure-fire prevention program for all potentially affected hospital employees.

The safety and health risks associated with work and the working environment can precipitate tensions and conflicts. No one asserts that owners or managers have a cavalier disregard for such risks. The issue is whether or not there is sufficient awareness. In addition, what are the relative costs and benefits of protecting employees' safety and health? Ideally, a 100 percent firewall of protection should be the standard. But the reality is that many occupations and workplaces cannot be so protected, because the costs of approaching that standard are simply prohibitive. Furthermore, for some jobs, the standard is simply not realistic; risks cannot be entirely eliminated. Therefore, there are bound to be some tensions over the degree and type of commitment to this kind of risk management.

Contingency Work. A medium-sized company, operating in an industry subject to wide market fluctuations, decides to lease many of its professional and technical employees when product demand rises rather than adding new employees to its core workforce. The leased employees, who do the same work as the core professionals and technicians, are actually employees of the lessor, not the lessee. The lessor pays the employees at scales it negotiates with the lessee. It is responsible for actually selecting these leased employees—i.e., making sure they are qualified. And the lessor is technically the employer who will handle performance or discipline problems on the job at the lessee's site.

Obviously, there is the potential for conflict over the interests, rights, and powers afforded to leased employees relative to the permanent workforce. If they are treated as more or less second-class employees but are doing the same work at the same level of quality, then there is potential conflict between them and the permanently "advantaged" workforce. Putting the shoe on the other foot, however, the permanent workforce could equally resent leased employees' being afforded the same rights, powers, and privileges. After all, should not those with a longer-term stake in the organization—those who live with the consequences of the actions taken—make the decisions rather than essentially temporary employees who will move on and not be stuck with the consequences?

As the workforce becomes increasingly contingent, these kinds of issues will surface and become stickier with greater frequency. Indeed, given the multiplicity of contingency work, there is the potential for multiple class frictions in the workplace. Leased employees are only one form of contingent worker. Others include part-time employees, temporaries, and independent contractors.

Supervision. A large, widely dispersed overnight mail delivery company's numerous agents operate face-to-face with customers in a steadily heavy flow of business. Serving the customer requires significant attentiveness and timeliness. Customer satisfaction depends on courteous, accurate, and timely service. To ensure that customers are satisfied and that costly errors do not occur, the company supervises these agents intensely. Rigid rules of service-providing are enforced. Extensive employee monitoring is required. Unannounced supervisory visits occur often. Performance reviews are intense and meticulous.

Needless to say, this is a company whose agents work under intense pressure. Strict supervision surrounds difficult work. Many supervisors have weak interpersonal skills, which aggravate already tense supervisor-employee relations. The end result is constant tension and systemic conflict—disagreement over how the organization treats its arguably most valuable asset (i.e., the agent), how supervisors are chosen and rewarded, and the extent to which the interests, rights, and powers of the agents should be formally protected. Numerous attempts at unionization have been made, and agent turnover has become a serious problem, especially as the job market has tightened (more jobs relative to recruits) in recent years.

The nature of supervision is partly a function of the kind of work and partly a result of the personalities chosen. Neither of these qualities is mutually exclusive. Certain personalities may be attracted to a particular kind of supervision. A certain kind of supervision can transform a personality.

Too often, organizations do not look closely enough at either the nature of supervision they impose or the caliber of supervisors hired. If supervision is stultifying and the supervisory class is neither the best nor the brightest, supervisor-employee conflicts will inevitably arise. These conflicts, moreover, will not be confined to the supervisor-employee relationship. They will be directed against management at all levels, including and especially at the very highest levels. Inevitably, tensions will affect how customers are treated, adding yet other layers of conflict.

Individual-Level Sources

At work, many of us operate under more or less similar circumstances. We may, for example, face a common set of environmental, workplace, and organizational contexts that invite cohesion rather than conflict. But even in such situations, conflicts will exist. Moreover, when confronted with comparable situations, people will respond differently. Some may react collaboratively or cooperatively to tensions whereas others may become confrontational, combative, or otherwise disagreeable.

For better or worse, we bring our personalities to work. And we know that a good deal of the conflict we encounter at work is due to personality clashes. These clashes are often unproductive and unhealthy: the situations that make us dread coming to work. Personalities may differ in numerous ways, but we often attempt to measure these differences along several common dimensions. The popular Myers-Briggs Type Indicators (MBTI) differentiate people on these dimensions: extrovert-introvert, sensing-intuitive, thinking-feeling, and judging-perceiving.

Another set of dimensions, referred to as the "Big Five" personality factors, includes extroversion, agreeableness, conscientiousness, emotional stability, and openness to experience. As personalities differ, the potential for conflict grows. As we will discuss later, some people cannot separate the person from the issue. Personalities clash, people dislike each other; and they act out their differences and dislikes by being conflictual in one way or another.

In addition to bringing their personalities to work, some, unfortunately, may bring psychological disorders. They suffer from depression, paranoia, bipolar disorder, or some other neurosis or psychosis. These individuals may find it extremely difficult to cope with circumstances that cause conflict. They may not be in full control of their thoughts or behaviors. Unfortunately, some of them can pose a danger to themselves and to others who occupy the common space of work.

Furthermore, others may suffer physical ailments that make it difficult to cope with the working environment. A person suffering a chronic backache or arthritis may be less agreeable than someone who is not so afflicted. To be complete, the diagnosis of conflict at work must account for such possibilities as well as the many others that trigger disagreement or render situations so intolerable that coping skills become inadequate.

Personalities. A chemicals company recruits a group of world-class scientists. In the main, these scientists are very introverted, analytical and critical, extremely conscientious, and mercurial. On top of this, the scientists' extensive education and training has reinforced this type of personality. Although the scientists have tended, in the past, to work well among themselves or alone, this cadre of new recruits is being charged to spearhead an interdisciplinary, cross-functional, team-based approach to new product development. In addition to the scientists, the teams include data-management experts, engineers, sales, marketing research, and operations members.

Although well-intentioned and conceptually charming, the teams have a hard time working together as a unit. Personality clashes abound. Team efforts seem to drag on endlessly or collapse from the weight of spent energy without results.

The case illustrates vividly how personalities can clash in unhealthy ways. The organization had sought the very best in scientific talent, as it arguably should have done. But it paid no attention to the personalities of those it hired. Nor did it give much attention to how team configurations of different personalities would work. It is almost a textbook case of organizational ineffectiveness.

Psychological Disorders. A veteran security manager for a major bank, whose track record has been superb, has shown some performance decay in the past year. He has become rather abrasive and curt with his direct reports, something way out of character for him. Previously an on-time, no-rework producer, he has recently submitted several important reports late and below his normal standards. This almost never unnerved security manager has recently become visibly piqued when queried by his vice president of organization security systems about his delays and other signs of deteriorating performance. He has also seemed to avoid contact with colleagues when facing deadlines or milestones in other projects.

After letting this matter go without a direct confrontation for several months, the vice president finally met with the manager. In this conversation, the manager revealed that his adult-age son had recently been convicted of drug possession. The manager had become extremely distraught over this unfortunate incident, and largely blamed himself because he had divorced his wife fifteen years ago, leaving her to rear the kids without much of his direct or even distant parental involvement. Upon hearing this, the vice president urged the manager to seek counseling immediately. He did so, was diagnosed as clinically depressed, and was put on antidepressant medication. For the most part, the performance problem disappeared within a few months after treatment commenced.

This situation is not an uncommon one. Events sometimes bring on unwanted psychological problems that affect performance adversely. In other instances, more systemic psychological disorders may also require treatment. Organizations need to be mindful that these disorders may sometimes be the underlying basis for conflict. In this context, they should be acutely aware of departures from normal behaviors or demeanor.

Physiological Condition. The president of a corporate foundation showed signs of extreme stress. She lost her temper with fundraisers who failed to meet their monthly goals. She became excessively demanding of clerical staff, intolerant of the slightest error, and dismissive of any personal concerns they might have had. She pushed clients hard for progress reports and threatened no future foundation support if end products were not up to snuff.

At her annual check up, her physician found that she had extremely high blood pressure. She was resultantly experiencing headaches. In addition, she had low blood sugar and was pained by arthritis.

Once again, the source of the conflicts she was creating was not work-related, except to the extent work that may have contributed to or aggravated her medical problems. More generally, individuals and organizations cannot be unmindful of the possibility that health-related problems may cause difficulties at work. They can trigger anger, depression, and other psychological states, which make an individual more prone to precipitate or exacerbate conflict. In this same vein, as just suggested, the physiological and psychological consequences of conflict cannot be escaped. A vicious downward cycle of "conflict-disorder-more conflict" may result.

It is important to emphasize that alcohol and drug abuse directly and indirectly contribute to workplace conflict. In a direct sense, such abuse can result in attitudes and behaviors that are both disruptive and disorderly, thereby triggering workplace conflicts. Indirectly, they can produce performance weakness and lapses, which strain other workers who must pick up the slack. At the same time, alcohol and drug abuse may be aggravated by workplace conflict, which creates a vicious cycle of abuse-conflict-abuse-conflict.

INDICATORS OF WORKPLACE CONFLICT

You see indications of conflict every day, even though you may not interpret them all as such. Conflict can be manifested in a variety of different ways. Some signs are outwardly visible, others are more repressed. You should look for various indicators of conflict to begin to assess the real costs and the potential benefits of managing them effectively. Too often, what appears on the surface as just another organizational problem is really a symptom of underlying conflict. Just as the stressors behind conflict can impinge on virtually every aspect of workplace life, the indicators of conflict may be as equally widespread. Thus, relying on the traditional signals—strikes, grievances, violence—leaves an incomplete if not outright false image of the degree of conflict that may be present in an organization.

In Figure 2.3, we provide a partial list of the indicators you can look for to reveal the extent to which conflict may be creating a problem in your organization. In looking at these indicators, however, you need to be careful not to presume conflict as a cause, although in some cases this may be a quite obvious and logical deduction. Instead, you need to look for their presence in the context of causal stressors. Also, you need to be particularly mindful of trends or departures from normal patterns. With these precautions in mind, we present the possible indicators of conflict—those things, in any event, you have a vested interest in tracking.

You are likely to see indicators of conflict in at least seven aspects

Figure 2.3 Indicators of Workplace Conflict

Type	Indicators
● Entry	✓ Recruitment ✓ Selection
● Maintenance	✓ Absenteeism ✓ Tardiness ✓ Turnover
● Performance	✓ Quality ✓ Productivity ✓ Innovation
● Employee/Labor Relations	✓ Grievances ✓ Unionization ✓ Work Stoppages ✓ Complaints
● Security	✓ Theft ✓ Violence ✓ Sabotage ✓ Espionage
● Decision-Making	✓ Delays ✓ Judgments ✓ Errors
● Quality of Work Life	✓ Health ✓ Safety ✓ Morale/Satisfaction ✓ Security

of workplace or organizational life: entry, maintenance of the workforce, performance, employee and labor relations, security, decision-making, and quality of work life. These are not mutually exclusive. Problems in one area can spill into the next. The effects are compounding. This is partly because each of these areas—e.g., entry, maintenance, and decision-making—is multifaceted and cross-cutting. In addition, individuals may find it well nigh impossible and certainly impractical to compartmentalize their feelings about and responses to conflict, be they negative or positive.

Entry

Companies that experience extensive conflict may find it difficult to recruit and select the candidates they want. If a company acquires a reputation as a difficult—highly conflictual—place to work, it may suffer tremendously in the recruitment process, especially where the word-of-mouth network is extensive or if the company has had considerable bad press. Two possible indicators of conflict or at least symptoms of conflict are:

- A shrinking pool of qualified job applicants
- A declining selection success rate—i.e., a declining ratio between accepted job offers and job offers made

Maintenance

Companies experiencing unwanted and unhealthy conflicts will find it increasingly difficult to maintain their workforce. This is analogous to trying to maintain a marriage in a constant state of disruptive conflict. Employees, like spouses, will resort to all sorts of coping behaviors. In substantial part, they may choose to avoid or escape the conflict and its source—the relationship to work or with a spouse.

Therefore, we would expect to see the effects of conflict manifested in behaviors associated with withdrawing from work: absenteeism, tardiness, and turnover—voluntary in a purely technical sense but involuntary from a psychological perspective.

Every workplace will have some expected, or ambient, level of absenteeism, tardiness, and turnover. These levels may or may not be problematic, from an operational or cost standpoint. But if they should change for the worse or show signs of exceeding industry norms, then companies need to look inward for the root causes, one of which may well be conflict. The possible indicators are:

- Rate of absenteeism
- Rate of tardiness
- Rate of turnover

Performance

Clearly, the above-mentioned indicators will affect performance at work. The inability to recruit qualified or optimally qualified workers will lead to performance problems relative to more successful recruiters. Temporary or permanent withdrawal can also be disruptive. In addition, there are likely to be even more direct performance effects.

For example, if a worker or workforce is experiencing a conflict with management, the quality and quantity of work produced might suffer. As a practical matter, both employees and managers are devoting time and energy to the conflict rather than concentrating on work. Each of us has experienced days at work when we have had a conflict with a colleague. If this conflict is intense and emotion-laden, the effect on us can be at least temporarily debilitating. We cannot focus on work. We go over the confrontation time and time again in our minds, like a video in constant replay.

On top of problems with respect to quality and quantity, or productivity, companies may suffer from a lack of creativity and innovation. In order to be creative and innovative, individuals need some psychological space—a zone of freedom of thought and expression. There needs to be a relative risk-free zone to challenge, question, probe, think outside of the box. To some such a zone can be threatening, especially when doubts are raised about the current accepted practice. Their reaction, therefore, would be to suppress free thought—an aggressive psychological or behavioral response to actual or potential disagreement. Under these conditions, employees may feel quite reluctant to venture forward—it becomes far more tolerable to ensconce themselves in the comfort of tradition.

In sum, the performance effects of conflict may be evidenced in the:

- Quality of production or service
- Quantity of production
- Innovation or creativity

Employee and Labor Relations

We commonly associate conflict in the workplace with indicators in this area. Indeed, employee and labor relations functions exist in large measure to resolve conflicts before they become disputes or something even more serious. In the United States, as well as many other countries, the labor relations system explicitly recognizes the presence of industrial or workplace conflict. Collective bargaining exists to help constructively channel such conflict. It is, in effect, a direct form of employee involvement. In the same vein, the employee relations function encompasses types of conflict that fall outside the sphere of labor relations. Included in this expansive set are an array of EEO concerns, ranging from sexual harassment to discrimination on the basis of age, race, gender, or religion.

Indicators in this area may fall into four categories: grievances, unionization, work stoppages, and nonlabor employee complaints.

Grievances. Employees or managers may be dissatisfied with personnel or organizational actions in the form of policies or more specific decisions regarding practices that affect them at work. They feel aggrieved or mistreated, and would like some opportunity to correct the situation. Or, alternatively, these aggrieved persons may simply want an opportunity to be heard, to address their concerns in a way that will be appropriately considered by the decision makers.

In general, we associate grievances with the unionized workforce. This is because the overwhelming majority of union–management-negotiated contracts have clauses that establish a formal grievance procedure, with stipulated steps leading typically to a neutral third-party arbitration.

But grievances are by no means confined to unionized settings. Even within a unionized employer, the nonunion employees, including managers, will have their grievances. And in some instances, the grievances can be vast in number and serious in nature.

Grievances result from disagreements. They are an embodiment of conflict. In and of themselves, grievances need not be unhealthy or counterproductive, though they can be difficult to manage effectively. Obviously, there does not need to be a formal mechanism for filing a grievance in order for one to exist. But a formal mechanism does provide a means of tracking the rate of such filings and how they progress through the settlement process. A critical aspect of grievances to watch for is the rate of change. Also, grievance levels in absolute terms can become a problem, quite apart from the causes underlying them. An organization that experiences an upswing in the grievance rate, or a general level consistently above industry or occupational norms, needs to look to see what is underlying these formalized complaints. Furthermore, companies need to be cognizant of how grievance levels vary internally—across divisions and units as well as among managers and supervisors—in order to pinpoint where the problem originates.

Unionization. It has been said that the presence of a union is a telltale sign of management failure. Without necessarily endorsing this view, we can say with more than a modicum of assurance that unions feed on conflicts. They exist as a collective means for employees to voice common concerns about how they are being treated. Unions can be expected to exploit grievances in order to gain advantage.

We expect that the threat of unionization, or the culmination of a recently successful unionizing effort, is a sign of deeper conflict in the workplace. That conflict, it is worth emphasizing, can be both substantive and process-oriented. Employees may have grievances about wages, benefits, and working hours or scheduling. They may also harbor resentment over their inability to articulate their concerns in a coherent, meaningful forum to which decision makers will pay genuine attention.

Work Stoppages. Work stoppages of various kinds indicate significant and most likely problematic conflict (though it is still possible to address this conflict constructively). Strikes represent a complete withholding of labor or work, which is the essence of a stoppage—a behavioral manifestation of conflict that may also be psychologically exercised (e.g., while I am physically at work, my mind is elsewhere). Other forms of stoppages include work slow downs, sick call-ins, and work-to-rule tactics. Such stoppages, regardless of the degree to which they are exhibited, translate into idle time.

Nonlabor Complaints. Finally, as suggested earlier, there are multiple types of nonlabor employee grievances besides those that fall under the ambit of labor relations. EEO, occupational safety and health legislation, and fair labor standards laws give employees considerable protections at work. If employees believe that their rights have been denied by their employer, they may avail themselves of judicial or regulatory recourse under these sundry statutes. To initiate these procedures, it is often necessary to file a formal complaint, though companies and agencies enforcing the laws may seek ways of resolving conflicts before formal complaints need to be filed. In any event, employee complaints, especially at rates that depart from normality or reveal upward trends, may suggest a serious conflict-based problem in the workplace.

To recap, there are four indicators of conflict in the domain of employee/labor relations:

- Grievances
- Unionization
- Work stoppages
- Nonlabor employee complaints

Security

Conflicts in the workplace may pose various security threats. They can result in physical or psychological harm to individuals and damage to property as well as breaches of confidentiality and intellectual property rights. In some instances, these threats may arise in the context of wider conflicts or disputes. For example, during the course of a bitter labor-management confrontation, strikers may attempt to intimidate those who cross the picket line.

Unfortunately, psychologically disturbed employees (current and former) may seek revenge or "remedy" through acts hostile to individuals at work or the company itself. In both types of situations, the retaliatory act results from a disagreement at work and becomes a psychological way of reconciling the matter, however distorted or disturbed the logic may be to a "normal" person.

Security threats may occur in a variety of forms. Among the more commonly witnessed acts are theft, assault (directed against persons or properties), sabotage, or espionage. Together, these workplace crimes result in untold losses. And, unfortunately, advances in technology are making it easier to perpetrate many of these crimes. Witness the potential harm done by those who plant computer viruses or penetrate electronic systems or databases to acquire confidential information, which they, in turn, use for illegitimate purposes. Obviously, the ease with which protected information—trade secrets or medical records—can be violated and disseminated without detection raises the danger of espionage compromising an organization's security. Companies necessarily respond by investing vast sums in erecting firewalls and taking a multitude of other technological and non-technological precautions to minimize their risks.

In short, conflicts at work can pose threats to company security. These threats may arise in otherwise legitimate disputes or disputes that are being otherwise legitimately contested. Threats may be made by disgruntled employees with an ax to grind. Or they can be the behavioral responses of the disturbed worker who believes that this is the only effective way of dealing with a problem at work. Unfortunately, to some, committing a threatening act—from stealing a computer or abusing a co-worker verbally to sharing trade secrets with competitors— becomes a way of evening the score. Possible indicators of escalating conflict are:

- Rising incidents of theft
- Increasing incidents of violence (property destruction, assaults, threats of bodily harm, harassment, etc.)
- Increasing incidents of sabotage
- Rising levels of espionage or evident breaches of confidentiality and loss of intellectual property

Decision Making

We may also expect conflicts, if not properly managed, to diminish the quality of decision making. Disagreements and disagreeing can serve the essential purpose of revealing new information or ensuring that decision makers hear what they need to hear but do not necessarily want to hear. We are all familiar with the fears and risks of being the messenger who brings bad news. But sometimes the bad news can prevent mistakes from happening.

Conversely, conflicts or the mere possibility of disagreement may be sufficient cause for some to avoid sharing information. In a slightly different vein, personality clashes may lead to distortions, both in terms of the presentation and interpretation of information. People will allow their likes and dislikes of others to affect how they view what is being said. They will also certainly allow these factors to affect how much and how well they listen. We have an amazing capacity to tune into people we like or to turn off those whom we dislike, not matter how relevant the message is.

Yet another twist is the very real possibility that those who are in the midst of conflict may withhold important information or tactically display data for unfair advantage. This can be a form of vengeance or a simple promotion of self-interest, analogous to the prisoner's dilemma phenomenon in which individuals pursue their own interests at the expense of the common good.

The fundamental point is that conflicts may corrode or corrupt decision making in organizations in several ways. Conflicts can distort communication, which is vital to effective decision making. These distortions may advertently or inadvertently delay decision, lead to poor judgments, or erroneous actions.

Illustratively, a company embroiled in a conflict with another over a possible joint venture may withhold critical information, effectively delaying the decision on how to proceed. A proponent of a proposed controversial acquisition may not convey an entirely truthful picture of the caliber of the management team in place at the targeted company in order to increase the chances of the acquisition taking place. As another example, a disgruntled executive could falsify information in a company's annual investors' report in order to create an embarrassing situation.

Obviously, it is often difficult to measure, let alone tie, bad decision making to conflicts at work. Again, however, the goal is to identify possible indicators of conflict, which include:

- Delays in decision making
- Misjudgments in decisions
- Bad decisions

Quality of Work Life

Because conflicts involve emotions, perceptions, and behaviors, they will affect the quality of work life (QWL). In other words, conflict can directly and indirectly affect our psychological and physical well being, which are core aspects of the QWL. Just consider momentarily how we feel when we are engaged in a disagreement with a boss, a co-worker, or a business partner. If things are not going well, we may feel hurt, angry, resentful, or extremely disappointed—let down, if you will. These kinds of feelings can lend themselves to temporary or more serious psychological or physical lapses.

Therefore, it is distinctly possible that conflict can affect our health, both from a physical and psychological standpoint. In may also affect safety at work. An individual preoccupied with a conflict may make a mistake that exposes another to danger. Think of a preoccupied pilot, police officer, fire fighter, or surgeon.

Similarly, conflicts at work can sap morale and erode satisfaction. They can cause people to not want to come to work. They can make people less motivated to perform while at work. The effects, moreover, of demoralization and dissatisfaction can be infectious.

Finally, conflicts may greatly affect the degree of security—in a psychological sense—one has at work. How secure do you feel in your job? If you are engaged in a conflict or a series of disagreements with superiors, co-workers, subordinates, or customers, you may have profound reservations about job security. Is your authority or power being challenged? Are you taking a risk in challenging a colleague or superior? Are you viewed as an iconoclast, malcontent, or dissenter? These are concerns that, if shared by others, can strike directly at our sense of security in an organization. If our security is threatened, then we can be expected to engage in all sorts of protective behavior, including looking for another job or being meticulously careful to avoid any controversy and stay out of the spotlight while at work.

In brief, conflicts can lead to:

- Escalating health-benefit uses, employee assistance program (EAP) referrals, and workers' compensation claims
- Increasing problems with or incidents of safety violations
- Decreasing employee morale and satisfaction
- Growing job insecurities

Together, the indicators can be very costly for an organization, and not just in terms of money.

THE COSTS OF WORKPLACE CONFLICT

Conflicts cost organizations. Simply put, conflicts consume resources that your company needs in order to produce goods and deliver services. Your organization pays for these resources to begin with, and the costs will be incurred regardless of whether they are being expended for productive purposes or unproductive conflicts. Conflicts may also produce so-called externalities. These are consequences which may extend beyond the individuals, units, or organizations involved. Your company pays lawyers to defend themselves in disputes litigated by employees. They pay at least part and in some cases most of the costs incurred when employees need health care as a result of conflict-induced ailments. Your company absorbs the costs of conflict resolution systems it may choose to design and implement. Along these same lines, your company pays for the additional risks it needs to manage as a result of the possibility of conflicts: more insurance, greater security, training, and technology-based protections.

In Figure 2.4, we identify three types of costs companies incur because of conflict: direct, indirect, and opportunity costs. (In this context, we are focusing on the negative effects of conflict, not the possible benefits from disagreeing with faulty policy or practice in an organization.) Some of these costs, obviously, are more readily measured than others, especially if their attribution to a specific conflict is to be factored more or less precisely into the calculation. Nonetheless, with the introduction of certain assumptions, it is possible to profile an organization's conflict-related costs.

Direct Costs

The direct costs of conflict include the following:

• *Labor.* The amount of time devoted to conflict, from its initiation to its escalation and resolution. This can be multiplied by a combined direct (wages) and indirect (benefits) factor to yield a labor cost.

• *Overhead.* Just as organizations pay overhead costs for productive activities, they also incur such costs for unhealthy activities, such as needless or destructive disagreement.

Figure 2.4 Costs of Workplace Conflict

Type	Indicators
• Direct Costs	√ Labor *Time & Compensation √ Overhead √ Litigation Settlements √ Replacement √ Workers Compensation √ Health Care √ Security
• Indirect Costs	√ Quality Defects √ Lost Productivity √ Lost Revenue √ Compensation Premium √ Excess Capacity
• Opportunity Costs	√ Missed Opportunities

● *Litigation.* When conflicts become disputes, the possibility of litigation looms. Companies pay the costs associated with investigations, evidentiary discoveries, preparing for trial, trial itself, post-trial appeals, should they occur, and any settlement terms owed.

● *Replacement.* Voluntary and involuntary turnover resulting from conflicts require that organizations seek replacements. The recruiting and selection processes must be recycled. Unfilled positions are like unwanted inventory, with companies absorbing the carrying costs. Finally, there are the sunk costs of training and education invested in this departing class of employees, which cannot be recovered.

● *Workers' Compensation.* Conflicts can trigger certain effects, such as workplace injury or stress, which necessitate seeking workers' compensation. Workers' compensation provides first-dollar medical coverage and stipends to protect a person during his or her period of incapacitation.

● *Health Care.* Similarly, conflicts can result in certain psychological or physical ailments that require treatment. To a substantial extent, these costs are borne by the company.

● *Security.* Companies will incur the costs of additional security steps needed because of the risks and dangers of conflict-related problems. The costs include the additional screening procedures needed to prevent maladjusted individuals from being hired, the costs of additional security personnel, the costs of additional security technology and equipment, and the costs of extended insurance coverage.

In essence, conflict at work, to the extent it results in the unproductive consumption of resources and various negative externalities, produces several major types of direct costs. You can convert these costs into monetary values in order to give your company a yardstick by which to compare itself to others and to monitor trends over time. Standing alone, however, these monetary values do not answer the question as to whether the costs are too high. The answer will depend on the contexts in which they are being incurred (e.g., is the company overall doing well vis-a-vis competitors?), the root causes behind the conflicts (e.g., bitter interdivisional feuds or class-action discrimination lawsuits), the manifestations of the conflict (e.g., violence, theft, or sabotage), and the short- or long-term nature of the conflict (is it something likely to recur or is it a rare occurrence?).

Indirect Costs

Organizations will also suffer various indirect costs from conflicts that create problems or that are otherwise poorly handled. These are the kinds of costs that exceed those more or less directly incurred. In this regard, the effects of conflict cannot always be confined to the principals or to those immediately surrounding them. In addition, the costs may compound over time. Furthermore, they may involve seemingly rational actions that are really perverse responses to conflicts. Take the case where a company reorganizes an office merely to separate two employees with an intense personality clash. The reorganization itself may be couched as an effort to achieve greater efficiencies when, in fact, it is an inefficient response to unproductive behaviors. Nevertheless, the change may be necessary to solve the problem.

In brief, indirect costs can be incurred in the form of quality defects, lost productivity (above and beyond the time and compensation of those directly involved), and lost revenue (in the form of sales never made, invoices never collected, and other billing errors). In addition, companies that experience high turnover and difficulties in successfully recruiting and placing employees—at least partly because of disturbing conflicts— may have to offer a compensation premium, i.e., pay more money than they would otherwise have to in order to fill slots.

Last, as suggested just above, companies may take what are in reality "perverse" steps to adjust to conflict or patterns of conflicts. It is conceivable that one such type of response is adding more capacity, or, in effect, excess capacity. A company may hire more people or use overtime in order to get work done that is not getting done because of unproductive conflict. If you cannot work through the problem, then work around it. The work does get done, but the company pays more to do it. Ultimately, the customer suffers, and the company may lose business, which further compounds the problem. In sum, the effects of conflicts can ripple through the value chain, adding more costs and detracting from the net value.

Opportunity Costs

Opportunity costs are the most intangible of all costs incurred. Yet, they are probably the largest, especially in relation to highly unproductive and unresolvable conflicts. A maxim of life in general is that what matters most is not always what happens to you but what fails to happen for you. When we are engaged in conflict, particularly of a bitter flavor, our energies are not positively directed. More important, our disaffection and hostility may be widely shared, infecting those outside the immediate circle embracing the conflict. We just cannot contain our feelings.

In these situations, we may do more harm than we realize. One result is that others may choose to distance themselves, to avoid contact, to seek safe haven. We miss opportunities to do business, whatever the business is. Consequently, our company suffers. It loses customers and revenues it might otherwise have gained. Unfortunately, we may never be aware of these lost opportunities. But if we are conflict prone and find, in comparing ourselves to the world outside, that business is passing us by, a logical inference is that we have missed opportunities because of conflict. This is why quality organizations often look for leaders to be repairers of the breach.

A MANAGER'S CONFLICT DIAGNOSIS

We have examined in some detail the various sources, indicators, and costs of workplace conflict. In doing so, we have adopted a global rather than narrow perspective. We believe that you will be far better equipped to deal with conflict if you appreciate the full breadth of its presence. If you do not comprehend the true scope of the causes and consequences of conflict at work, you will unavoidably miss opportunities to resolve it effectively. Perhaps worse, you will allow it to fester and often unintentionally exacerbate it. Some argue that denial is what contributes most to the escalation of disagreement into formal disputes and beyond.

To provide a relatively simple and quick way for you to diagnose the possible causes, indicators, and costs of workplace conflict, examine the following three checklists. Walk through them so that you can gauge the scope of conflict in your areas of work. A useful extension of the exercise is to compare where you are to where others (e.g., comparable organizations or competitors) are and to where you want to be.

Manager's Checklist 2.1: Conflict Stressors

Think in terms of the extent to which these conditions are present in your organization. Then sum the totals of the number of items checked multiplied by their respective values.

Stress or Conditions	Extent of Presence			
	To what extent are they present in your organization? (Check one)			
	Not Present (0)	Low (1)	Medium (2)	High (3)
Downsizing	☐	☐	☐	☐
Litigation Ongoing	☐	☐	☐	☐
Diversity in Workforce	☐	☐	☐	☐
Changing Employee Social Expectations	☐	☐	☐	☐
Shifting Product Demand	☐	☐	☐	☐
Profit Losses	☐	☐	☐	☐
Merger or Acquisition	☐	☐	☐	☐

	# Checked * 1	# Checked * 2	# Checked * 3	# Checked * 4
Change in Business Strategy	☐	☐	☐	☐
Change in Management Philosophy	☐	☐	☐	☐
Change in Business/ Management Leadership	☐	☐	☐	☐
Change in Key Organizational Policies Affecting Employees	☐	☐	☐	☐
Extensive Work Redesign	☐	☐	☐	☐
Expanding Workload	☐	☐	☐	☐
New Work Technology Being Introduced	☐	☐	☐	☐
Safety/Health Hazards	☐	☐	☐	☐
Use of Contingency Workers	☐	☐	☐	☐
Strict Supervision Practices	☐	☐	☐	☐

**CONFLICT
POTENTIAL SCORE:**

Total 1 + Total 2 + Total 3 + Total 4 = Overall Total

Checklist 2.2: Conflict Indicators

Think of the extent to which the following possible indicators may be a problem in your organization. Then sum the totals of the number of items checked multiplied by their respective values.

	Extent of Problem (check one)			
Conflict Indicator	Not a Problem (1)	Somewhat of a Problem (2)	A Serious Problem (3)	A Very Serious Problem (4)
Recruiting New Hires	☐	☐	☐	☐
Absenteeism	☐	☐	☐	☐

	# Checked *1	# Checked *2	# Checked *3	# Checked *4
Tardiness	☐	☐	☐	☐
Turnover	☐	☐	☐	☐
Product/Service Quality	☐	☐	☐	☐
Customer Satisfaction	☐	☐	☐	☐
Productivity	☐	☐	☐	☐
Innovativeness	☐	☐	☐	☐
Grievances	☐	☐	☐	☐
EEO Complaints	☐	☐	☐	☐
Theft	☐	☐	☐	☐
Violence	☐	☐	☐	☐
Employee Morale	☐	☐	☐	☐
Employee Satisfaction	☐	☐	☐	☐
Quality of Teamwork	☐	☐	☐	☐
Project Delays	☐	☐	☐	☐
Group Decision-Making	☐	☐	☐	☐
Workplace Accidents	☐	☐	☐	☐
Workplace Injuries	☐	☐	☐	☐
Disciplinary Actions	☐	☐	☐	☐
Workers' Compensation Claims	☐	☐	☐	☐
Employee Assistance Program Referrals	☐	☐	☐	☐

**CONFLICT POTEN-
TIAL SCORE:**

Total 1 + Total 2 + Total 3 + Total 4 = Overall Total

Manager's Checklist 2.3: Conflict Cost Calculator

This is a very simple back-of-the-envelope checklist to use to calculate (roughly) the cost of a conflict in your organization. Consider a situation in which you have been involved in a conflict with another (perhaps an employee who reports to you). Calculate the amount of time that you spent on the conflict, that the other person spent on the conflict, and that others (if any) might have spent who were involved in the conflict. Then calculate the hourly compensation allocated to each person, including yourself, and multiply that number by the total number of hours involved and sum across individuals.

Conflict Situation

Individuals Involved	Number of Hours Spent	Compensation (Direct and Indirect)/ Hour	Hours times Hourly Compensation
Yourself	_____	_____	_____
Employee	_____	_____	_____
Others	_____	_____	_____
Person X	_____	_____	_____
Person Y	_____	_____	_____
Person Z	_____	_____	_____
# People	# Hours	Total Compensation/ Hour	Total Compensation Cost

Chapter 3

Dealing with Conflict

"Flight Attendants' union approves tentative agreement with American Airlines."

"Cathay Pacific Airways fires forty-nine pilots."

"Ford retreats on tough white-collar performance appraisal system in face of lawsuit."

"Coca-Cola faced with bias lawsuit."

At work as in life, you handle conflicts with people differently. Some you want to avoid. Others you try to accommodate. Occasionally, you may get angry and aggressive. Alternatively, you may try to cooperate with people to find a mutually agreeable solution. Sometimes, you may simply split the difference or find a happy medium.

How you respond depends partly on your natural style. It also depends on learned behavior—you learn what works best for you. In addition, your response varies with the situation and context. Who is involved? What are the consequences of conflictual exchange? What does your organizational culture condone? Does it promote competition or cooperation?

You experience workplace conflict daily. You know it affects you both personally and professionally. Conflict affects how you think, behave, and feel. Sometimes with painful memory, you can recall instances in which you wish you had handled the situation better. When you or someone else mishandles conflict, you will suffer consequences. Broken relationships. Distrust. Vengeance. Squandered time. Divisive meetings.

If mismanaged, conflict at work costs you. It also costs your organization. It wastes time and money. It burns energy. It exhausts good will and morale. General Motors lost $2 billion when last struck by the United Auto Workers. How much do you think it suffered in damaged relationships, trust, and esprit de corps?

Consider these other pertinent facts as just examples that prick the surface of the costs of mishandling conflict in the workplace:

- *Fortune* 500 senior executives spend 20 percent of their time on litigation-related activities.
- One hundred twenty-six thousand grievances and arbitrations are pending at the U.S. Postal Service alone.
- Up to 30 percent of a typical manager's time is spent on interpersonal conflict.
- One out of four workers has been attacked, threatened, or harassed at work.
- It takes 216 days, on average, to resolve a charge at the Equal Employment Opportunity Commission (EEOC).

Your own self-interest and your company's well-being depend on dealing with conflict effectively. This obviously begs the question of what we mean by effective conflict management. How can you handle conflict in a way that benefits you personally, professionally, and organizationally?

CHAPTER OBJECTIVES

In this chapter we address the issue of what effective conflict management means and other related questions. More specifically, this chapter:

- Identifies the goals you should seek when handling conflict
- Presents you with strategic choices on how to deal with conflict
- Unfolds a nine-step guide to collaborative conflict resolution
- Maps the logical extensions of collaboration at work
- Gives you options if collaboration "fails"

- Shows you how to select and sequence alternative conflict resolution methods consistent with the goals of effective conflict management
- Identifies the core competencies that you and your colleagues at work will need to deal with conflict better

WHAT DO WE MEAN BY DEALING WITH CONFLICT EFFECTIVELY?

Scenario

You are a facilities manager for a large financial institution with the title of director of corporate amenities and recreation. You handle the cafeteria, the health spa, the corporate library, and corporate travel arrangements, including hotelling. You want to expand your portfolio of responsibilities so that you can one day rise to the position of vice president of corporate services. You have submitted a reorganization plan that would give you additional responsibility for site security. Your immediate superior, however, does not appear convinced you are ready, and has therefore held up the reorganization plan. This hesitation bothers you more than a little. You are preparing for a meeting to convince your superior to go ahead with the recommended reorganization and give you responsibility for site security. Your superior is known to be temperamental, sometimes difficult, often acerbic, and sometimes obstinate. How do you approach him? What do you do if he balks, gets angry, says "no" dismissively? What are your options to deal with this potential conflict?

Exercise 3.1: List Your Options

Think of a recent conflict you have had with a peer, superior, or subordinate. Jot down what the conflict, briefly, was about. Then list the various ways you could have handled it. Finally, identify how you did handle it and why it worked or did not work.

Conflict situation:

_____

_____

Approaches to deal with conflict:

1. _____

2. _____

3. _____

4. _____

5. _____

Which one did you use? Did it work? Why or why not?

_____

_____

You might think that dealing with conflict effectively means reaching an agreement. But this is far too simplistic. Agreements can be meaningful or not. They can be enforceable or not. They can actually solve underlying problems or not. They can build or damage relationships. They can prevent or invite future conflicts.

You should think of effective conflict management as consisting of several related goals:

- Preventing escalation
- Solving the real problem
- De-personalizing the disagreement

- Inventing solutions
- Building relationships
- Achieving workplace goals

First, you know that escalated conflicts will often result in disruptive behaviors. You may become involved in a pointless shouting match. You might sulk. You might harbor anger and resentment that clouds your thinking and judgment. All of this because you allowed the situation to spin out of control. Dealing with conflict effectively means avoiding those actions that fuel the fire. Think before you act. Thomas Jefferson said that when he was angry he counted to ten before he responded. When he was really angry, he counted to one hundred. Do not respond in anger, for that will likely set off a chain of reactions that make you even angrier.

Second, you want to solve the real problem. Think about how many disagreements you have had that have been wall-papered or disguised as something else. Visualize a subordinate who habitually shows up late to meetings. You extract a promise that this tardiness will not happen again. Problem solved? No! The real problem is that the subordinate disrespects you, lacks confidence in you. Showing up late merely manifests this disdain. Unless you deal with this problem, you will not avert future conflicts, though they may masquerade in different costumes, such as undermining you in the eyes of other colleagues.

Third, you must avoid personalizing the situation. Admittedly, this is easier said than done. When anger is being tossed at you, when criticism is being leveled against you, when a person is being obstinate and contrary, do not take it personally. Do not respond tit for tat. Count to ten or one hundred. Think empathetically. Remember you do not have to deny your interests, reach an unwise agreement, or tolerate abuse. Stay in control of yourself. If you think in terms of the situation rather than how hurt your feelings are, your response will be more effective. You must apply the breaks on conflict escalation to create an opportunity for meaningful dialogue.

Fourth, to manage conflict well, you must often invent where invention seems impossible. You need to think outside the box. What are the possible options? Imagine facing an employee disgruntled because he or she was denied a desirable assignment. You value the employee, but had to choose a more deserving candidate. You can understand the employee's anger and frustration. To deal with this, you could say that you will make the employee "happy" in the future. A better approach, however, is for you to deal promptly and openly with the underlying interest, which is recognition and opportunity for the employee. Do not let the discontent fester; neglect is the parent of outburst. Brainstorm possible approaches to give recognition and create opportunity. By approaching the matter inventively, you can defuse the anger, involve the employee, and show your respect.

Fifth, in dealing with conflict, you absolutely do not want to miss opportunities to build relationships. Sometimes you may not be able to satisfy everyone's needs or allay all relevant concerns. But you can make a good faith effort that inspires trust, belief in your sincerity, and appreciation of the realities you confront. You create mutual understanding and respect—the building blocks of sound relationships.

Sixth, in a workplace context, effective conflict management requires you to keep an eye on the broader mission. Conflict resolution is a process—a means to an end. You are at work to perform, to help the company achieve its mission, to help others serve the mission. You cannot "solve" conflict by taking actions that are contrary to the goals and interests of the organization. You should not set harmful precedents, create inequities, falsely raise expectations, or squander resources in order to fix a problem. You may be tempted to appease a malcontent with a favor. But favoritism breeds envy and anger. Simply put, you should not deal with one conflict in such a way that invites many others that are even more serious. Figure 3.1 summarizes the goals of effective conflict management. To a large extent, you will find them mutually supportive.

Figure 3.1 Goals of Effective Conflict Management

● Prevent escalation.	Avoid actions that escalate the conflict, forcing a response—counterresponse chain reaction of negative behaviors.
● Focus on the real problem.	Get to the bottom of the situation. Do not mistake symptoms for causes. Probe the underlying issues.
● Avoid personalization.	Try not to take things personally. Think emphathetically and sympathetically. Speak in objective, situational terms.
● Invent solutions.	There is more than one road to Rome or path to success. Think broadly and creatively. Do so even when you think it might not be absolutely necessary.
● Build relationships.	Never miss a chance to build a relationship. Share interests, concerns. Inspire trust.
● Achieve workplace goals.	Managing conflict does not occur in a personal vacuum. How you deal with it has broader professional and organizational implications. Never lose sight of the fact that how you deal with something today can come back to haunt you tomorrow.

STRATEGIC APPROACHES TO DEALING WITH CONFLICT AT WORK

Scenario

You are an HR professional assigned to the organizational effectiveness staff at the research and development site of a global food manufacturer. One of your responsibilities is to work with newly created cross-discipline product development teams consisting of scientists, engineers, market researchers, and information systems analysts. Nominally, the scientists head the teams, but the groups are expected to function collaboratively. Your job is to see to it that they have the support from organizational effectiveness to work collaboratively.

One team in particular is encountering problems, which are affecting harmony in the ranks. The head scientist is a bit authoritarian and elitist. Interpersonal relations are not his strong point. You have been asked to "coach" the team and the scientist. You have had one preliminary telephone conversation with the scientist, who said that "his team" did not need your interference and that it was doing just fine without "organizational effectiveness." It is now two days later, and you are on your way to your first in-person meeting with the scientist. What approach should you take?

In theory and reality, you do have options, but they are not likely to be equally effective. You have five choices on the menu: accommodation, avoidance, collaboration, competition, and compromise (see Figure 3.2). You should view these as strategic choices. That is, you decide which one to use. You should bear in mind that you can switch choices as circumstances dictate. In addition, you may choose to act mildly or strongly one way or another. You do not have to be purely competitive or compromising. Also, none of these approaches requires you to be adversarial, disrespectful, hostile, or inciting, although competition is often associated with these behaviors.

Thus, as the HR professional, you may choose to accommodate, avoid, collaborate, compete, or compromise. Let's see how you would exercise your options. If you were to *accommodate*, then you would defer to

Figure 3.2 Alternative Strategic Approaches to Conflict

Strategy	Behavior
Accommodation	A party concedes to the other's position. Is not assertive of own interests or needs or positions.
Avoidance	A party ignores, denies, escapes. Is proactive in avoiding confronting the other party or issue.
Collaboration	A party seeks a win–win outcome that is naturally satisfactory. Is assertive of own interests and empathizes with the other party's.
Competition	A party is selfishly motivated and behaving. Is interested in winning, pure and simple.
Compromise	A party is willing to settle for half a loaf. Is inclined to split the difference to get the matter settled if not resolved.

the scientist. You would not challenge him to take a different tack. By no means would you be confrontational. In so doing, you would not deal with the problem, which is the scientist's unwillingness to be a team player. Most likely, you would only postpone a more difficult encounter by being an accommodator.

Alternatively, you could behave as the HR professional escapist—the consummate *avoider*. In this role, you would try to avoid the in-person encounter. Assuming, however, that the encounter occurred, you would try to avoid the subject. You might concoct an artificial agenda to deflect attention from the real issue. Most likely, you might find neutral territory to occupy, discussing innocuous topics. Once again, you have not addressed the problem. More disturbingly, you have given your approval, however tacitly, to the scientist's conduct. Consequently, you will find it more difficult to correct in the future if compelled to do so.

Using your third option, you could approach the scientist *collaboratively*. You would attempt to identify the underlying interests and needs of the scientist. You would not deny or fail to assert the organizational interest in product development teamwork. But you would look for ways to serve that purpose while simultaneously satisfying the scientist's needs. Simply put, you look for ways to make his teamwork useful to him. You might appeal to his position as a role model and the critical leadership he provides because of his professional stature.

If you were to *compete* or try to dominate—your fourth option—you would be interested in controlling the exchange. You want to win an argument. You're interested in convincing the scientist he must change. Its "my-way-or-the-highway." No need to explore options, identify needs, or achieve mutual satisfaction. In the short term, you may get what you want: submission. But you will probably provoke resentment and invite vengeance.

Your fifth choice is *compromise*. In this case, you might attempt logrolling, giving one thing in exchange for another. You seek a temporary truce. You could, for example, ask the scientist to temper his style in exchange for a plum future assignment or a new team complement. In so doing, however, you have not solved the problem. Instead, you may have created a monster by setting a dangerous precedent.

WHICH STRATEGY SHOULD YOU USE?

We advocate collaborating. We also advocate acting collaboratively when you might be thinking competitively. In the case above, the HR professional should try to collaborate with the head scientist, no matter how difficult the process or the person.

Collaboration fits nicely with the goals of effective conflict resolution. It emphasizes getting to the real problem, exploring options, meeting interests, and building relationships. In other words, collaboration is outcome and relationship focused.

Figure 3.3 presents the "dual-concerns" model of conflict resolution. It suggests that the preferred strategy depends on two concerns: one, the degree to which the relationship is valued, and two, the degree to which

Figure 3.3 CR Strategy Outcome–Relationship Graph

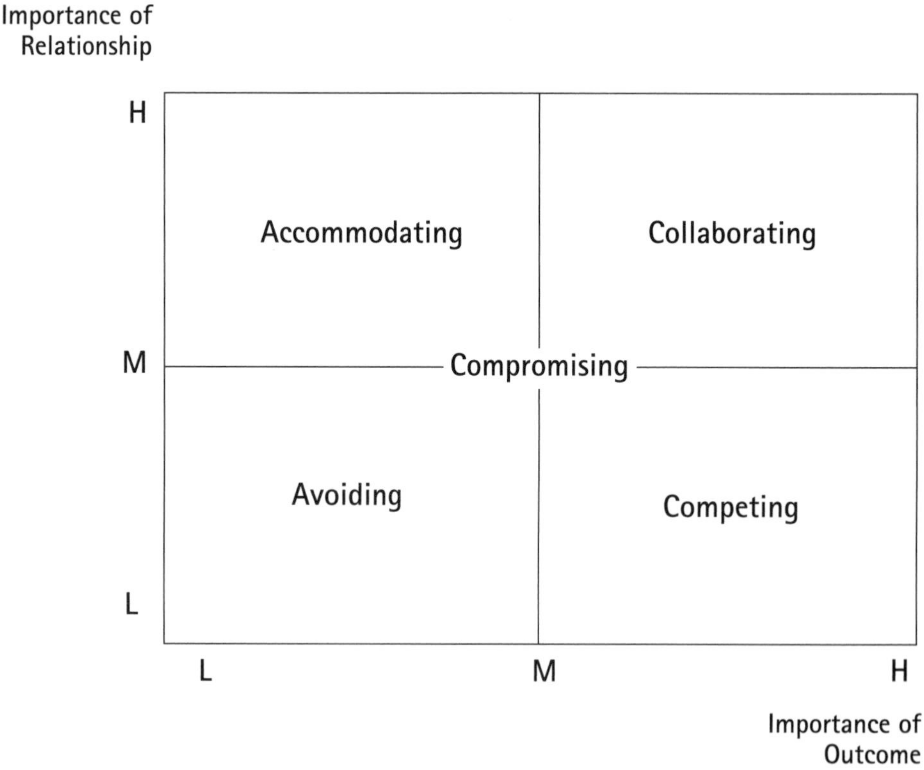

Importance of
Relationship

H	Accommodating	Collaborating
M		Compromising	
L	Avoiding	Competing

L   M   H

Importance of
Outcome

the outcome is valued. When the outcome and relationship are highly valued, collaboration emerges as the preferred choice.

At work, your willingness to collaborate is important because relationships are often long-term and unavoidably proximate. The corporate push for teamwork reinforces this tendency. Also, you should not underestimate the importance of workplace outcomes to employees, no matter how minor or trivial they may appear at first glance. Sometimes the smallest recognitions, rewards, or opportunities can be valued quite highly, because they affect relative status or one's sense of fair treatment.

More specifically, collaboration is preferable when:

- Relationships are important
- Relationships are interdependent
- Mutual interests exist
- Outcomes are important
- Maintaining teams is important
- Creating a team-based working environment is important
- The nature of work is integrated
- Cultural, professional, and occupational differences exist
- The parties want to achieve better outcomes
- The potential for escalated conflict is high

At the same time, you should be aware of what collaboration is *not*. Collaboration does not mean:

- Being overly nice
- Agreeing for the sake of getting things settled
- Jeopardizing important interests
- Sacrificing rights or principles
- Tolerating unacceptable or inappropriate behavior
- Avoiding difficult topics or people

THE NINE STEPS OF COLLABORATION

Figure 3.4 illustrates the nine steps of collaboration. Before diving in, you should know that this is not a lockstep procedure. Collaboration should

Figure 3.4 The Collaborative Approach
A Nine–Step Guide

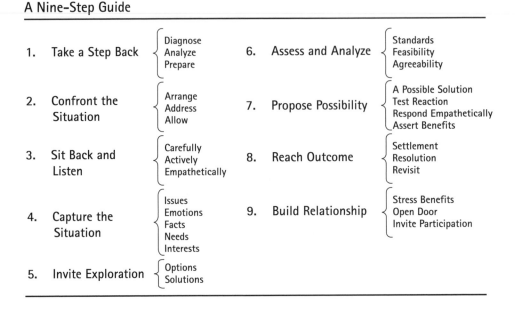

1.	Take a Step Back	Diagnose / Analyze / Prepare	
2.	Confront the Situation	Arrange / Address / Allow	
3.	Sit Back and Listen	Carefully / Actively / Empathetically	
4.	Capture the Situation	Issues / Emotions / Facts / Needs / Interests	
5.	Invite Exploration	Options / Solutions	
6.	Assess and Analyze	Standards / Feasibility / Agreeability	
7.	Propose Possibility	A Possible Solution / Test Reaction / Respond Empathetically / Assert Benefits	
8.	Reach Outcome	Settlement / Resolution / Revisit	
9.	Build Relationship	Stress Benefits / Open Door / Invite Participation	

be dynamic, fluid, and flexible, rather than rigid, mechanical, or linear. Feel free to move forward or backward as needed. Just keep your eye on the goal: effective conflict management. And remember the person with whom you are dealing may see the world, at work and elsewhere, quite differently from you. That is one reason why opening a dialogue and listening are so essential to making the process work.

Step 1: Take a Step Back

The first thing you want to do wherever you can is to take a step back—give yourself some time to think. In the scenario involving the HR professional and the head scientist, you would want to spend some time diagnosing the situation, analyzing the problem, and preparing some solutions for discussion. What interests are involved from each party's and the organization's perspectives? Is the head scientist in over his head? Is the team poorly comprised or equipped? Are there personality clashes at play? Is the concept of the team threatening to professional independence and stature? Has the organization done the necessary groundwork to prepare people for teams? Is the HR system—in terms of selection, compensation, and performance management—aligned with teamwork?

You also want to assess the nature of the issue: Are there principles or rights involved? Are the stakes high?

Step 2: Confront the Situation

You want to arrange a meeting. By going to the head scientist's office, you are signaling your respect. Find a mutually comfortable time. Break the issue situationally, asking if there is anything that organizational effectiveness can do. Give the head scientist an opportunity to explain the situation. Do not present the issue in a threatening, accusatory manner by saying something like: "You have presented me with quite a problem. What are you going to do to get yourself and me out of this predicament?" You may choose to say something more like: "Teams are challenging and we are interested in making certain that they can benefit from your talents. How might we help you?"

Step 3: Sit Back and Listen

This is the golden opportunity you want to make happen. You must listen actively and empathetically. By listening actively, you hear not only the words but also the feelings, emotions, and thinking process behind what is being said. By listening empathetically, you put yourself in the other person's shoes. You comprehend what he is saying from his perspective. In other words, you are no longer filtering what he is saying through your own perspective of the world. Instead, you see it from his viewpoint. This is an important distinction because much of conflict is about perception: What makes no sense to you makes a lot of sense from another perspective because that person perceives the world differently.

Going back to the HR professional and head scientist, they undoubtedly have different personal, professional, and organizational perspectives. The HR professional has a responsibility to help teams work collaboratively. The scientist sees his contribution more in terms of applying scientific knowledge to inventing new products. When both parties realize that they are personally and professionally served by supporting an organizational climate conducive to teamwork that still respects everyone's contribution, you have the basis for making distinct progress.

Step 4: Capture the Situation

Once you have listened intently, you want to capture the situation. Think in terms of taking a moving picture and a snapshot. What has been said? What are the core issues (e.g., professional integrity versus forced conformity)? What interests and needs are being raised? What are the facts surrounding the situation? Is the team actually performing as badly as portrayed? Is the team really an outlier or is the problem more system-wide? Is the head scientist as authoritarian and elitist as described? Sometimes we enter meetings like this one between the HR professional and head scientist misinformed about the real situation. Be open to changing your perception of the situation if contravening data are presented.

Step 5: Invite Exploration

You need to create an environment in which the parties to a conflict (at whatever stage it might be) are open to exploring options to address the issues raised. You should, however, avoid the mistake of proposing the solution early on the session or meeting. Coming to the meeting with a preordained conclusion or solution closes your mind to better options. Also, you tell the other person that his or her thoughts really do not matter. You know what is right. When this happens, you may find the person disagreeing simply because of having been excluded.

What you want to do is discuss possible options and possible solutions. Brainstorm. Encourage creative ideas. And listen. Do not reject ideas just because they do not square with your thinking. You will be surprised at how inventive people can be if given the freedom to let their intellectual juices flow.

Step 6: Assess and Analyze

Once you have generated a list of options to meet the underlying interests, you need to assess them. This requires that you come up with some reasonable analytical criteria. Reasonable means in the eyes of both parties, not just one side's. Feasibility is a possible criterion. Another is whether or not the solution proposed is really a mutually agreeable one. Relative costs and benefits can also be explored more or less precisely. In short, you want to come up with a set of standards by which to assess the options.

For example, it might have been proposed that the head scientist's team invite a facilitator to help things work more smoothly. Is there precedent for that within the company? Are facilitators available? How much does a facilitator cost and is that cost affordable? Is the head scientist comfortable with that option—is he willing to let it work?

Step 7: Propose Possibilities

In this step, you want to steer the meeting toward a set of possible solutions. The analysis conducted in the preceding step should have weeded out some of the options. Now you can focus on the possible solutions in more depth. But these are possibilities, not decrees. Respond empathetically to possibilities offered by the other side. Identify their possible benefits before laundering the costs. Test reactions to your suggestions. This is an opportunity for trial balloons. You are fine-tuning the collaborative process.

Step 8: Reach Outcome

After you have proposed possibilities and explored their benefits and costs against various decision-making standards, reach a consensus. Reach a settlement or, ideally, a resolution. If facilitation is the basis for an agreement, discuss how it will work, how the facilitator will be selected, and what you expect to achieve. If you are uncertain that the proposed settlement or resolution will work, then propose revisiting the matter to assess progress in a timely manner.

Step 9: Build Relationship

To a certain extent, you have been trying to do this throughout the process. Too often, however, exchanges like these end with the settlement (outcome) highlighted and the relationship undernourished. After reaching an agreement, spend some time on relationship building. Stress the benefits of the exchange—getting an opportunity to see different perspectives to generate new ideas, to understand the situation better, and to build a strong professional relationship. Open the door for future discussions on this and other matters. Invite continuing participation in the teamwork development process. This, as previously said, is an opportunity you do not want to miss.

COLLABORATIVE APPLICATIONS

The collaborative approach can be applied widely in the workplace. As we said earlier, it can be applied in conflicts involving interests, rights, and power, although it may need to be combined with other dispute resolution methodologies when issues involving rights or power struggles exist. (It becomes more difficult as a resolution technique standing alone when the conflict involves a contest of will or a fundamental right or principle.) In the vein, you can view workplace collaboration as the hub of the wheel. It can be used to address a myriad of workplace issues that may cause disagreement between those with a workplace nexus.

From this hub, you can draw several spokes to explain the business-related applicability of collaboration. As you can see in Figure 3.5, the spokes lead you in several important directions, which are central to work. These applications become increasingly more important as the nature of work and the workplace itself become more seamless. They become more relevant as the whole value chain of production becomes more integrated. And, they become more important as the nature of the employment relationship becomes more varied, less permanent, and more flexible.

In short, you can avail yourself of the collaborative approach in a host of business interactions. Build an encompassing corporate capability in this regard with extensive internal and external applications. Think of collaboration as a way of building relationships between yourself, your team, your unit, and your company, on the one hand, and, on the other hand,

Figure 3.5 The Hub and Spoke of Workplace Collaboration

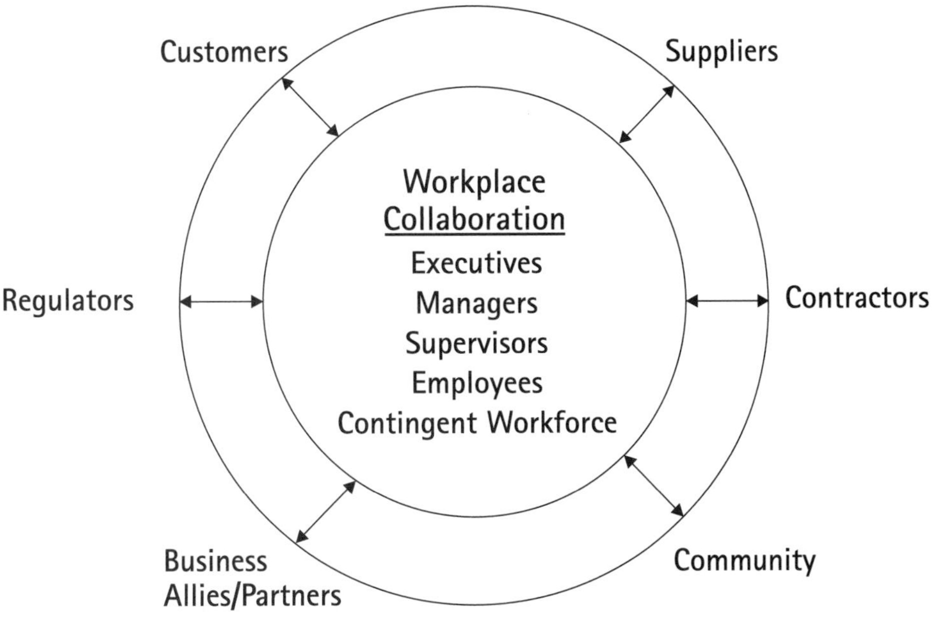

your customers, your suppliers, your contractors, your regulators, and your community.

WHAT IF COLLABORATION "FAILS?"

In collaboration, the principal parties to a disagreement remain in control over the process, outcome, and their relationship, to the extent the context allows. But you know that collaboration, however desirable it may be, does not always succeed. Sometimes it "fails." What do you do then? You can look at this question from both a personal or professional level and an organizational viewpoint.

You should know, however, that we use the term "fail" advisedly. You should not think that collaboration has failed because a settlement or agreement was unobtainable. This is particularly true in the initial stages of collaboration. Do not view collaborating as a discrete, one-shot attempt. It is a process. Moreover, by trying to collaborate, the parties may have avoided escalation and moved closer to agreement or resolution than would have otherwise been the case. And their relationship may be better off for having made the effort, even though settlement proved elusive. The situation is not hopeless and the parties are not hapless when collaboration falls short of agreement.

You should view collaboration between the principals as the first step of what is sometimes a long journey. A good conflict resolution system opens the door for other alternative dispute resolution procedures (see Figure 3.6).

If you do not achieve a settlement or resolution (one that hopefully addresses the real problem in a mutually satisfactory way), you may have entered a phase in the conflict resolution process where you are at an impasse, stalemate, or deadlock. For whatever reason, be it interpersonal conflict or division over fundamental principles, you cannot resolve matters in disagreement. But you are still interested in pursuing agreement without resorting to arbitration, litigation or something even worse, such as sabotage, public embarrassment, or exodus. You need assistance. You want to salvage the effort and relationship before things break down to the point where litigation, striking, or quitting the organization are the only options the parties can see.

When the principals struggle with seeming futility, inviting further decay in the relationship, they need to think about third-party interven-

Figure 3.6 What If Collaboration "Fails"

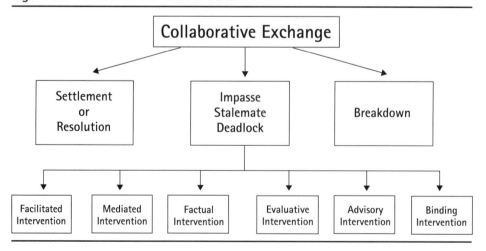

tion. These interventions can be distinguished by the nature and extent of the third party involved. Figure 3.6 presents these interventions in what you may view as a progression in decision-making involvement.

Facilitated Intervention

In this case, a facilitator or conciliator becomes involved in trying to improve the flow of information between the disputing parties. The facilitator, as we will discuss more fully in Chapter 5, focuses on process not outcome. The rationale is that by improving information exchange, you will be better able to find your way to agreement.

Mediated Intervention

To some, this is a notch above facilitation. In traditional mediation, the neutral mediator works with the parties to fashion an agreement. The mediator, like the facilitator, does not have authority to impose an agreement. But the mediator's involvement may be more substantive than that associated with the facilitator.

Factual Intervention

In this arena, you may call upon varyingly neutral and impartial factfinders, investigators, or ombuds to conduct an investigation to gather the relevant facts in a workplace dispute. These investigators do not have the power to impose settlements, though they may be empowered to recommend solutions and work toward a facilitated or mediated resolution. The principal expectation is that gathering the facts and portraying them in an objective light will motivate the parties to resolve the conflict themselves.

Evaluative Intervention

In this methodology, you are moving closer to decision making. This approach is sometimes referred to as neutral evaluation or early neutral evaluation. Essentially, before you go to a decision-making venue (e.g., litigation or arbitration), you ask the neutral to opine about how such a decision might come out if pushed to a higher level, so to speak. Presenting the neutral with the facts and arguments behind a dispute, you invite his or her informed evaluation or forecast. This is another way of trying to get the parties to assess realistically the risks and costs of going to court. Again, bear in mind you are pursuing means of alternative dispute resolution.

Advisory Intervention

Advisory intervention moves you another step closer to decision making. You empower a neutral or panel of neutrals to issue an advisory judgment. The neutral hears the evidence, then presents a recommended settlement. The disputing parties are not bound by the advice, but they are expected to give it serious consideration. Otherwise, a lot of time and effort have simply gone down the drain. Advisory arbitration fits this bill of particulars.

Binding Intervention

At this stage, you invite a binding decision. The process is typically structured to be adversarial, though not as formalized or costly as litigation. Once again, a neutral or panel of neutrals is commissioned to hear a dispute and then render a judgment. Unlike advisory judgments, these judgments are binding on the parties. Binding arbitration is an increasingly prevalent alternative to litigation in the area of employment or workplace disputes.

THE BUILDING BLOCKS OF CONFLICT RESOLUTION

You now have the basic items on the conflict resolution menu. First, you may work with the disputing party through one or more of the conflict resolution strategies. Second, if you, as one the principals, cannot resolve the matter in conflict, you may avail yourself of a host of third-party interventions shy of litigation or some other extreme measure. Now, the question you face is how to organize these options in a sequence or order that makes sense.

Figure 3.7 diagrams a few alternative ways to sequence the building blocks of conflict resolution. As you can see, the alternatives vary according to the basic nature of the dispute. We advise that this is only one approach. As we will discuss in the last part of the book, you want to build a model that serves your organizational needs consistent with certain legal and moral principles.

To refer to the conflict-type classification we presented earlier, you can group most conflicts as those involving interests, rights, and power. (You realize, however, that conflicts may fall into more than one category and evolve into multifaceted disputes over time.) *Interest-based conflicts,* which cover a wide spectrum of workplace disputes, can arise over the

Figure 3.7 The Building Blocks of Conflict Resolution

Conflict Type	Non-Intervening	Non-Decisional Involvement	Decisional Intervention

Interest-Based
  Physiological
  Psychological
  Emotional
  Professional
  Occupational
  Social
  Spiritual
  Economic
	Collaboration	Facilitation
		or
		Investigation
		or
		Mediation
			Advisory

Rights-Based
  Equity
  Justice
  Procedural
	Collaboration	Facilitation
		or
		Investigation
		or
		Mediation
			Binding

Power-Based
  Abuse
  Dereliction
  Inappropriate Use
	Collaboration	Facilitation
		or
		Investigation
		or
		Mediation
			Advisory
			or
			Binding

need to satisfy certain psychological needs and the adequacy of basic workplace safety and health conditions to the need for appropriate recognition and reward. Involving basic interests, these types of conflicts are often viewed as quite amenable to collaborative resolution, if the parties are willing to make the effort. In any event, noninterventionist strategies to resolve these conflicts—collaboration, bargaining, etc.—are preferred as a first step to give the parties control over the processed outcome.

If that fails, then a non-decisional intervention may be employed. In this vein, facilitation or mediation become viable steps. These conflict resolution alternative procedures do not impose settlements but they hopefully improve the process of interaction to make settlement or resolution possible.

Last, if this intermediate stage fails, the parties may resort to an advisory decisional mechanism, such as advisory arbitration. Here, they are given the benefit of a neutral's advice in the form of a formal recommendation. But they are free to reject it. Thus, they still retain ultimate control over the outcome.

Rights-based controversies arise over matters involving equitable treatment, justice, and procedural fairness. For example, employees may feel that they were denied promotions because of their age, race, gender, or disability, all of which situations are protected by law. These conflicts can often be very contentious, emotional, and wrought with core principles. They can lend themselves to adversarial confrontations. To the extent, however, that they involve misunderstandings or underpinning interests, then it makes sense to try to resolve them collaboratively or, if that does not work, through nondecisional interventions such as mediation. (This is the philosophy behind the Equal Employment Opportunity Commission's mediation program, which we take up in Chapter 10.) However, because rights are involved, it is important that the parties know that the ultimate settlement will not depend upon a contest of power or the whim of the organization. That is why a binding, neutral decision is often desirable as a last step. This binding process can be structured so that it is much less expensive and time-consuming than litigation. But the opportunity for finality through a balanced, neutral process is critical when one party, e.g., a disgruntled low-ranking clerical worker, might feel either overpowered or oppressively disadvantaged.

Power-based struggles are more difficult to get a handle on because the term is so nebulous. But power conflicts can range from a pure contest of will (where collaboration can seem hopeless or pointless) to questions about whether power has been abused, or inappropriately used. Very often these questions will also involve rights or interests. For instance, a supervisor who fails to promote an employee may be charged with discrimination or the inappropriate use of power, if the seemingly objective criteria used to make the decision were improperly applied.

Accordingly, there are circumstances in which the parties may be encouraged to resolve the disagreement collaboratively and that nonbinding third-party interventions be made available to clear the air and get to the bottom of the situation. If that fails, then you may want to consider advisory or binding arbitration of the dispute. Sometimes, power-based controversies can boil down to managerial or organizational discretion. If the goal is to preserve such discretion while offering the aggrieved some recourse, then the advisory option gains favor.

In sum, you can arrange conflict resolution options, from collaboration to binding arbitration, to give your organization multiple venues in which to resolve disputes. The availability of a sequence of options can permit the early resolution of conflict while avoiding litigation should the principals' efforts fail to yield a settlement. The sequencing can also be used to reinforce the basic rights of employees and to arrest the abuse or misuse of power.

CORE COMPETENCIES

To manage conflict effectively, you need more than awareness of the menu of options and knowledge about the technique of collaboration. You need to develop certain core competencies that will improve your overall conflict resolution capability. Such development benefits you personally and professionally, increasing your satisfaction at work and your value to the organization.

As a key organization player, you can help build an organizational capability to handle conflict constructively. You may help design a training program to develop employees' core competencies in this area. You can also serve as a role model for others at various organizational levels to emulate. By broadening the capability of others to manage conflict, you benefit in two specific ways. First, you reduce the number of conflicts into which people will drag you because they cannot deal with them by themselves. People will manage their own conflicts better, freeing you to do other things of more strategic value. Second, your company's environment as a whole should improve. It will reflect a greater capacity to manage relationships internally and externally. The costs of doing business should go down, releasing resources that can be more productively spent. If your company is saddled with huge conflict-related costs (e.g., litigation fees, turnover, workers' compensation, formal complaints), it has less to devote to other things, from hiring needed personnel to rewarding current employees adequately. Conflict resolution affects the bottom line.

Figure 3.8 identifies five sets of core competencies associated with conflict resolution. You first need a good set of interpersonal skills, which include being able to communicate verbally and in writing, to listen ac-

Figure 3.8 Conflict Resolution Core Competencies

Interpersonal	Managerial	Analytical	Personal
Communications	Coaching	Logic	Self-Confident
Listening	Delegating	Judgment	Patient
Empathy	Meeting Management	Comprehension	Persistent
Team-Oriented	Time Management	Problem-Solving	Stamina
Discretion		Synthesizing	Risk-Tolerance
		Brainstorming	Tolerance
			Flexibility
			Humor
			Assertive

Technical
Subject Area Expertise
Information Technology

tively and empathetically, to work as a member of a team playing various team roles, and to exercise discretion in dealing with others.

You also need to be developed managerially. To the extent that you can coach others, delegate tasks, manage time, and manage meetings, you can be instrumental in handling conflict. Think of the number of meetings in which conflict has arisen because the sessions have been poorly managed. Think about the number of tight spots you have gotten into because you have not managed your time well or ignored matters that would eventually come back to haunt you.

Third, your ability to handle conflict is enhanced to the extent that your analytical skills are developed. How good are you at problem-solving, synthesizing information, brainstorming, thinking things through logically to reach viable decisions? How well do you comprehend the contexts, subtleties, and nuances of conflict? These are important elements to possess to deal with conflict at work.

Fourth, as a person you are helped if you possess certain traits. Are you self-confident and assured? Are you patient, persistent, tolerant, and flexible? Are you assertive? Do you have a sense of humor to help deflect anger and defuse hostility? These qualities can contribute to effective conflict management.

Finally, in some instances, you may be aided by possessing relevant technical knowledge or expertise. This is particularly important when the source of conflict is over technical problems or a debate as to which technical approach is best. Are you capable of speaking the language of people with technical specialties? Can you relate realistically to what they are saying? Furthermore, do you have ability to use information technology to reduce and manage conflict? Can you use information technology to present data in a way that clarifies issues rather than creating confusion that spawns more disagreement? As misinformation is often the cause of conflict, effective use of information technology can help you address this difficulty.

Manager's Checklist: Dealing with Conflict

You want to take stock of your and your organization's ability to deal with conflict effectively. Ask yourself these questions:

1. What is your preferred style of managing conflict?
2. Does your organization have a dominant conflict resolution style?
3. Are people in your organization sufficiently developed in core competencies of conflict management?
4. Does your organization experience too many problems in handling conflict?
5. Do you spend too much of your time on managing others' conflict?
6. How well does top management handle conflict?
7. Are there areas at work where conflict appears to be more of a problem?
8. Does your organization have a formal conflict resolution system?
9. Does the approach your organization takes to conflict achieve the goals of effective conflict management?
10. What would you do to improve your company's ability to manage conflict?

Exercise 3.2: Resolving a Complex Conflict

You are the vice president of engineering for a major transportation equipment manufacturer. At forty-three years of age, your climb to this high-level position has been nothing short of meteoric. You are focused, assertive, aggressive—a Type A personality. You have fifteen direct reports and over 120 engineers in your area of responsibility at corporate headquarters. You report directly to the CEO.

One of your direct reports, a senior manager with twenty-seven years of experience with the company, has had some serious reservations about a major restructuring you recently initiated. He believes that the plan is harming morale and places too much emphasis on productivity indicators as a way of evaluating and rewarding engineers, who are "professionals." You vehemently disagree. You believe the senior manager, at the age of fifty-nine, has too much invested in the status quo. He has been, in your judgment, reluctant to change and unwilling to "go along with the program."

Recently, your concerns reached a head when you gave the senior manager his annual performance review. One of the evaluative criteria is "adaptability: willingness to change as the organization requires." You gave the manager low marks on this dimension, which caused him to become perturbed. His response was that he was being judged unfairly because of his age and tenure. You suspect he thinks he should be the vice president (he was an unsuccessful candidate for the position when it was open a couple of years ago). A low performance evaluation on this critical dimension will negatively impact the senior manager's chances for plum project assignments, his expected general pay raise, and his bonus and merit raise. You suspect that he is conferring privately with an attorney about bringing an age discrimination charge against you and the company. You know, through information received from peers and other direct reports, that the senior manager has voiced his accusations and otherwise tried to drum up support for his position.

How are you going to handle this situation? What options do you have available? What do you do if a collaborative approach does not succeed? How important is it to avoid or mitigate the likelihood of litigation, or at least a formal charge being brought to the regional Equal Employment Opportunity Commission? Your company is covered by the Age Discrimination in Employment Act (ADEA) and other federal antidiscrimination laws and regulations.

PART 2

ALTERNATIVE MEANS OF RESOLVING CONFLICT: From Negotiation to Alternative Dispute Resolution with Third Parties

If your workplace situation is typical, you face an increasing number of employment conflicts and disputes, with dispute inferring a more intensified and formalized conflict. The causes of this increase vary: competitive pressures to raise productivity, relentless downsizing and restructuring, spiraling mergers and acquisitions, workforce and cultural diversification, rising employee expectations, and the explosion of new workplace technologies. Unfortunately, a growing number of these employment disputes get resolved in courts or other governmental venues. When this happens, your company's costs and risks rise. You lose control over the process of managing conflict and the outcome. A class-action discrimination suit or a single wrongful discharge suit can cost a company millions. The law has expanded the sphere of employee rights and broadened the scope of relief the aggrieved may seek.

For these reasons, your company has probably begun exploring its options in the area of alternative dispute resolution (ADR). The alternative means alternative to litigation or some other formalized, governmental adjudication. Your exposure to ADR may inform you that it includes such procedures as mediation and arbitration, which is true. We adopt a broader view of ADR, but one that is neither unconventional nor radical. We define ADR as *those procedures or methodologies of resolving conflict that are alternative to litigation and the like.* ADR encompasses a myriad of conflict resolution approaches that range from negotiation and facilitation to mediation and arbitration. In the mix, you will find minitrials, partnering, conciliation, neutral evaluation, final offer arbitration, variants of mediation, ombuds, and peer reviews. Without question, ADR is growing in variety and application, in employment and other business contexts. We will guide you through this increasingly murky field in this part of the book.

More specifically, Part 2 consists of five chapters under the heading of ADR. Chapter 4 covers the essentials of negotiation, the most common but often undervalued form of conflict resolution. It guides you through the increasingly popular methodology of interest-based negotiation, which is akin to collaborative dispute resolution.

Chapters 5 through 7 guide you through facilitation, mediation, and arbitration. In each chapter, our main goal is to give you an understanding of how to use these procedures, when to use them, and what their relative costs are, especially from an organizational standpoint. Chapter 5 gives you the basic knowledge you need to apply facilitation. It shows you how it fits into the schema of conflict resolution. Chapter 6 walks you through the operational mechanics of mediation. It informs you on when to use mediation, how to get a mediator, what happens in a mediation session, and how much it might cost you. Also, it compares transformative mediation to conventional or traditional mediation. The former has gained stature in the ADR/conflict resolution field, and it has been used to handle equal employment opportunity (EEO) claims.

Chapter 7 presents similar kinds of information about arbitration. What is it? When do we use it? How does arbitration work? How do we select an arbitrator? The final chapter in this section, Chapter 8, walks you through an assortment of other ADR techniques. It tells you a little bit about each technique, how it works, and when you might use it. The techniques covered include fact-finding, peer review, early neutral evaluation, and ombuds.

We suggest that you use the following five chapters as guides to inform you personally as a professional or manager. In addition, you can use them as organizational guides, providing information to inform your company about what its options are in the realm of conflict resolution. This sets you up to play an instrumental role in designing and implementing a conflict resolution system for your company, a topic to which we will turn in Part 4.

Chapter 4

Negotiation

The dictionary defines negotiation, the main technique of conflict resolution, by saying that it is the action or process of negotiating and that to negotiate is to confer with another so as to arrive at a settlement of some matter.

Theodore W. Kheel, 1999.

Negotiation is undoubtedly the most common methodology used to resolve conflicts, whether you realize it or not. Everyone at work negotiates. Interestingly, the Spanish word *negocio* means business. As the workplace is the central to the world of business, negotiation is an integral aspect of doing work. If you were unable to negotiate at work, your business would be literally undoable. How could you move beyond one conflict at a time if the solution always required enlisting the aid of third parties or resorting to measures more costly and drastic than negotiation, such as litigation, a strike, or turnover?

You may often associate negotiation in a workplace setting with union-management relations. Indeed, collective bargaining, a form of negotiating, is a statutorily protected means of resolving workplace conflicts that might otherwise result in bitter strikes and violent confrontations, both of which have blemished union-management relations in the United States and elsewhere. But we are not talking here specifically about union-management relations or collective bargaining. We are speaking more generally about how you can apply the principles of negotiation to a variety of workplace conflicts. Those conflicts may arise in the routine course of hiring employees, conducting performance evaluations, determining pay raises and other rewards, and allocating work. However, you can take these same tools and apply them to a unionized setting, recognizing, of course, there are certain differences, many of which stem from statute and the nature of unions as institutions.

CHAPTER OBJECTIVES

The overall objective of this chapter is to present the essentials you need to negotiate effectively at work across the vast expanse of conflicts that arise. More specifically, the chapter gives you guidance on:

- What negotiation is
- What you negotiate for
- The core elements of a negotiation
- How adversarial bargaining differs from collaborative negotiating
- How to negotiate using the interest-based model
- How to get ready quickly for a negotiation
- The key competencies you need to be an effective negotiator
- Tips you can follow to negotiate more effectively at work and in business generally

> ### Remember This Essential Point
>
> Negotiating gives those involved in the world of work a voice to influence those matters that affect them: It is the principals' pulpit.

WHAT IS NEGOTIATION?

Chester L. Karrass's (1996) aptly titled book, *In Business as in Life—You Don't Get What You Deserve, You Get What You Negotiate*, makes an important point. You might modify that statement to fit our context: *In work as in life—you don't get what you deserve, you get what you negotiate*. If negotiation is in fact so important, you need to be clear about what it is. Definitions abound, but can be boiled down to the following essence in a workplace context:

> Negotiation is a process whereby the parties in conflict attempt to reach an agreement on issues on which they presently or potentially might disagree.

We add these other properties to describe negotiation:

First, the parties themselves determine the nature of the negotiating process, within relevant organizational and environment constraints.

Second, negotiation does not require agreement in a formalized contractual sense to accomplish its goals.

Third, negotiation allows the parties to reach an agreement of their own accord. But there may well be adverse consequences if agreement is not reached.

Fourth, negotiation is about giving employees at various levels, including managerial and executive ranks, a "voice," an opportunity to decide jointly the conditions and terms under which they work.

To put negotiation into a broader conflict resolution context, look at the methodologies shown in Figure 4.1. You may choose to avoid conflict, hoping it will go away. Alternatively, as a manager, you may exercise your prerogative to settle the matter unilaterally. You decide. End of story. But you know that it is not always a viable or desirable option, particularly as your organization tries to empower and involve the workforce more purposefully.

You have another set of alternatives, as we discussed in Chapter 3. You may go directly to third-party intervention if you so design a system for resolving conflict. Once you go directly to these options, however, you can begin to see control over the process of conflict resolution slip away from your grasp.

Another option is litigation. You may choose to go to court to set an example, deter future misconduct, or establish a managerial principle. Aggrieved employees may exercise the same option. Prospective or current

Figure 4.1 Conflict Resolution Methodologies

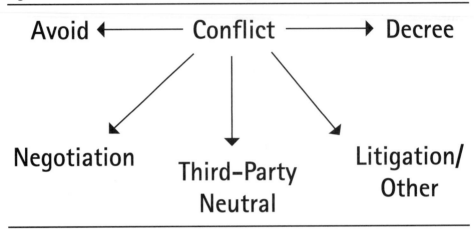

employees may allege biased treatment, claiming your company discriminated against them on account of age, gender, disability, race, or religion. The involuntarily removed senior executive may sue your company for wrongful discharge. The likelihood of this option being pursued grows as other alternatives shrink. Once you enter this sphere, your direct control really has slipped away—a judge, jury, or administrative official will decide for you.

From this vantage point, you begin to see the appeal of negotiation. By creating a workplace climate amenable to negotiation, you give yourself and your workforce the opportunity to work things out by themselves. You and others become more approachable, more amenable to collaboration. You effectively change the culture of a company from one in which employees feel powerless, management decides, and the only way change occurs is through litigation (or worse) to one in which you and others are empowered to make your own decisions. This is the virtue of negotiation in comparison to the other alternatives.

WHY SHOULD YOU NEGOTIATE?

You negotiate for three important and interrelated reasons. First, you negotiate to resolve a disagreement. Workplace disagreement runs the gamut, from disputes over performance ratings to the description of jobs. These disagreements can be resolved by the parties themselves through negotiation.

Second, you negotiate to reach agreements that will prevent conflict. Think about an occasion in which you have hired a new employee. You are negotiating compensation, performance expectations, and work responsibilities. If you fail to clarify these matters or agree on what they really mean, you certainly have opened yourself up to conflict in the future. Agreements are intended to affect current and future behavior. One of the principal reasons why you should negotiate is to reach agreement on these behavioral expectations so as to prevent conflict.

Third, you negotiate to avoid the serious consequences of not giving employees a voice or an effective alternative to more disruptive and unproductive behavior. You can think of this in terms of the classic exit-voice model. If employees have no means to express concerns at work, their only option to better their situation is to leave (exit). They exercise their voice by quitting or, until they can quit, withdrawing as much as possible from the life of the company. According to this model, if you give people a "voice" alternative, they do not have to exit. They will become more involved and empowered by being able to negotiate important workplace matters.

In sum, you need to resolve existing disagreements, to prevent new ones (many of which are highly predictable), and to give employees (at all levels) an alternative means of resolving disagreements—alternative to potentially costly conflictual actions.

WHEN SHOULD YOU NEGOTIATE?

You should negotiate when it is in your and others' best interest to do so. A pivotal point in negotiation is that there be some sense of mutuality or reciprocity, though symmetry in interests and needs across negotiating parties is not required. You want to work purposefully to create a climate that promotes negotiation, not hand-to-hand combat.

More specifically, you should negotiate when:

- You have mutual interests
- You are willing to change or give something up
- You think a positive difference can be made
- You want to build relationships
- You have your emotions under control
- You are willing to live with an agreement reached
- You want to give someone a chance to express views or concerns
- You want to avoid escalation or more serious confrontation
- You believe the company can benefit from listening and being open to change

Not all of these conditions need be present, but your negotiation will benefit to the extent that they exist.

> Your goal in negotiating is to reach an agreement that will positively affect workplace relations and redound to the benefit of the company.

THE CORE ELEMENTS OF A NEGOTIATION

To negotiate effectively, you need an appreciation of the structure of the negotiating process. Fisher and Ertel (1995) have captured the structure of negotiation in seven core elements: interests, options, alternatives, communication, relationships, legitimacy, and commitment. You prepare for, conduct, and follow up on a negotiation with these elements in mind. By being conscious of these elements in the preparation, bargaining, and post-settlement phases of a negotiation, you elevate your capacity to succeed. And success will be more readily shared with your negotiating partner.

- *First, you diagnose the negotiating parties' interests*. What needs must be met? What interests correspond or overlap? Which are in discord?

• *Second, what are your options?* What are the various means of serving underlying interests and needs? You want to be open to new ideas or creative variations of old ones.

• *Third, you want to think about your alternatives* if the negotiation does not produce a satisfactory agreement. Your real power in a negotiation rests on your willingness to walk away. You are not there to give away the company store. Both sides' interests, including your own, need to be met. You must think in terms of what you can do if accord is not possible. Think in terms of your best alternative to a negotiated agreement (BATNA).

• *Fourth, you need to be concerned about the element of communication.* You and an employee, for example, might disagree over something. The employee may question why a request for time off was denied, why a transfer was made, why a positive performance review did not translate into an anticipated pay raise. You may attempt to allay these concerns in a meeting or negotiation of sorts. The employee may not be entirely satisfied with your explanation, but you have opened the lines of communication. You have tried to establish a dialogue to enable you and the employee to discuss issues and concerns openly, without fear of recrimination, to your mutual advantage. Conversely, in a negotiation, you can do irreparable harm if you fail to pay attention to how to communicate. If you dissemble, mislead, lie, or distort the truth, trust will evaporate. And, while it is often useful to vent in a negotiation, you must be prepared to be the repairer of the breach if you recklessly insult or denigrate someone else. In workplace conflict, the aphorism that "sticks and stones may break my bones but words can never hurt me" is patently false. You will pay for what you say.

• *Fifth, you want to negotiate with relationships in mind.* Negotiations are about interpersonal relations. At work, relationships are critical. On many occasions, in fact, you will find that the important consideration is not the outcome of the negotiation but rather how well the relationship emerged from the process. No matter how much we may struggle to insulate ourselves, we depend on others to achieve our goals and the broader goals of an organization. We diminish our capacity—individually and institutionally—to do so when we damage relationships.

- *Sixth, by looking for touchstones of legitimacy* you can bolster the acceptability of a proposed solution. The standards of legitimacy are best if they derive from agreeing on external measures. If you are negotiating salary with an employee, your proposed offer is imminently more defensible if grounded in market-based information. Imagine how the credibility of your offer will dissipate if you justify it strictly in terms of what *you* think is best.

- *Seventh, you need to focus on commitment.* Are you and the others prepared to abide by an agreement, to live up to its terms?

WHAT'S THE DIFFERENCE BETWEEN ADVERSARIAL BARGAINING AND COLLABORATIVE NEGOTIATING?

Scenario

An office manager of a clerical unit in a hospital has been experiencing difficulties with one of his administrative assistants. He is disturbed that she has been showing up late on occasion and asking to leave early with growing frequency. She, a single parent, has also been making a sizable number of personal phone calls at work. Otherwise, she has an excellent work record, and has been a dependable and trustworthy administrative assistant. The office manager has heard through the thick grapevine that she wants a different work schedule. How would his approach differ if he were to negotiate a solution adversarially vis-a-vis collaboratively?

Obviously, since you negotiate to prevent and resolve conflict, you find similarities in the strategies and styles exhibited in negotiation and conflict resolution per se. In fact, we often refer to conflict resolution and negotiating strategies/styles interchangeably. But we will be a little more precise in a negotiating context, showing how too often juxtaposed approaches differ. We will show you how adversarial bargaining (or negotiating) differs from collaborative negotiating. Once you appreciate these differences, you will see clearly how the manager in the scenario above would handle the situation differently using these alternatives.

As we mentioned earlier, you are probably most familiar with the adversarial approach in a collective bargaining context (hence we chose the term adversarial bargaining). Union-management negotiations are often characterized as involving bitter disputes over wages, pensions, job security, and work rules. The sides are willing to go to the mat and risk it all in this adversarial climate. Although this is not an accurate portrayal of union-management relations generally, you have enough specific knowledge, awareness, or experience to know that adversarialism can and does occur in unionized contexts. More important, however, you know from your own bank of experiences that any type of workplace negotiation can be adversarial, even extremely adversarial. Indeed, that is why collaborative alternatives have gained such favor as a means of dealing with employment disputes.

So, how does adversarial bargaining differ from collaborative negotiation? We distinguish the approaches on five dimensions (see Figure 4.2).

> *First,* they differ in terms of their basic operating *assumptions*. If you
> negotiate adversarially, you view the pie as fixed. The negotiation
> is characterized as win-lose or zero-sum: Whatever you get, the

Figure 4.2 Comparing Adversarial Bargaining to Collaborative Negotiation

Dimension	Adversarial Bargaining	Collaborative Negotiation
Assumption	Fixed Pie Win-Lose	Expandable Pie Win-Win
Focus	Winning Position	Satisfying Mutual Interests
Emphasis	Outcome	Relationship and Outcome
Information-Sharing	Strategic Selective	Open Sharing
Tactics	Hard-Nosed Aggressive Dominating Borderline	Probing Listening Brainstorming

other side cannot. Or, if you consider the pie as fixed, you assume the negotiation will be adversarial. Whichever way you view it, your frame of mind is nonetheless set.

On the other hand, in the collaborative approach, you view the pie as an accordion. It is expandable. You look for ways to grow the pie to create win-win scenarios. In the scenario above, instead of viewing the situation as lending itself to only one solution—adherence to one schedule—you look for options to give the administrative assistant more flexibility while ensuring that her performance lives up to organizational standards.

Second, the approaches differ in *focus* or objective. In the adversarial negotiation, you want your position to win. The office manager wants conformity to the standard schedule. Your position will dominate. In fact, winning is what motivates you.

Taking a collaborative approach, you focus on satisfying mutual interests. Based on prior performance, the administrative assistant wants to be a good employee. She may need some accommodation in scheduling or day-care for performance to rise to previous levels. It is in your interest to achieve that goal, so you look for a solution.

Third, the *emphasis* differs. Adversarial bargaining is supremely outcome focused. Collaborative negotiation is both relationship and outcome focused. Both approaches can result in the same outcome. For example, they might both yield a more flexible work schedule. But the process of getting there will have been different. One might have soured the relationship while the other elevated it.

Fourth, the *information-sharing* process differs. In adversarial bargaining, you keep your interests and information close to your vest. You reveal things selectively and strategically. In collaboration, you are more open and sharing. The office manager invites the administrative assistant to tell her story in her own way. The manager will then reveal his and the organization's concerns and their interest in working toward a satisfactory agreement.

Fifth, these approaches or strategic choices tend to involve different types of *tactics*. If you are negotiating adversarially, you are more prone to be tough, hard-nosed, aggressive, dominating, and ethically borderline in your conduct. You might (dishonestly) tell the administrative assistant that there is no alternative but shaping up and conforming to the standard schedule. You have proven yourself tough, and you have unhesitatingly presented your case.

When you negotiate collaboratively, these tactics become much less thinkable. You probe for an understanding of what the problem is. You listen to the assistant's story. You are empathetic, not contradictory. You brainstorm for options. How can we work this situation out in a mutually positive way?

Undeniably, we have juxtaposed extremes. You will find many negotiations involving elements of both. But you should keep in mind that even when issues involve distributing fixed sums, your tactical approach to resolving the dispute can be more collaborative than adversarial.

PRINCIPLES OF INTEREST–BASED NEGOTIATION

Scenario

A high school principal has an upcoming performance appraisal session with a social studies teacher. The evaluative criteria are: student test scores; quality of instruction; collegiality; and overall contribution to the school. The teacher, who has worked at the school with the principal for eight years, has tended to fall in the "satisfactory" performance category on these dimensions. He believes that his contributions have been underassessed. He believes he deserves an "excellent" rating on most if not all the dimensions. (The rating categories are: outstanding; excellent; satisfactory; below satisfactory; unacceptable.) Ratings affect pay raises and eligibility for plum assignments. The teacher, who can be abrasive and accusatory, is deeply disturbed and has been vocal in his discontent. The principal is preparing for her meeting. How might she anticipate applying the principles of interest-based negotiating?

Just as in resolving conflict collaboratively, you will find a technique to collaborative negotiation. As a manager or professional, you can benefit from mastering this technique because negotiation comprises a good portion of your interactions at your workplace and with others at their workplaces (i.e., internal versus external negotiating). Fisher and Ury (1981) popularized the technique in the best-seller, *Getting to Yes*. Their technique includes four core principles (see Figure 4.3). They advocate a principled versus positional approach to negotiation. Interest-based negotiation (IBN) is the label commonly attached to this approach. Many believe, as do we, that IBN can yield more fruitful outcomes and strengthen relationships.

• First, you must *separate the people from the problem*. In negotiating collaboratively at work, you must concentrate on "the problem" and not allow personalities or clashes between personalities to cloud the problem, except, obviously, to the extent that personalities are the problem. Even then, however, the focus must remain on dealing with the problem and not attacking the person.

• Second, you *focus on the parties' interests*. Positions, demands, or fixed opinions detract from this quest. Therefore, you continually frame and re-frame the discussion in terms of interests, which can be psychological, physiological, social, or economic in nature.

• Third, to get away from fixed situations, where resource constraints become barriers to solutions, *you explore options*—multiple ways to address issues. If, for instance, the social studies teacher's interest is increased recognition, there are several ways, apart from a pay raise, to meet this need. They may include a change in title, a new office assignment, or providing another student teacher or classroom aide.

Figure 4.3 Key Principles of Interest–Based Negotiating (IBN)

People:	Separate the people from the problem.
Interests:	Focus on interests, not positions.
Options:	Generate a variety of possibilities before deciding what to do.
Criteria:	Insist that the result be based on some objective standard.

Source: Roger Fisher and William Ury. 1981. *Getting to Yes.* New York: Penguin Books.

• Finally, *you employ criteria* to legitimize options that materialize through brainstorming.

Let's play out these principles using the scenario with the principal and the social studies teacher.

Separate People from the Problem

The problem in that scenario is that the social studies teacher does not believe his ratings are valid. The principal's task is to convince the teacher that they are valid, if in fact they are. The teacher could be defensive, irritable, or confrontational in the performance review session. The principal should deflect that behavior and not focus on him but on why his performance assessment is valid. (Be open to the possibility that it may not be valid.) Then the principal should explore ways to improve performance. There may be circumstances beyond the teacher's control that are affecting performance. Get to the crux of the matter. This is especially important when personalities may have clashed in the past. Remember that the principal and the teacher—who is probably tenured and represented by a union like the American Federation of Teachers—will have to work together in the future.

Focus on Interests, Not Positions

The teacher may come in with a loaded tongue. He may demand a higher rating. That is his position. The principal may challenge that position, asserting authoritatively that the rating stands. This response could trigger an acrimonious escalation. What the principal should do is focus on what lies underneath the demand. Does the teacher feel neglected? Does the teacher feel unappreciated? Are there personal or other problems affecting performance? Is the teacher really interested in a reasonable explanation, thinking the only way to get one is to be demanding? You should never confuse a position with an interest.

Generate Options

The key is to explore options to improve the situation. Suppose the teacher claims that his performance has not been better because his classes have been too large, that he has not had sufficient student-teacher or teacher-aide assistance, and that he has not had access to the technology needed to make his class more interactive and real-world. From this point, the principal and teacher might explore ways to address these issues. If resources permit (always, unfortunately, a big if), the teacher might be given the help he needs to show his claim is true. A plan might be developed to review the teacher more frequently after the changes have been made to see whether performance has improved.

Use Legitimate Criteria

In this case as in other workplace contexts, the parties need to believe that the criteria used to make a decision are valid. If the principal were to assert that her evaluation was based largely on her own more or less subjective readings, she invites trouble. Has quality of instruction been measured according to acceptable professional standards? Are objective measures or objective evaluation procedures used? You want external validation of the approach taken. And both parties must see the wisdom of it.

GETTING READY TO NEGOTIATE

Scenario

A plant manager is under direct corporate orders to slash payroll by 10 percent in the next three months. A company devotee, he accepts this challenge loyally. He has scheduled a meeting with various line managers to announce the plan and enlist their support to achieve the necessary reductions in head count to meet this goal. He knows that he can expect resistance because the line managers are very close to those who will inevitably lose their jobs. The plant has already undergone several downsizings in recent years. A commonly expressed opinion is that the plant is operating about as lean as possible. As the plant manager, how would you get ready for your upcoming negotiation with the line managers?

In the real world of work, you often do not have a whole lot of time. Unfortunately, time is the most finite of all resources. You will often have to get ready for a negotiation in a hurry. But get ready you should still do, even if you have only a few minutes.

To help you organize your thoughts efficiently, use the template presented in Figure 4.4. Keep a pad of blank "getting ready to negotiate" sheets at your disposal. Use them when negotiating, whether on the

Figure 4.4 Getting Ready to Negotiate

Step 1:	The Issue	Cutting Line Managers' Payroll Head Count
Step 2:	The Interests	
	Yours	Reducing payroll Improving productivity Supporting lean operations Following corporate orders Saving company
	Theirs	Getting work done Preserving employee morale Preserving jobs Improving productivity Saving company Following company orders
Step 3:	The Options	Firings Buy-outs Reassignments Retraining Restructuring
Step 4:	Criteria	Savings Productivity Measures Employee Morale Compliance

phone or face-to-face. With some practice, you will become proficient at IBN.

Using the payroll scenario, you should boil down the issue to its essence in Step 1. The issue or problem is cutting head count and payroll.

In Step 2, enumerate your interests and the line managers' interests. You're interested in reducing payroll, improving productivity, supporting lean operations, following corporate orders, and keeping the company alive. The line managers are interested in getting the work done, preserving employee morale and jobs, improving productivity, saving the company, and being good company citizens. There is more overlap than you might have initially realized.

In Step 3, consider some options. Are there ways to reduce payroll without reducing head count? Are there relatively painless ways to reduce head count? Can certain employees be re-trained to make them useful in other areas where shortages exist? Be creative and open-minded.

Finally, in Step 4, jot down some criteria that have to be met to legitimize the possible solution. Criteria might include payroll savings expected, anticipated productivity enhancements, impact on employee morale, and degree of compliance with a corporate mandate.

We strongly recommend that you get into the habit of getting ready to negotiate. Time you spend in this effort can save you time at the meeting itself by helping to focus discussion.

CHARACTERISTICS OF AN EFFECTIVE NEGOTIATOR

What's a good negotiator? Chester Karrass provides a grand slam answer by saying that "If I were to restrict my answer to a single trait, it would be the ability of negotiators to deal with people in their own organization."[*]

Your ability to deal with people and therefore be an effective negotiator is promoted by the traits listed in Figure 4.5.

[*]Karrass, Chester L. *In Business as In Life—You Don't Get What You Deserve, You Get What You Negotiate*. Los Angeles: Stanford Street Press, 1996, p.98.

Figure 4.5 Characteristics of an Effective Negotiator

• Visionary	• Patient	• Confident
• Communicator	• Persistent	• Thick-Skinned
• Listener	• Team-Oriented	• Empathetic
• Assertive	• Risk-Tolerant	• Open-minded

1. You need to have a vision of where you want to go. Otherwise, the negotiation will wander and flounder.

2. You have to be able to communicate, verbally and in writing. You should also know how to communicate nonverbally. Body language is important.

3. You must listen well—actively and empathetically.

4. You must be assertive. You must be willing to assert your needs and interests and to walk away if they are not going to be met satisfactorily.

5. A good negotiator is patient. You will make more mistakes when you are hurried or in a hurry.

6. You should be persistent. "No" does not always mean "No."

7. You should be team-oriented, willing and able to work with others and build a complementary negotiating squad when necessary.

8. Good negotiators are tolerant of taking measured risks. But they are not risk-prone or reckless.

9. You have to be confident. This does not mean being closed-minded, but rather confident that your approach is reasonable and justifiable. Although willing to listen, you will return to your message if convinced it is a worthy one to deliver.

10. You need a thick skin. This is imperative if you want to be able to separate people from the problem.

11. You need to think not just sympathetically but also empathetically. You should be able to sing as well as hear the other side's music.

12. You have absolutely got to be open-minded.

Because you must increasingly be a good negotiator to be a good manager, both in terms of your relations at work and with others at their workplaces, you want managers who possess an adequate complement of these qualities. And, from an organizational perspective, you want to develop these qualities throughout your ranks.

NEGOTIATING TIPS FOR MANAGERS

You will confront countless situations in which your immediate task is to negotiate an agreement. Negotiating enables you to preserve control over the situation. You and your negotiating parties are the arbiters of your own fates (see Figure 4.6).

The following set of tips or guidelines for you to follow at work are offered for situations that arise hurriedly or that permit considerable preparation.

- Prepare for the session by examining the principals: Who are they? What do they do? What is their negotiating style? What are their likely interests and needs?
- Use considered responses. That is, listen to what the other side is saying. Listen to their thoughts, emotions, and cues. Consider what they have to say before responding.
- Focus on building broad-based relationships and networks. Do not wait until confronted with a conflict or negotiation to do so. Even if you cannot get to know the other principals before a confrontation or session, you may get to know people who know them and who can influence them.

Figure 4.6 Key Tips on Negotiating at Work

• Prepare	• Identify Agreed-Upon Standards
• Use Considered Responses	• Emphasize Relationship
• Broaden Networks	• Accept Responsibility
• Deflect Attacks	• Be Creative
• Reframe	• Be Patient
• Be Flexible	

- Deflect personal attacks and verbal assaults. Look at the underlying problem(s).
- Re-focus on the real issue at hand and keep personalities at bay.
- Be flexible. Explore options with the other side.
- Look for agreed-upon rationales. Find mutually acceptable reasons for committing to a particular solution.
- Repeatedly emphasize the salience of the relationship (even when it is a one-shot deal) and how both sides need to benefit if an agreement is to be sustainable.
- Accept responsibility. If something goes wrong in the session or negotiation, do not blame the other side. Laying the blame on others compounds rather than solves problems.
- Be creative. Think outside-of-the-box. Invite different approaches. Remember, one of the objectives that negotiating serves is to give the parties a voice—an opportunity to express themselves and to expound upon their thoughts.
- Be patient. Time *is* money. It is often worthwhile to invest the time to look for new solutions, to probe underlying interests, and to build trust. By doing this, we create opportunities to anticipate and prevent new problems. We also enable ourselves to design real rather than illusory solutions.

Manager's Checklist: Your Organization's Negotiating Capability

Your interest is not only in developing your own negotiating skill but also in building negotiating as an institutional capability. The checklist below is intended to help you assess the extent to which such a capability exists in your organization and, by inference, how much needs to be done to realize that objective.

To what extent does your company, or relevant division/ unit therein *(please check one):*	Not at All	Very Little	A Little	Some	More than Some	A Lot	Don't Know
Reward managers on the basis of effective negotiation skills	☐	☐	☐	☐	☐	☐	☐

Emphasize effective negotiating skills in evaluating managers for promotion	☐	☐	☐	☐	☐	☐	☐
Encourage negotiating as a way of resolving workplace conflict	☐	☐	☐	☐	☐	☐	☐
Train managers generally on negotiations skills	☐	☐	☐	☐	☐	☐	☐
Train employees generally on negotiations skills	☐	☐	☐	☐	☐	☐	☐

Exercise 4.1: Negotiating a Salary Raise

As the head of a department, you have responsibility for allocating merit pay raises. This year, your merit budget, as usual in recent times, is modest. The average pay hike for merit will be 2 percent. The range will be 0 percent to a high of 10 percent. One of your direct reports, an excellent, hard-charging project manager, wants 10 percent, or so you have heard. You are concerned she might leave if not properly recognized and rewarded. You have planned a 7 percent merit raise for her. She is known to be a highly sensitive person who can easily feel slighted. She has asked for a meeting to discuss ("to negotiate") her merit raise. How would you prepare for a meeting to discuss the merit raise? What is the issue? What are your options? How would you assess the options?

Exercise 4.2: Negotiating a Reassignment

You are the senior vice president of marketing for a mid-sized steel manufacturer. You have been charged with restructuring the sales force. Downsizing, consolidation, and reassignment are entailed. You have decided to reassign one of your stellar performers, who is senior, from a region that has been profitable to a much less profitable region. In addition to being less profitable, the region to which the senior sales manager will be reassigned is aesthetically much less appealing. The sales manager has requested a meeting to discuss or negotiate an alternative for reassignment. How will you prepare for this negotiation? What are the issues likely to come up in your meeting? What are the interests? What are the options? How do you assess the options?

Exercise 4.3: Negotiating a Job Reduction

You are a senior vice president of human resources. You have problems with one of your HR managers. A historically outstanding performer who has made a long and significant contribution to your Fortune-ranked company, he has fallen on hard times. He recently got divorced and has suffered from depression. During the past year, his performance deteriorated markedly. He has fallen behind, ignored his mentoring role, and let projects slide.

You have to deal with the situation. You have decided to work with him to reduce his sphere of duties so that he can focus better and improve his record of performance and thereby stay somewhat on track for a future promotion. You are pleased that the manager has availed himself of the help offered by the Employee Assistance Program and that he has begun taking an antidepressant. You know your plan will not be received with welcome arms, and you want to avoid making a difficult situation even worse. How do you prepare for this negotiation? What are the issues? What are the interests? What are your options? How would you assess those options?

Chapter 5

Facilitation

Conflict at Yahoo: "The 'perfect' match between a big-picture CEO and practical president turns 'toxic.' " (*Business Week,* May 21, 2001)

Conflict at Xerox: "Downfall of Xerox due to executive discord that approached 'civil war.' " (*Business Week,* March 5, 2001)

You may be skeptical about the practicality and utility of the collaborative approach to negotiation. IBN sounds too good to be true. The technique looks so silky smooth that it appears borderline unctuous. You have undoubtedly tried collaboration only to be disappointed by the results or process. Too many people simply will not cooperate. On some occasions, you may have outright rejected collaboration because it seemed inappropriate or undesirable. Why should you collaborate with a disgruntled employee whose thirst for complaining is unquenchable?

We advocate IBN and collaborative conflict resolution methodologies not because we are naive about their ease or probable success. We urge collaboration because we believe that, on average over time, you will benefit from it. The benefits include stronger relationships, broader networks at work, and superior agreements or outcomes. Your benefits will rise commensurately with your proficiency in using collaborative techniques. But you cannot and should not expect to succeed every time. Even when you do not succeed, you will often be glad that you were collaborative.

Indeed, you know that some of your collaborative endeavors will prove less successful than desired. In fact, some negotiations, regardless of whether they are collaborative or adversarial, will result in impasses, inconclusive results, or complete breakdowns. In reality, the principals involved in negotiation (or any set of workplace sessions—e.g., meetings—that amount to a negotiation) will sometimes find themselves incapable of making headway. You can relate to many of the possible reasons for negotiating shortfalls:

- Personality clashes
- Poor meeting management
- Recalcitrance
- Too much emotion
- Dominating personalities
- Too many players
- Lack of preparation
- Lack of focus
- Dilatory tactics
- Insufficient information
- Absence of key decision makers
- Insufficient time
- Poor timing
- Bad location

When this happens, you beg for help. Just as a sick person calls a physician, you, as a manager, may want to call a facilitator, who may come from within or outside the company. When doing so, you should know what to ask for, when to ask for it, and what you expect to achieve.

CHAPTER OBJECTIVES

After reading this chapter, you will appreciate how you can use facilitation to prevent, resolve, and work through conflict. You will better understand how facilitation can be used generally in your company to achieve these goals. You will also (we hope) be more attuned to how important facilitation is to your professional and managerial roles. One of the critical functions a manager can perform is to facilitate others to success. An HR department can greatly extend its organizational value by offering facilitators to deal with the myriad of workplace conflicts that surround it.

More specifically, this chapter examines the following issues:

- What is facilitation?
- How does it differ from other ADR techniques?
- What are the critical steps to effective facilitation?
- What are some effective facilitation tools?
- What competencies should you look for in a facilitator?
- How do you measure the results of facilitation?
- How do you measure the costs of facilitation?

In addition, we briefly describe a technology developed by the Federal Mediation and Conciliation Service (FMCS) to promote facilitation in the workplace, called the Technology Assisted Group Solutions (TAGS) system. Furthermore, we offer a manager's checklist and a few exercises.

WHAT IS FACILITATION?

Scenario

You are an HR manager for a retail corporation. Your company's sales and market share have fallen significantly in the past three years because of new and more convenient types of competitors entering the market. Your company has a problem with customer satisfaction. You know that employee satisfaction is a strong predictor of customer satisfaction and critical repeat business, a dimension on which your company fares poorly. A high-level corporate team has been created to analyze the problem and come up with a plan in three months. One month has gone by and the nominal head of the team, the vice president of customer relations, has asked for help. The team, so far, has accomplished nothing. With nine other members on the team, meetings are often unruly, and there is too much bickering.

Meetings drift back and forth among topics with no closure. The vice president has asked for your help. How do you respond?

You may think of facilitation, mediation, and conciliation as being one in the same. As a practical matter, facilitators can and should wear several hats. They may serve as logistics coordinators and information sources. They may play the role of counselor. Facilitators may also teach others how to communicate. And they must be willing to intervene as mediators or problem-solvers when necessary to keep the parties on track.

FACILITATION IN ADR PERSPECTIVE

Still, facilitation is a distinguishable form of ADR. Obviously, it is one of many possible third-party interventions. But it is a relatively and intentionally mild form of intervention. Like other ADR techniques, facilitation is intended to avoid litigation and other adverse consequences of workplace conflict. You should appreciate the fact, however, that when you use facilitation you are generally not avoiding the issue or problem or operating unilaterally. You will find that facilitation often goes hand-in-glove with negotiation. Thus, its advantages and disadvantages closely resemble those of negotiation. The hope is that some mild prodding and shift in the dynamics can get you over the hump.

You will discover that what distinguishes facilitation is its relative emphasis on process. The U.S. Office of Personnel Management (OPM) offers a precise definition:

> Facilitation involves the use of techniques to improve the flow of information in a meeting between parties to a dispute. The techniques may also be applied to decision-making meetings where a specific outcome is desired (e.g., resolution of a conflict or dispute). The term "facilitator" is often used interchangeably with the term "mediator," but a facilitator does not typically become as involved in the substantive issues as does a mediator. The facilitator focuses more on the process involved in resolving a matter.

The facilitator generally works with all of the meeting's participants at once and provides procedural directions as to how the group can move efficiently through the problem-solving steps of the meeting and arrive at the jointly agreed upon goal. The facilitator may be a member of one of the parties to the dispute or may be an external consultant. Facilitators focus on procedural assistance and remain impartial to the topics or issues under discussion.*

Two observations are noteworthy. First, facilitation focuses on information-sharing and -processing as means of moving the principals toward resolving their workplace conflict or reaching an agreement. Second, using a set of more or less standard tools, facilitators can operate in a variety of workplace contexts and deal with a wide range of conflicts.

HOW DOES FACILITATION DIFFER FROM OTHER ADR TECHNIQUES?

You can see more clearly how facilitation differs from other ADR techniques by looking at Figure 5.1. Specifically, we compare facilitation to negotiation, mediation, and arbitration on five dimensions:

1. The principals' control over the outcome
2. The focus on outcome or settlement
3. The focus on the process of interaction among the parties
4. The emphasis on conflict prevention
5. The opportunity for early resolution of conflict (and resolution at a level close to where the conflict originated)

You should keep these comparisons in mind when considering which technique to use, the order in which they may be sequenced, and the opportunity to move forward or backward among these alternatives.

You can see that the principals' control over the outcome is high in both negotiation and facilitation. This is important for two reasons. First,

*U.S. Office of Personnel Management, Office of Workforce Relations. *Alternative Dispute Resolution: A Resource Guide.* Washington, D.C.: OPM, July 1999, pp. 4–5.

Figure 5.1 Negotiation, Facilitation, Mediation, and Arbitration

Dispute Resolution Method	Principals' Control Over Outcome	Focus on Outcome/ Settlement	Focus on Process	Conflict Prevention	Early Resolution
Negotiation: Involves an attempt by the principles to reach agreement and/or resolve conflict.	High	High	Low–Moderate	High	High
Facilitation: Involves the use of process techniques to improve the flow of information in a meeting between the parties to a dispute.	High	Low	High	High	High
Mediation: Is the intervention into a dispute or negotiation of a neutral and impartial third party whose objective is to assist the parties in voluntarily reaching an acceptable resolution of the issues in dispute.	High–Moderate	Moderate–High	High	Low	Moderate
Arbitration: Involves the presentation of a dispute to a neutral and impartial third party for issuance of a decision.	Low	High	Low	Low	Low

Source: Adapted from U.S. Office of Personnel Management. 1999. *Alternative Dispute Resolution: A Resource Guide.* Washington, DC: OPM.

the parties preserve ownership of the end result, which will often make them more committed to faithful implementation. Second, they have not bound themselves to the deal-making prodding or chancy ruling of a third party. When you venture into mediation, particularly that of a traditional sort (as we will discuss in Chapter 6), you risk losing some control. The degree of risk depends upon your sophistication and the understanding of what mediation is really intended to do. You lose complete control when an arbitrator decides, except to the extent that the arguments you presented may have been persuasive.

You can also see that facilitation, like negotiation, can be used to prevent conflict, brace its escalation, and promote its early resolution among those closest to its origin. Mediation and arbitration are tools employed when the chances of early resolution by the parties themselves are receding.

As a process, however, facilitation, unlike negotiation, is not focused on the outcome. The role of the facilitator, as will become even clearer, is process-oriented. Facilitators do not push the parties to settlement. They strive to improve the process of exchanging information so as to raise the chances of achieving positive results. In contrast, negotiation is typically about achieving an outcome of sorts. If the parties cannot settle, reach an agreement, or resolve a conflict, they often become frustrated, disappointed, dejected, or even angered. They are then likely to resort to other ADR techniques or more extreme forms of conflictual behavior. Likewise, negotiation is only concerned about process per se to the extent the parties themselves make it an issue (which they often do). The negotiators control the process and outcome. A facilitation, by definition, is concerned about process.

When to Use Facilitation

Because of its mild interventionist quality, you may think of facilitation as innocuous. You should not be so deceived. Anytime you introduce a third party, you change the dynamics.

The parties need to be ready for a facilitator. They should understand the role. They should not expect facilitation to be an elixir or panacea.

Figure 5.2 identifies what you should consider when making a decision about introducing facilitation.

> *First*, if emotions are running high, wait until they cool down before you try facilitation. There is no point in forcing people together when they are so emotionally charged that they cannot think straight enough to communicate coherently.
>
> *Second*, facilitation is more likely to work in helping the parties make headway when they are not extremely polarized. If you have parties with fundamental differences in principle, facilitation may serve no other purpose than restating the obvious. Keep in mind that facilitation is not costless. As we will discuss below in the context of the facilitation calculator, the costs extend far beyond the fees charged by the facilitator.

Figure 5.2 When to Use Facilitation

When To:	*When Not To:*
• The parties' emotional intensity is not too high	• The parties are blinded by emotion
• The parties are not to polarized	• The parties are far apart on critical issues
• The parties are relatively trusting of each other	• The parties are highly distrustful of each other
• The parties share common interests and will benefit mutually from a resolution	• The parties have deep divisions on interests
• The parties do not need a near-term resolution	• The parties need a final resolution
• The parties need to explore interests, options, and possible solutions	• The parties need to sharpen and focus on their differences
• The parties are having difficulty communicating with and understanding each other	

Source: Adapted from U.S. Office of Personnel Management. 1999. *Alternative Dispute Resolution: A Resource Guide.* Washington, DC: OPM.

Third, for facilitation to work, the parties need at least some a measure of trust. They must have enough confidence in each other to share information. One objective of the facilitator, however, is to create a climate that fosters trust-building.

Fourth, facilitation will prove more useful when the parties do in fact have mutual interests, even though these common concerns might not have been the key topics of discussion between them. A facilitator can get them to explore their mutual concerns and interests and help them appreciate better their genuine interdependence.

Fifth, facilitation can be a long-term process, particularly when introduced after difficult negotiations or among parties that have had a history of clashes and breaches of trust. If you want a quick settlement, this is often *not* the route to go, unless things seem likely to fall into place with a little boost from the facilitator.

Sixth, as is the case with negotiation, you may be just as interested in building the relationship as achieving an outcome or settlement. Sometimes it helps to get the parties together periodically, in the calming presence of a facilitator, to explore their interests, options, and possible solutions. In this context, facilitated meetings can be highly exploratory in nature.

Seventh, when the parties are having difficulty communicating, because of cultural, professional, or organizational barriers, you may want a facilitator.

A STEP-BY-STEP GUIDE

As a process, facilitation should be flexible, adapting to the needs of the parties. Likewise, facilitators need to be flexible and appreciative of the audiences. You definitely want to avoid a facilitator who has a lengthy rulebook and a mechanistic approach. However, you will find it useful to sequence the principal phases of facilitation that you may want to use to build a team, help a project group achieve its mission, or assist an ad hoc task force with a special assignment, such as improving customer satisfaction. Figure 5.3 presents a seven-step guide to facilitation that you can reference.

Step 1. Organize the Meeting

A lot of meetings or negotiations go badly because they are poorly organized. You have been to meetings in which the parties have been inadequately prepared, needed materials have been unavailable, the setting has been adverse to work, and the agenda has not been appropriately developed. One of the reasons why this may occur is that no one has taken responsibility for the necessary but mundane tasks of organizing the meeting. A facilitator can be assigned these important and often time-consuming tasks, which include setting the time and location, distributing materials, compiling agenda items, ensuring adequate facilities, and helping the parties to get the right complement of attendees.

Figure 5.3 Step-by-Step Guide to Facilitation

Step 1: Organize the Meeting
- Materials
- Equipment
- Preparation
- Agenda-Setting
- Attendees
- Facilities
- Location
- Time

Step 2: Structure the Meeting
- Introduction
- Familiarization
- Amenities
- Norms
- Roles
- Goals
- Procedures

Step 3: Apply the Tools
- Generate Ideas
- Assess Ideas
- Make Choices

Step 4: Keep the Flow Going
- Maintain Focus
- Ensure Decorum
- Prevent Disruption
- Allocate Opportunity

Step 5: Exchange Hats
- Resource
- Teacher
- Mediator
- Challenger

Step 6: Close Session
- Summarize
- Emphasize
- Point Forward
- Suggest

Step 7: Post-Session
- Evaluate
- Feedback
- Follow up

Step 2: Structure the Meeting

Particularly in the early stages of the process, the facilitator will want to lend some structure to the meetings. The core structural elements, besides providing proper introductions and familiarizing the parties with the locale and amenities available, include the norms, roles, goals, and procedures to be assigned or followed. These are the basic ground rules, and they should be kept simple and flexible.

For example, one norm may be that everyone listens while someone else is speaking. You may need to assign chairs and co-chairs, note takers, presenters, etc. The facilitator will also help you set the goals of the meeting and establish procedures for you to follow in making decisions.

Step 3. Apply the Tools

Here we get into the technology of facilitation. Facilitators, who focus on information exchange and process, will want to help groups generate ideas, assess ideas so that they can focus on those most meritorious, and make decisions or selections. There are specific methodologies that can be used to generate ideas (e.g., brainstorming) and to make assessments and selections (rank orderings and voting procedures).

Step 4. Keep the Flow Going

You can probably recall far too many occasions when meetings were unruly, unfocused, indecorous, and disruptive. A facilitator's job is to keep these things from happening. The facilitator should give the parties the latitude they need to generate and evaluate ideas, but keep them focused on the goals and stop discourteous, offensive, or otherwise counterproductive behavior. A facilitator should also make certain that everyone has an opportunity to participate and that a few dominating personalities do not hog the whole show. In scheduling, it is also important to give the parties enough time so that they are not hurried.

Step 5. Exchange Hats

You want facilitators who are versatile. A good facilitator should be able to wear several hats. Perhaps above all, the facilitator can be most useful as a teacher, showing, by example, how the parties can communicate better, which includes listening actively, not passively. A facilitator may also be useful in challenging the parties to continue, to explore further, to go the extra yard or two when they feel like stopping. In addition, the facilitator can help as an information clearinghouse—making certain the parties know where to go to find out things they need to know to make decisions. Finally, as a mediator, the facilitator will intervene to resolve personality clashes that detract the parties from making progress. The goal is not to suppress but rather to reframe and redirect constructively.

Step 6. Close Session

A facilitator can be helpful in knowing for how long a time period a meeting should be scheduled and, once underway, when it should be closed. Many groups do poorly in closing meetings, and mistakes and misunderstandings occur as a result. People start scattering and stop listening toward the very end. A facilitator recognizes the importance of closing effectively. Key points need to be summarized. Accomplishments or milestones need to be highlighted. Future direction must be provided. Also, suggestions for improvement in the meeting process may be needed.

Step 7. Post-Session

A facilitator can be the thread that helps bind the group together between meetings. Often, facilitators will be needed for several sessions. Between sessions, they can ensure the distribution of minutes, follow up on tasks assigned, compile items for the next meeting's agenda, and provide more formal feedback if desired to improve the quality of the next session.

FACILITATOR COMPETENCIES

We have already mentioned a few of the qualities or competencies that you want in a facilitator and hinted at others. A more complete list is in

Figure 5.4. The qualities you want are pretty straightforward and do not require much elaboration. But you should not treat the decision of selecting a facilitator lightly. It is an important one.

More specifically, you want a facilitator who can communicate effectively and read an audience. You want a facilitator who is adept at listening, composed, confident, and impartial. In addition, you want one who knows how to manage meetings and is willing to be assertive enough to keep groups on track. A facilitator also needs to know the idea-generation and decision-making technologies. Furthermore, there may be occasions on which you want a facilitator with some subject-matter expertise or familiarity with the culture and operations of the organization. Finally, experience is probably something you want to be mindful of in selecting a facilitator.

Here are some things you definitely do not want to find in a facilitator:

- Overly inclined to opine
- Excessively talkative
- Confrontational and combative
- Biased toward an outcome or solution
- Impatient for settlement or closure

IMPORTANT TOOLS

Facilitators have a battery of tools or technologies available to help groups work effectively (see Figure 5.5). As mentioned, a facilitator will help your group generate ideas and evaluate and select the best ones (or the ones your group thinks are best). Several common techniques are used for these purposes. To generate ideas, the facilitator will employ brainstorming, the

Figure 5.4 Facilitator Competencies

• Communicator	• Technique	• Expertise
• Listener	• Experience	• Familiarity
• Composure	• Impartiality	• Assertive
• Confidence	• Meeting Management	

Figure 5.5 Facilitation Tools

What For:	How To:
• Generating Information and Ideas	Brainstorming Nominal Group Technique Gallery Method
• Evaluating and Selecting Ideas and Strategies	Consensus Decision-Making Plus-and-Minus Technique Priority Analysis

Source: Adapted from Dennis Kinlaw. 1996. *The ASTD Trainer's Source-book: Facilitation Skills.* New York: McGraw Hill.

nominal group technique, and the gallery procedure. To filter ideas and help the group make decisions, facilitators may use consensus decision making, plus-and-minus, or priority analysis techniques. Consensus decision making is an interactive process in which the parties attempt to reach universal agreement on something that each can support. Building consensus focuses on including everyone, especially those who may be hesitant, difficult, or doubtful.

Obviously, the quality of a decision will only be as good as the caliber of ideas generated. Therefore, *brainstorming* is the bedrock of facilitation in many sessions, particularly when groups are starting or have stalled. Although intended to stimulate creative thinking, brainstorming is not an unstructured mind dump. As shown below, the technique is operationalized as an interactive process that is intended to be inclusive and iterative. Certain rules of conduct may be laid down by the facilitator to create a climate conducive to generating ideas and thinking outside of the box.

Brainstorming

1. Clarify the ground rules for brainstorming.
2. Define the topic or information subject.
3. Sequentially solicit the ideas of each participant.
4. Record all ideas.
5. Ask for one more round of ideas.
6. Review ideas and clarify.
7. Collapse ideas into discrete categories.
8. Review, clarify, and finalize.

In so doing, follow these rules:
- Consider one idea at a time.
- Limit discussion to review stages.
- Disallow personal criticism.

MEASURING RESULTS

You want to consider several factors to measure the success of a facilitator and the facilitation process (see Figure 5.6). Among these factors are the rate and speed of settlement. While facilitation is about process, the intent is to get the parties to the point where they want to go but obviously cannot or will not if left unassisted. Facilitation should help the parties reach agreement and do so more expeditiously than if left to their own devices in which case they would likely flounder and eventually collapse.

Other possible success criteria include the parties' satisfaction with settlements reached, the parties' satisfaction with the facilitator and the facilitation process, whether the parties' ability to communicate has improved, the parties' understanding of each other and the issues at hand, and the costs of the settlement (or lack thereof) and the facilitation process itself—especially vis-a-vis alternative forms of third-party conflict resolution. You want to look broadly at what success means. It is not simply a matter of direct financial cost-benefit calculations. From an organizational standpoint, you are interested in the communication competency and relationship-building, which can yield a high return on the investment over

Figure 5.6 Measuring Results

- Settlement Rate
- Settlement Speed
- Parties' Satisfaction with Settlement
- Parties' Satisfaction with Facilitation Process
- Parties' Satisfaction with the Facilitator
- Cost of Facilitation/Cost of Alternative (e.g., litigation, mediation, arbitration)
- Parties' Ability to Communicate Effectively
- Parties' Understanding of Competing Interests, Rights, and Powers
- Cost of Settlement

time. Also, by using multiple criteria, you can make better comparisons across other ADR procedures.

THE FACILITATION CALCULATOR

Regardless of the success criteria chosen, you want to know how much facilitation costs. The facilitation calculator, shown below in Figure 5.7, provides you with a baseline formula to use.

Several possible elements capture the various costs of facilitation. They include the administration fee when an outside agency is used to provide a facilitator, the facilitator's time and expenses, the participants' costs, an estimated administrative overhead cost, the cost of a facilitated settlement, and the costs of implementation. Together, these dimensions cover both the individual and organizational costs.

TECHNOLOGY ASSISTED GROUP SOLUTIONS SYSTEM

Advances in telecommunications and computing technologies have yielded innovations that can make the facilitation process even more ver-

Figure 5.7 The Facilitation Calculator

1. Administration	Fee
2. Facilitators' Time and Expenses	[Rate × Time] + Expenses
3. Participants' Cost	[Time × Compensation (Direct and Indirect)] + Expenses
4. Overhead	[Clerical Support + Copying + Rentals, etc.]
5. Settlement Cost	Actual Cost
6. Post-Settlement Costs	Sum of Costs of Post-Settlement Implementation and Review

Total Cost = [1 + 2 + 3 + 4 + 5 + 6]

satile and efficient. We mention briefly the Technology Assisted Group Solutions (TAGS) system developed by the Federal Mediation and Conciliation Service (FMCS). You should keep such a technology in mind to help facilitate meetings in this era of distance conferencing.

TAGS is a computer software program designed to assist facilitators (and mediators) in running meetings. It can be used in face-to-face meetings and distance-based interactions. Through computer interactions, the parties to a meeting participate electronically in group activities, which greatly expedite the process of recording and analyzing information obtained in various group interactions.

The FMCS has recommended and used TAGS for the following types of facilitated or mediated sessions:

- Interest-based negotiations
- Traditional bargaining
- Strategic planning
- Alternative dispute resolution
- Collaborative initiatives

TAGS has the capacity to assist these and other types of meetings—whether occurring on-site or through electronically linked remote sites—through a software that enables:

- Brainstorming ideas
- Recording ideas
- Categorizing ideas
- Processing ideas
- Evaluating ideas and making decisions
- Developing action plans

Manager's Checklist: Using Facilitation

If you are considering making facilitation a part of a systemic approach to conflict resolution, or using it on an ad hoc basis in response to particular disagreements, you should go through the following checklist:

What is the nature of the conflict to be addressed?
What are the desired results of facilitation?

- Settlements
- Improved Communications
- Improved Relationships

How shall the facilitation process be triggered?
What criteria will be placed on the usage of facilitation?
How will the facilitator be selected?
What is the facilitator's stipulated role?
Who is eligible to be a facilitator?
Must the parties agree to facilitation and the facilitator?
May the parties object to the facilitator?
Is a facilitated agreement binding?
Are facilitated sessions confidential?
Are written agreements required before the initiation of the facilitated session?

Obviously, facilitation is a broadly applicable methodology that can be used for various purposes. In many cases, however (such as facilitating a strategic planning session, which can still involve considerable conflict), the formal approach suggested in the above checklist may be unnecessary and even undesirable. But where facilitation is the method used to address specific workplace conflicts that have the potential to rise to formal disputes, we highly recommend that you use the checklist.

Exercise 5.1: Facilitating an Executives' Meeting

The CEO of a small company ($10 million annual sales) has called a meeting of his five direct reports. He is interested in exploring ideas to reduce cycle time and enhance product innovation. Relatively new to the position (and from the outside), he suspected that there may be some tensions between himself and the group. He has asked you, the senior HR manager, for your advice on whether the meeting should be facilitated. What is your recommendation? What would you look for in the facilitator? What would you expect facilitation to accomplish and, conversely, not to accomplish?

Exercise 5.2: Facilitating a Meeting with a Group of Professionals

A major health insurance company employs a set of full-time physicians to screen patient treatment claims. The company's executive team, composed of nonphysicians, has pushed the physicians conducting claim reviews to be more selective and rigorous in their approvals. The physicians are disturbed about this "push." They have more general concerns about their professional independence in the company. Also, some issues of employment treatment have emerged as troublesome among this group. The CEO has asked you for your advice on how to handle the situation. Would you recommend a facilitated meeting? Why or why not? If yes, what would you expect it to accomplish?

Chapter 6

Mediation

"The U.S. Navy convinced HR specialists that mediation is the better way to go to resolve discrimination claims among civilian employees." (*www.mediate.com*, 2001)

"The Equal Employment Opportunity Commission (EEOC) operates the largest workplace voluntary mediation program." (*www.mediate.com*, 2001)

"Mediation collapses between the Central Intelligence Agency and current and former employees alleging that the CIA violated their right to private counsel." (*Washington Post*, April 3, 2001)

Mediation has become an increasingly popular method of resolving conflicts in numerous settings, ranging from family disputes to international hostilities. In the workplace, you may connect it with labor-management disputes. Congress created the Federal Mediation and Conciliation Service (FMCS) and the National Mediation Board to promote the mediation of labor disputes and thereby reduce the likelihood of costly strikes. But mediation has grown in popularity in the workplace to cover a variety of nonlabor disputes. A similar trend has been observed in other business contexts, including commercial, environmental, and intellectual property disputes.

A study by Lipsky and Seeber (1998), *The Appropriate Resolution of Corporate Disputes: A Report on the Growing Use of ADR by U.S. Corporations*, shows that most of the Fortune 1000 firms surveyed reported having use mediation to resolve employment disputes. In fact, 79 percent of 601 responding firms claimed having had at least some experience using mediation to resolve these workplace conflicts. Lipsky and Seeber observe that mediation will gain even greater acceptance in a variety of business-related areas because of its flexibility and other advantages.

We concur. Recent legal and public-policy developments, in conjunction with concerted efforts to expand the field and practice of ADR, make it much more likely that you will be exposed to mediation in employment and other business-related contexts as well. Your interest in mediation, however, should not be driven only because of the increased likelihood of exposure. You will find mediation a potentially powerful and versatile conflict resolution tool. While we will focus on the more formalized use of mediation in which an independent neutral third-party is retained, you can mediate conflicts informally without having to retain the services of an independent neutral person. Furthermore, even when using independent neutrals, you can structure mediation to operate expeditiously and informally.

CHAPTER OBJECTIVES

After reading this chapter, you will know how mediation works. You will appreciate what mediation is intended to achieve, when to use it, how to select a mediator, and how it fits into the bigger picture of conflict resolution. The chapter addresses the following topics:

- What is mediation?
- How does mediation fit into ADR?
- The advantages of mediation.
- When to use mediation.
- How to choose a mediator.
- How the mediation process works.
- What a mediation session looks like.
- What is the difference between "transformative" and "traditional" mediation?

- How do you measure mediation results?
- Calculating the costs of mediation.

WHAT IS MEDIATION?

Scenario

You work for a high-tech company in the Silicon Valley of the Washington, D.C. area: Fairfax, Virgina. You have a senior sales manager who has just been informed that he was not selected for the company's leadership development review program. This means, for all practical purposes, that his career has reached a plateau. The senior manager, age 55, does not want to quit. He believes that the rejection or denial is a ruse—disguising a real attempt to get him to quit. He recently refused an early retirement buy-out. The employee believes the sales vice president, who is 40, has an age bias against older managers. The VP and senior sales manager have been unable to work out the situation themselves. As the HR vice president, you anticipate an age discrimination claim. Would you recommend getting the parties to submit their disagreement to mediation? (We give an answer later in this chapter.)

Mediation, like facilitation, often gets misconstrued. You may be even more confused by the fact that mediators play different roles, even within the same mediation, and that they exhibit different styles. Some are relatively passive information transmitters, while others become aggressively involved in driving the parties toward settlement. Also, relatively new thinking in the field of mediation urges a significant shift in the emphasis away from settlement to developing the disputing parties to improve the way they interact. This model, called "transformational mediation," will be discussed later in the chapter. For now, we focus on traditional mediation.

One of the foremost neutrals in the field of workplace dispute resolution, Theodore Kheel, encapsulates the essence of mediation, arguing that

"Negotiators, mediators, and arbitrators have the same goal—to resolve the dispute. . . . The mediator is simply called upon to assist the disputants in agreeing with each other" (Kheel 1999). In traditional mediation, the mediator focuses on settlement. Thus, it is a more interventionist form of third-party involvement than facilitation. Unlike arbitration, however, the mediator does not render a decision, though he or she may well be instrumental in reaching the final outcome.

The following definition of mediation used by the U.S. Office of Personnel Management (1999) demonstrates this intended intensification of involvement. It also shows the variability in styles mediators may use. Both of these aspects—intensified involvement and stylistic variability—have implications for the degree of care you should take in selecting a mediator. A mediator is in a powerful and influential position. You can ill afford ethical breaches, incompetence, or lapses in judgment in a mediator.

Mediation is the intervention into a dispute or negotiation of an acceptable, impartial and neutral third party who has no decision-making authority. The objective of this intervention is to assist the parties in voluntarily reaching an acceptable resolution of issues in dispute.

Mediators differ in their degree of directiveness or control while assisting disputing parties. Some mediators set the stage for bargaining, make minimal procedural suggestions, and intervene in the negotiations only to avoid or overcome a deadlock. Other mediators are much more involved in forging the details of a resolution. Regardless of how directive the mediator is, the mediator performs the role of catalyst that enables the parties to initiate progress toward their own resolution of issues in dispute.

In brief, traditional mediation exhibits these fundamental properties:

- Use of a neutral, impartial third-party to aid the principals in reaching agreement or resolving disputes
- Voluntary as opposed to imposed settlements

- Emphasis on problem-solving and resolution when directive in nature

Your ability to use mediation effectively depends upon understanding these properties and how the mediation process works. As a principal involved in a dispute, you retain decision-making power with the other disputant. You do not forfeit it to the mediator, unless you mistakenly choose to do so.

Within such a directive or problem-solving mode, mediators play different roles to promote resolution. Kheel (1999) identifies five distinctive ones: housekeeper, ringmaster, educator, communicator, and innovator. You will find these roles akin to the facilitator's hats, for they concentrate on shaping the process of interaction toward an end. As *housekeeper*, the mediator sets the tone, takes notes, and clarifies his or her role as well as the purpose of the mediation. As *ringmaster*, the mediator keeps the process on track, keeping time, caucusing privately, transmitting information, and recessing and resuming discussions when necessary. As *educator*, the mediator may help clarify language, assist in interpreting information, and offer suggestions on how to couch arguments. But these intrusions must be made carefully so as not to violate confidences or unwisely invade the parties' decision-making prerogative and space. As *communicator*, the mediator shares information with the parties as a transmitter or messenger. Finally, as *innovator*, the mediator may suggest options, usually in the presence of both parties so that the appearance of fairness and impartiality is maintained.

In traditional mediation, you can expect mediators to play different roles. Use them to your advantage. You can also expect the focus to be on getting you to resolve the conflict, but you retain the right to choose whether to do so or not. And, you can expect different degrees of directiveness. You can influence the extent of involvement by what you tell the mediator and what you give the mediator permission to say to the other side, as well as how responsive you are to his or her suggestions. Maintain control of yourself, but allow the process to work.

How Does Mediation Fit into ADR?

You may comfortably view mediation as a form of dispute resolution that logically follows negotiation. It occurs when the negotiation, whether it be collaborative or adversarial, has not resulted in an agreement or resolution. But the parties are still willing to talk, albeit with the aid of a neutral. In some situations, like labor-management disputes in the airline and railroad industries, which are covered by the Railway Labor Act, mediation is mandatory. In other cases, governmental agencies or other forces may encourage the parties to try mediation, explaining the advantages, especially relative to litigation or other adverse consequences, such as a strike in a union setting. Generally speaking, mediation is a voluntary process. There are advantages to keeping it so, as the parties retain control over which process to use to resolve their disputes. Given that mediation requires the good-faith efforts of the disputants, you may wonder how realistic this is if mediation is made compulsory.

If mediation does not result in agreement, however, you have not reached the end of the ADR spectrum. Arbitration is a logical next step. Furthermore, mediation can be coupled with early neutral evaluation to induce the parties to settle themselves and avert either litigation or arbitration, where the parties relinquish control over the process and the decision.

The Advantages of Mediation

Mediation has grown in popularity. The previously cited survey of Fortune 1000 companies conducted by Lipsky and Seeber reached this pertinent conclusion:

Mediation has been used to resolve all types of disputes in corporate America. . . . Our [corporate] respondents . . . expect the use of mediation to grow significantly across the board.*

*Lipsky, David B. and Ronald L. Seeber. *The Appropriate Resolution of Corporate Disputes: A Report on the Growing Use of ADR by U.S. Corporations.* Ithaca, NY: Cornell/PERC Institute on Conflict Resolution, 1998, p.31.

Why such an expectation? You will find the answer in the comparative advantages of mediation (see Figure 6.1). As mentioned earlier, mediation is used extensively in employment disputes. Its popularity stems from its advantages in the areas of efficiency, process, relationship-building, and outcome attainment. These advantages are illuminated most brightly when mediation is compared to litigation.

First, you expect to derive some efficiencies. You use mediation because it is less expensive and speedier than litigation. In addition to saving money, it helps to avoid the often enormous costs of damaging publicity because it is a confidential proceeding.

Second, by involving an impartial, neutral third-party with facilitative skills, you promote meaningful communication, reduce barriers to understanding, and renew the parties' commitment to resolving conflict. Still, you retain control over the outcome. Mediation does not impose a settlement, but mediators may push the parties hard in that direction.

Third, you have an opportunity to stress mutual interests in mediation. By improving communication, the mediator should help you understand not only what those various interests are but also how the other side sees the world. In arbitration and litigation, you focus on the differences, justifying why your position is the superior one.

Figure 6.1 Comparative Advantages of Mediation

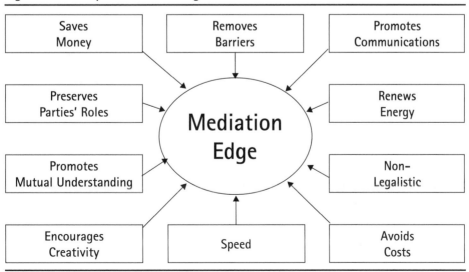

Fourth, by helping you to think more clearly and empathetically, mediation is intended to improve the quality of a settlement. Prior to mediation, you were stumped and stultified. Introducing the mediator helps get your creative juices flowing. If you focus more on exploring options than justifying irreconcilable positions, then your chances of creative decision making rise.

In short, you use mediation because it is speedier, more informal, less adversarial, and less costly than litigation. You should benefit from enhanced communications and richer understandings. As a result, you should be more satisfied with the process itself and the outcome. Lipsky and Seeber found that the most frequently mentioned reasons companies used mediation were that it (1) saves money; (2) allows the parties to resolve the disputes themselves; (3) results in a more satisfactory process; (4) saves time; and (5) yields more satisfactory settlements.

WHEN SHOULD YOU USE MEDIATION?

Figure 6.2 offers some guidelines for when to use mediation. You want to use mediation when it is most likely to produce the results you want (e.g., a settlement) and when it is better than the alternatives (e.g., no resolution or litigation). You should consider mediation when:

- The issues are too emotional to discuss without the calming influence of a third party.
- You are too exhausted to go on further without some prodding or encouragement.
- You want to maintain a good relationship or avoid further damages.
- You really do want to solve the problem or reach an agreement.
- You have difficulty communicating with the other side, regardless of whose fault that is.
- You want to avoid costly, protracted, formalistic procedures that invite adversarial representations of the dispute.
- You may fear further direct exchange without another party present.

Figure 6.2 Considerations About When to and Not to Use Mediation

Considerations To:	Considerations Not To:
Issues are too emotional to discuss calmly	Parties want a final, binding decision
Parties are psychologically exhausted	Parties are not interested in addressing or solving problems/issues
Parties' relationship is important	Parties are highly imbalanced
Parties want to solve a problem or address issues	Conflict involves issues of salient principle
Parties face difficult communications barriers	Parties want to set precedent for future
Parties want to avoid formal proceedings	Parties are unwilling to abide by possible resolutions
Parties are willing to explore options	Parties will not honor the confidentiality of the process
Parties fear direct confrontation without other presence	Parties' impasse results from lack of expertise or absence of information neither has to share
Parties have cultural barriers or differences	
Parties understand mediation process	

- You have cultural differences that impair communications and un-derstanding.
- You understand the mediation process, what it is supposed to do, and what your role is in the process. (For example, you should not expect the mediator to decide for you or the other side.)

Conversely, you will regard mediation less favorably when you want a final, binding decision. You may find it less appealing, particularly as the last step of a conflict resolution system, when important rights or princi-ples need to be settled. Similarly, your reservations may build if the parties seem imbalanced in terms of power. In this context, mediation may simply be viewed as a procedural extension of the imbalance present in a negotia-tion. Also, if the parties are extremely polarized, emotional, or hostile, you may have doubts about trying mediation, unless emotions or hostilities have had some time to settle. But good mediators can sometimes help you find the forest in the middle of the trees and enable you to work past these complications.

How to Choose a Mediator

If you intend to use mediation to resolve a particular workplace dispute or plan to introduce it as an organization-wide ADR option for employment disputes, you confront two immediate issues. First, where do you find a mediator? Second, what competencies do you want in a mediator?

As to the first question, you could look internally within your company for an "impartial person" or attempt to cultivate your own corporate cadre of mediators. This option may not be viable when you need the services of a mediator quickly. Also, internal sources are not independent, which may raise serious questions about their perceived or real impartiality and neutrality. Some organizations address this issue by drawing from internal sources located at different sites and establishing procedures to promote the autonomous stature of the internally sourced mediators.

You should consider going outside your organization. We generally recommend this approach (another one of our biases), especially when questions raising employment rights are connected with the dispute to be mediated. You have plenty of sources to go to, which you may find locally, regionally, or nationally in terms of geographic coverage. Figure 6.3 lists several organizations that can assist you. The American Arbitration Association (AAA) is one of the most prolific referral sources. It, like other dispute resolution providers, maintains a roster of qualified neutrals. You can specify your needs and request appropriate referrals. Although nongovernmental organizations charge a fee for their services, their fees are not exorbitant. They want the business, and many operate not-for-profit.

We recommend contacting one or more sources to see what services they offer and how they can help you evaluate the qualifications of their neutrals (e.g., mediators). Many providers, such as the AAA and the CPR Institute for Dispute Resolution, have plentiful information on the web about how they work, where they can be contacted, and relevant guidelines on how mediations should be conducted.

Figure 6.3 Where to Find a Mediator

- American Arbitration Association
- American Bar Association Section on Dispute Resolution
- Construction Mediation Inc.
- Dispute Prevention/Resolution Services
- Equal Employment Opportunity Commission
- Federal Mediation and Conciliation Service
- Global Arbitration Mediation Association
- International Academy of Mediators
- JAMS/Endispute
- Society of Professionals in Dispute Resolution
- CPR Institute for Dispute Resolution
- World Intellectual Property Organization Arbitration and Mediation Center

With a little bit of effort, you should not have much difficulty locating a supply of mediators that you can call upon as needed. Your bigger difficulty will be in satisfying yourself that you are getting a qualified mediator. The professionalism of a provider is a critical factor in making this judgment. Obviously, the more experience you have had with mediation and mediators, the less difficulty you will have in assessing qualifications. Regardless of whether you are experienced or a novice in using mediation in employment disputes (or any other type of business dispute for that matter), you want a mediator who represents the traits listed in Figure 6.4. In this regard, you need to do more than get the "right" person. People must be confident that the process you used is a fair and reasonable one.

First, you want a mediator who is impartial, neutral, and fair. Perhaps even more important, you want one who is perceived as such. If a

Figure 6.4 Qualifications of the Ideal Mediator

- Impartial and Fair
- Perceived as Impartial and Fair
- Personal Stature and Respect
- Inspires Trust
- Understands People
- Sets Civil Tone
- Good Listener
- Capable of Understanding Issues and Facts
- Good Analytical Skills
- Creative and Imaginative
- Articulate
- Patient and Flexible
- Energetic
- Experienced
- Expertise

mediator is independent of your company and comes with a favorable reputation, then the chances grow that he or she will have the personal stature and respect needed to inspire the trust of all disputants.

Second, apart from having sufficient cognitive and analytical capabilities, you want a mediator who understands and relates to you. You want a mediator who can communicate clearly and diplomatically. A mediator must have well developed listening skills. And he or she must be able to keep a civil tongue, in the face of emotion and combativeness, while ensuring that the parties do not allow their emotions to boil over and endanger the process. But the parties need opportunities to express their feelings.

Third, because mediations are intellectually intensive, and some can last for hours on end, you need a mediator who is patient, energetic, and creative enough to keep things going when the parties hit the doldrums. A mediator must be flexible. The needs of the parties come first.

Finally, in some instances, the mediator may need subject-matter expertise. For instance, if you are involved in a mediation to resolve a labor-management dispute, you will want someone who understands labor relations. If you are in an industry in which understanding acceptable conduct or practice requires knowledge of that industry, then you will look for a mediator with such familiarity. In situations where the mediator will address issues affecting employment rights, such as in the area of equal employment opportunity, you will look for mediators who have an understanding of what the law means in this complicated arena. Experience handling these types of cases is often a must.

Should You Mediate?

Returning to the Senior Sales Manager Scenario mentioned above, we recommend that you consider mediating this conflict before it spills into costly litigation. Ask the parties to submit voluntarily to a mediation session. Select a mediator from an independent organization's roster. Request one competent in EEO law and age discrimination specifically. Have the parties sign an agreement stating that they will abide by any settlement agreed to at the mediation, though agreement is not required. Allow the parties to bring legal counsel to the session.

HOW MEDIATION WORKS: THE PROCESS

We have divided the mediation process into six steps (see Figure 6.5). In Step 1, you agree to mediate. You may have entered into a pre-dispute agreement, in which you have agreed, at the request of any party, to submit a dispute to mediation before it arises. The American Arbitration Association has constructed a model pre-dispute clause for employment:

If a dispute arises out of or relates to this [employment application; employment ADR program; employment contract] or the breach thereof, and if the dispute cannot be settled through negotiation,

Figure 6.5 The Mediation Process

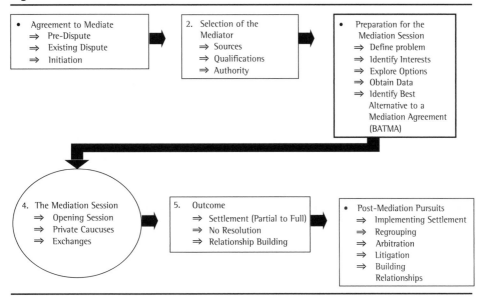

> the parties agree first to try in good faith to settle the dispute by mediation administered by the American Arbitration Association under its National Rules for the Resolution of Employment Disputes, before resorting to arbitration, litigation, or some other dispute resolution procedure.

Or, alternatively, you may agree to submit a current dispute to mediation, if you do not have such a pre-existing arrangement.

Once a dispute has arisen, the parties may initiate mediation by requesting it. The request, made in writing, states the nature of the dispute and the parties involved.

In Step 2, you select the mediator. A mediator may be selected in a variety of ways. Through joint agreement or company procedure, you may request an independent organization, such as the AAA, to draw a list of acceptable mediators from a pre-existing roster. Alternatively, you may privately contract the services of a mediator, e.g., a private attorney who mediates. Or, you can use an internal pool of mediators if the company has an in-house program.

In selecting a mediator, you want to be careful to stipulate the qualifications you need. You may ask for a particular type of expertise, educational background, or record of experience. You may also ask for references to be provided. Check the references.

It is important for the parties to define the authority of the mediator. They should understand that the mediator does not have the power to force a settlement. But an agreed-to settlement may be binding upon the parties, unless there is evidence of corruption or misconduct on the part of the mediator. Also, you may require the designated mediator to complete a conflict-of-interest disclosure form. The parties may be permitted to object on conflict-of-interest or competency grounds. Some independent organizations have already established procedures whereby the parties may challenge a mediator on selected grounds before having to go to the session.

In Step 3, you prepare for the mediation. We recommend that you prepare for a mediation like you would for a negotiation, but with the aid of your legal counsel, especially if issues involving employment rights are raised. You should define the issues in dispute; the relative interests involved; the options for possible resolution; and the standards by which to assess these options. One last point: you should identify the best alternative to a mediated agreement (BATMA) just as you look for a best alternative to negotiated agreement (BATNA) in the negotiating phase preceding mediation. What do you do if mediation does not result in a settlement?

In Step 4, you're in an actual mediation session, which is described below in more detail.

Step 5 is the outcome of the session. If you reach an agreement, the outcome is a cosigned settlement, which can be made binding on the parties. Alternatively, you may not agree. In that case, the dispute may go to arbitration or some other procedure. You should consider the implications of not reaching an agreement on your relationship with the other party.

Finally, in Step 6, you may seek implementation if an accord has been mediated. You should begin to rebuild your relationship with the other party, regardless of how happy you may be with the settlement. Post-settlement conduct is an important but frequently overlooked part of the mediation process. It is vital that the parties live up to their agreements if the process is to have integrity and inspire confidence.

THE MEDIATION SESSION

No two mediation sessions are exactly alike. But mediations are not random events with no common features. Figure 6.6 illustrates a typical traditional mediation session. The session will vary in formality depending upon the nature of the issue, the interests of the parties, and the style of the mediator. You can prestructure mediation to be less or more formal. Often, you will want legal representation, especially if questions pertaining to employment rights are involved. A typical mediation session may last two to three hours, though some can go on longer. Sometimes, multiple sessions are required. Nine common steps in the session are:

1. Pre-meeting arrangements: Set session and agree to counsel.
2. Opening statement by mediator: Set ground rules.

**Figure 6.6 The Traditional Mediation Session
(2–3 Hours)**

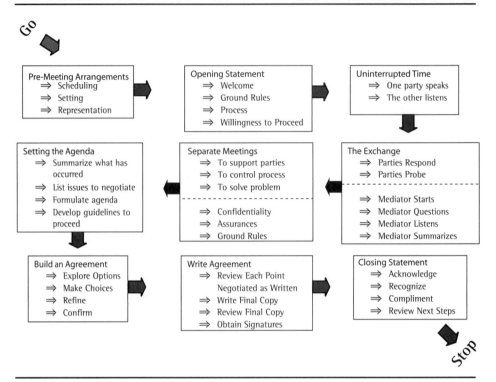

3. Parties' statements, uninterrupted: Present your side.

4. Mutual agenda setting: Decide what to decide.

5. Separate back-and-forth caucuses: Think creatively and privately.

6. Mediator transmittals to caucuses: Communicate options.

7. Building an agreement: Review, consolidate, find common interests.

8. Written agreement: Review and sign.

9. Closing statement: Mediator congratulates parties, reviews next steps.

Unlike facilitation, the parties will often separate for private caucuses and meetings with the mediator. These private sessions can be invaluable in helping you explore options while avoiding committing to particular solutions in the presence of the other side.

TRANSFORMATIVE MEDIATION

You need to be aware of a relatively recent development in mediation as an employment dispute resolution procedure. Several academics and practitioners have attacked traditional mediation for its problem-solving orientation and settlement-driven bias. Mediators advertise their settlement rates, and ADR advocates emphasize that mediation has produced high rates of settlement (usually 70 percent or better) in employment disputes.

But in a major departure from this line of thinking, Bush and Folger provide an alternative way of using mediation. In their judgment, traditional mediation does not really represent an *alternative* dispute resolution procedure at all. Instead, it has evolved into a quintessential adjudicative process:

> The problem-solving approach to mediation does not offer a meaningful alternative to adjudicative forums. Reaching settlements through mediation as currently practiced is, in a fundamental sense, not that different from settling disputes through arbitration.*

Consequently, Bush and Folger advocate a different model of mediation—the transformative one. The transformational view of mediation emphasizes changing and developing the parties to improve the way they think, behave, and interact. You no longer judge the success of mediation by its settlement rate, but rather the extent to which it enables the parties to handle conflict better themselves. The goals become *empowerment and recognition.*

In transformative mediation, you "aim higher." You seek benefits that accrue to a broader array of workplace interactions, because the disputants are transformed or improved. In addition, you benefit over the long term, not just by a short-term settlement. As a manager, you will have fewer conflicts to deal with because your employees and co-workers can deal

*Bush, Robert A. Baruch and Joseph P. Folger. *The Promise of Mediation: Responding to Conflict Through Empowerment and Recognition.* San Francisco: Jossey-Bass, 1994, pp. 283–284.

with them without you. In this process, you know that you have been *empowered* if you

- Reach a clearer understanding of what is important and why
- Understand your goals and interests more clearly
- Become aware of possible options to secure goals

You achieve *recognition* (of the other party) when you can

- Reflect on the other side's human predicament
- Focus on what the other party is experiencing
- Desire to focus on the other party's situation

In essence, transformative mediation rests on a different set of assumptions from traditional mediation (see Figure 6.7). It views conflict as an opportunity to develop, not a problem to solve. It focuses on building capability rather than constructing a settlement. It stresses empowerment and recognition, not agreement. And the mediator focuses on a relationship-building rather than a short-term directive process. In transformative mediation, you are deeply interested in the postmediation results. Are the disputants better at dealing with conflict as individual employees and members or citizens of an organizational community?

In the real world, the U.S. Postal Service has emerged as one of the

Figure 6.7 Traditional vs. Transformative Mediation

Dimension	Traditional	Transformative
Assumption	Conflict is a Problem to be Solved	Conflict is an Opportunity To Develop People
Focus	Getting a Settlement	Developing People to Cope with Own Conflicts
Goal	Formal or Informal Agreement	Empowerment and Recognition of Parties
Mediator's Role	Directive/Problem-Solving	Process

Source: Robert A. Baruch Bush and Joseph P. Folger. 1994. *The Promise of Mediation: Responding to Conflict Through Empowerment and Recognition.* San Francisco: Jossey-Bass, Inc.

leading users and proponents of the transformative model. In 1994, it launched its Resolve Employment Disputes, Reach Equitable Solutions Swiftly (REDRESS) program on a pilot basis to handle EEO complaints. Since then, it has taken the REDRESS program nationwide.

Although the program is explicitly interested in resolving disputes, it is also concerned about using the process to produce positive "longer-lasting upstream effects in the workplace" (Hallberlin 2000). Representatives of the U.S. Postal Service have testified to the apparent success of REDRESS, both in terms of resolving conflicts and achieving these "upstream" effects.

Although it offers an appealing promise and enjoys strong advocates, transformative mediation has been criticized and questioned. According to Zumeta (2001): "Detractors say that . . . transformative mediation takes too long, and too often ends without agreement. They worry that outcomes can be contrary to standards of fairness and that mediators in these approaches cannot protect the weaker party."

MEASURING RESULTS

How can you measure the success or effectiveness of a workplace mediation program? We recommend that you use the same basic approach taken to assess the effectiveness of facilitation as an ADR procedure. That is, rely on multiple indicators. Thus, you focus on the following as possible measures: the ratio between the cost of mediation to alternatives, the settlement rate, the parties' satisfaction levels, empowerment and recognition effects, cost and attitudinal measures compared to industry benchmarks, and the level of education and understanding with respect to conflict resolution engendered by the program.

THE MEDIATION CALCULATOR

Irrespective of the type of mediation you choose, your company should track the costs of mediation relative to alternative conflict resolution procedures. Figure 6.8 provides a formula for calculating the costs of media-tion. The costs include the administration fee (if any), the charges of the mediator, the parties' representational costs, the parties' costs in terms of compensated time, an overhead factor, the price tag of the settlement (if reached), and postsettlement implementation costs. This summation can be benchmarked against alternatives. You can make comparisons across mediators, types of cases mediated, and mediation styles, should your company, for example, be interested in comparing the cost of a transform-ative model to a more traditional problem-solving one.

In this area of costs, you should be aware that the issue of who pays for the mediator is a nontrivial one. It has implications for the affordability of the program and the perceived impartiality of the mediator. We will address this issue in more detail in Chapters 6 and 13. Suffice it to say that the conflict resolution program you adopt should be structured to make it affordable and ensure the appearance of impartiality. Splitting me-diator fees is one way to promote perceptions of impartiality.

Figure 6.8 The Mediation Calculator

Cost Item	Cost Calculus
1. Administering Organization Fees	As Stipulated
2. Mediator	[Fee × Time] + Expenses
3. Parties' Representation • Pre-session prep • Session • Post-session	(Number of billing hours × Representation hourly rate) + Chargeable expenses
4. Parties' Costs • Pre-session prep • Session • Post-session	(Number of hours × Direct and indirect compensation per hour normally paid to parties) + Parties' expenses
5. Overhead	Clerical Fees, Copying, Rental Fees, etc.
6. Settlement	The dollar value or in kind equivalent of the settlement (if reached)
7. Post-Settlement	Sum of post-settlement costs.

Total Cost = [1 + 2 + 3 + 4 + 5 + 6 + 7]

Manager's Checklist: Using Mediation

Use the following checklist when considering a mediation program:

1. Is the mediation program pre-dispute or ad hoc (e.g., case-by-case)?
2. What cases are eligible for mediation?
3. Who is eligible for the mediation program?
4. How will mediators be selected?
5. How will mediators be compensated?
6. What style of mediation is preferable?
7. How will the process be triggered?
8. How timely will the process occur?
9. Are the parties entitled to legal representation?
10. Shall the costs incurred by the parties be subsidized?
11. Should the parties be required to sign confidentiality agreements?
12. Is mediation the last stage of a conflict resolution system or are there backward- and forward-movement options (e.g., forward to arbitration)?

Once your program has been adopted and implemented, you should undertake periodic evaluations, measuring costs and satisfaction levels.

Exercise 6.1: Mediating a Promotion Dispute

You are a head of a department of architects. You have recently gone through a round of performance reviews and promotions. You recommended promoting two persons to the project director level. You rejected a third person's promotion application. The rejected architect has expressed deep reservations about the fairness of the process and the merits of the decision. You have entered into an agreement to mediate this dispute. If a settlement is reached, it will be binding. How would you prepare for the mediation? What are your options? How would you present your case? How would you deal with the issue of relationships versus outcomes?

Exercise 6.2: Mediating a Workplace Conflict

Think of a recent workplace conflict that you have been involved in that did not get resolved satisfactorily. Could it have been better addressed through mediation? If you had used mediation, how would you have prepared?

- Describe the conflict.
- What were the interests involved?
- What were the possible options?
- How would you have evaluated the options?
- What was your best alternative to a mediated agreement?

Chapter 7

Arbitration

American Air Accepts Arbitration: "American Airlines agreed to binding arbitration to resolve an impasse with its flight attendants' union." (Reuters, May 24, 2001)

Arbitration Results in $50,000 Wage Hike: "New Brunswick government and the province's 1,300 physicians agreed to an 18 percent pay increase for physicians as recommended by an arbitrator." (*Yahoo Headlines*, April 18, 2001)

High Court Upholds Forced Arbitration: "Companies can require workers to submit job-discrimination claims to an arbitrator and waive their right to file suit." (*Washington Post*, March 22, 2001)

Scenario

You are the supervisor of a clerical pool. In your company, clerical employees are expected to show up on time, dress according to code, and maintain a professional attitude. You have had recurring problems with one of your assistants. He shows up late once or twice a week. He violates the dress code. And, in your judgment, his attitude is a bit too chilly to be professional. You have written him up on all three counts twice. Just recently, you suspended him for three days without pay for continued violations of company policies. The assistant has filed a grievance under your company's in-house dispute resolution program (the company is nonunion). The grievance has gone through the first three steps, being decided at each against the employee, upholding the suspension. The employee has decided to take it to arbitration. What can you expect? What should you do to prepare?

Arbitration, like mediation, has long been used to resolve workplace disputes. You hear about it typically in union-management contexts, where it has become standard operating procedure. Familiar headlines include arbitrated settlements of professional athletes' salary disputes with club owners; teachers' contract disputes with school boards; and police and firefighters' disputes with cities. Arbitration makes the news because it is consequential.

You use arbitration to resolve rights-based and interest-based controversies, as well as differences over the use of power. When you use it to resolve a salary dispute, you are using it in an interest-based context. When you arbitrate a dispute over whether or not someone has been discriminated against, you are using it in a rights-based context. In both situations, you may have power imbalances between the grievant and the corporate authority (e.g., club owner or supervisor). From the standpoint of the grievant, you may prefer arbitration because of its organizational autonomy and impartiality. It becomes an equalizer in dispute resolution.

Recently, federal courts have given a big boost to arbitration as an alternative to litigation in resolving employment disputes that involve statutorily protected rights. As an employer, you may require that employees, as a condition of employment, agree to arbitrate disputes over issues involving legal rights and essentially forfeit the right to pursue litigation. In sanctioning this requirement, the U.S. Supreme Court, in its March 2001 *Circuit City* decision, has elevated the arbitration of nonlabor disputes to the position accorded arbitration as a feature of dispute resolution in unionized workplaces with collective bargaining agreements that have grievance procedures culminating in binding arbitration.

CHAPTER OBJECTIVES

At the end of this chapter, you will know when and how to use arbitration to resolve employment disputes. You will appreciate the imperative of being careful in selecting these adjudicators, and you will better understand why it is important to exhaust other ADR procedures before resorting to arbitration. This chapter presents the following topics:

- What is arbitration?
- How does arbitration fit into ADR?
- The advantages of arbitration.
- When to use arbitration.
- How to choose an arbitrator.
- The arbitration process.
- Standards of conduct.
- Varieties of arbitration.
- Measuring arbitration results.
- The arbitration calculator.

WHAT IS ARBITRATION?

Several arbitral forms have developed over time to resolve employment and other business-related disputes. You have a choice in deciding which type to use. At the core of these variants is the ultimate call for a judgment to be rendered by an arbitrator or panel of arbitrators. You presume that the arbitrator or panel is impartial and neutral.

Perhaps the most fundamental distinction for you to keep in mind in choosing arbitration is whether or not the arbitrator's judgment is binding or advisory. Because of the deference courts commonly accord arbitration, binding decisions entail a real sense of finality, one courts will enforce if called upon to do so. Nonbinding or advisory arbitration, while perhaps resulting in an intellectually compelling or even mutually agreeable judgment, does not commit you to accept the decision.

With this distinction in mind, we offer two definitions of arbitration, as provided by the U.S. Office of Personnel Management.

Binding arbitration involves the presentation of a dispute to an impartial or neutral individual (arbitrator) or panel (arbitration panel) for issuance of a binding decision. Unless arranged otherwise, the parties usually have the ability to decide who the individuals are that serve as arbitrators. In some cases, the parties may retain a particular arbitrator (often from a list of arbitrators) to decide a number of cases or to serve the parties for a specified length of time (this is common when a panel is involved). Parties often select a different arbitrator for each new dispute. A common understanding by the parties in all cases, however, is that they will be bound by the opinion of the decision maker rather than simply be obligated to "consider" an opinion or recommendation. Under this method, the third party's decision generally has the force of law but does not set a legal precedent. It is usually not reviewable by the courts.

Nonbinding arbitration involves presenting a dispute to an impartial or neutral individual (arbitrator) or panel (arbitration panel) for issuance of an advisory or non-binding decision. This method is generally one of the most common quasi-judicial means for resolving disputes and has been used for a long period of time to resolve labor/management and commercial disputes. Under the process, the parties have input into the selection process, giving them the ability to select an individual or panel with some expertise and knowledge of the disputed issues, although this is not a prerequisite for an individual to function as an arbitrator. Generally, the individuals chosen are those known to be impartial, objective, fair, and to have the ability to evaluate and make judgments about data or facts. The opinions issued by the third party in such cases are non-binding; however, parties do have the flexibility to determine, by mutual agreement, that an opinion will be binding in a particular case.*

HOW DOES ARBITRATION FIT INTO ADR?

Because of its decision-making nature, you will find arbitration at the end of the ADR spectrum. In companies with multiple ADR procedures (negotiation, mediation, factfinding, and arbitration), you will typically find arbitration as the last available option. This, obviously, is no coincidence.

Although it often does, arbitration does not have to follow mediation or facilitation. You could opt to go directly to arbitration after negotiation. On some occasions, in fact, you may want to do this. Hence, you want to be flexible in sequencing the venues of dispute resolution.

*U.S. Office of Personnel Management, Office of Workforce Relations. *Alternative Dispute Resolution: A Resource Guide.* Washington, D.C.: OPM, July 1999, v. 3, p. 7.

Once you resort to arbitration, however, your options thereafter are limited. If you have chosen binding arbitration, you will be bound by the arbitrator's decision. The courts accord considerable deference to arbitration, limiting legal appeals of arbitral rulings. If you want to keep the doors to litigation open, you should avoid binding arbitration.

THE ADVANTAGES OF ARBITRATION

Because of its relative finality, you may have reservations about going to arbitration or offering it as a standard option in your company's conflict resolution menu. But you must make your decisions relative to various possibilities, including litigation. As you get closer to arbitration, the controversy most likely is getting more litigable. Compared to litigation, arbitration offers several advantages. This explains why Lipsky and Seeber (1998) found that 80 percent of the major companies they surveyed reported having used arbitration to resolve a multitude of business disputes. Fully 62 percent reported using arbitration to resolve employment disputes.

Figure 7.1 illustrates some of the general advantages companies see

Figure 7.1 Comparative Advantages of Arbitration

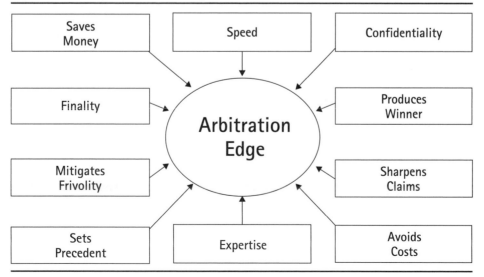

in arbitration. It is cheaper, less formal, speedier, confidential, and final (i.e., you generally do not have mountains of appeals). Figure 7-2 compares arbitration to mediation on selected dimensions. While the principals lose control vis-a-vis mediation, they gain finality. It has the advantage of mitigating frivolous claims, producing a "winner" (which is sometimes desired by one or the other party), and sharpening arguments surrounding the claims in dispute (see Figure 7.2).

Another important advantage of arbitration relative to litigation for you to keep uppermost in your mind is that you have some choice in choosing the arbitrator. You can structure the process to expand your range of choices and ensure the opportunity to object to designated arbitrators before you go to a hearing. In fact, one of the main reasons why federal courts have deferred to labor arbitration is because of the expertise these arbitrators bring to the adjudicatory process that cannot be found in the general courts. Furthermore, while arbitrators' decisions do not usually establish precedents with the compelling force of court rulings, they nonetheless may suggest guidelines to follow in subsequent interactions at work.

Interestingly, some of the reasons Lipsky and Seeber (1998) found to explain why companies use arbitration (except when it is required by contract), are that it saves time, saves money, results in a more satisfactory process, and uses the expertise of a neutral. But you do lose control of the process and outcome, particularly when the decision is binding. As mentioned, this is why some people may feel uncomfortable with arbitration. Lipsky and Seeber say that their corporate respondents "are uneasy about arbitration in part because they believe they are less able to control the process."

Figure 7.2 Arbitration, Mediation, and Litigation

Dispute Resolution Method	Speed	Cost	Finality	Principals' Control	Confidentiality	Precedent
Arbitration	Moderate	Moderate	High	Low	High	Moderate
Mediation	High	Low	Moderate	High	High	Low
Litigation	Low	High	High	Low	Low	High
			(If not appealed)			

WHEN TO USE ARBITRATION

Figure 7.3 gives you some guideposts for when to use arbitration.

> *First*, when you need a decision to get a dispute behind you, you may
> want to use arbitration. You can structure a process that is not
> prone to delay or that allows for expedited arbitration.
>
> *Second*, arbitration gains appeal when you have exhausted other
> means. There is no point in trying to beat a dead horse to death.
> Nor is there much point in going over the same arguments repeat-
> edly with no end in sight.
>
> *Third*, you may want an impartial decision, for the benefit of the dispu-
> tants and the company, but want to avoid the expense and public
> injury of litigation. Once you go to court, you really lose control.
> Corporate affairs become an open book. Lawyers push for victory.
> Larger issues and principles take over the situation and may swamp
> your interests as well as the interests of the other party.
>
> *Fourth*, you use arbitration when you (or others) have doubts about
> the objectivity and fairness of kicking the dispute to a higher rein of
> management. A grievant may perceive that managers scratch each
> other's backs, following an unspoken code of loyalty. By resorting
> to arbitration, you signal to employees the impartiality and fairness
> of your company's dispute resolution program. Your concern is
> more than mere window-dressing. You want substantive impartial-
> ity. Your commitment of substantive impartiality and procedural

Figure 7.3 When to Use Arbitration

- The parties in an employment dispute need a decision.
- The parties have exhausted efforts to resolve the employment dispute themselves.
- The parties need an impartial decision but want to avoid litigation.
- The parties lack confidence in the impartiality or fairness of submitting the dispute to a higher organizational level for a decision.
- The parties need external guidance or expertise on how to resolve the employment dispute.

fairness lends credibility to corporate assertions that employment disputes can be resolved without prejudice, a claim highly relevant when employee rights are involved.

Fifth, you may find yourself in some situations where you lack the expertise or knowledge to render a reasonable decision. Have an employee's contractual or legal rights been violated? Are your managerial actions consistent with standard or acceptable industry practice? Sometimes you need the benefit of an observer's interpretation of the facts, law, and contractual language. There is an old Chinese proverb to the effect that the observers of a chess game have a better view than the players. The same case can be made here.

HOW TO CHOOSE AN ARBITRATOR

This is really a three-part question: How do you want the process administered? Where do you find an arbitrator? What qualifications do you look for in an arbitrator?

Administration

First, do you want an administered or self-administered process (see Figure 7.4)? If you use an administered process, an external organization like the AAA will set up and administer the procedure according to its rules,

Figure 7.4 Arbitrator Selection Issues

Issues	Options
● Administration	√ Independent-Organization Administered √ Self-or-Non-Administered
● Number	√ Single √ Tribunal or Panel
● Methodology	√ Pre-Existing Rosters √ Private Referrals

for a fee. Such organizations will provide you with a list of arbitrators from which to choose. The list is drawn from a pre-existing roster. You can specify certain qualifications, and may challenge arbitrators on selected bases (e.g., conflict of interest). The organization works with you to make the necessary arrangements and can run a lot of interference between the parties on establishing ground rules. You can also receive a lot of technical and background information to get you prepared. And, you have ready-to-go standards of conduct.

If you opt for a self-administered or nonadministered process, you may still go to organizations like the CPR Institute for Dispute Resolution to obtain a list of qualified arbitrators. Under this arrangement, you have greater control over the mechanics of the process. However, as a general rule we recommend that you use an administered process when you are inexperienced or when you are uncertain about the qualifications of arbitrators. The administering organization not only can provide the arbitrator but can also deal with whatever difficulties you might encounter with that person in the course of the arbitration process. These organizations tend to have a strong interest in protecting the integrity and competency of the process. Furthermore, when you use an administered process with a previously established set of practices and guidelines, you foster the appearance of independence and impartiality that is so important to the parties' ultimate satisfaction with the process.

Another issue you need to address is whether to use a panel or a single arbitrator. A panel might consist of two arbitrators appointed by the respective disputing parties. A neutral third arbitrator would be selected by the two parties' designees or by an independent organization. Having three arbitrators may add to the cost of arbitration. For three arbitrators to make a decision, at least one of the parties' designees must side with the neutral third arbitrator.

Panels have been suggested as being most useful in interest disputes where a compromise is needed. According to Kheel (1999), "They are less useful in disputes over the meaning and application of law or contracts. In such disputes they rarely add anything more to the arbitration than cost and time."

Where to Find an Arbitrator

Just as was the case with mediation, you can go to several organizations for assistance in locating an arbitrator (see Figure 7.5). Together, the American Arbitration Association and the Federal Mediation and Conciliation Service maintain rosters of about 3,500 arbitrators, although only a relatively small percentage of these individuals are full-time arbitrators. Many work in other capacities—as lawyers or academics—and moonlight as arbitrators.

You will find the AAA among the best known in this area. It offers mediation and arbitration services in a variety of areas besides employment. The AAA was formed in 1926. It has thirty-seven offices nationwide and it has arbitral agreements with institutions in numerous other countries.

The AAA administers the arbitration. To promote consistency and integrity, it has issued the following publications: a *Guide for Employment Arbitrators*, the *Code of Professional Responsibility for Arbitrators of Labor-Management Disputes*, a handbook on *Resolving Employment Disputes—A Practical Guide*, and a compendium *National Rules for the Resolution of Employment Disputes*. According to the AAA:

> To resolve workplace conflict, more than 500 employers and 5 million employees worldwide turn to the AAA. The AAA's National

Figure 7.5 Where to Find an Arbitrator

- America Arbitration Association
- American Bar Association Section on Dispute Resolution
- Conflict Resolution Center International
- CPR Institute for Dispute Resolution
- Dispute Prevention/Resolution Services
- Federation Mediation and Conciliation Service
- Global Arbitration Mediation Association
- International Court of Arbitration
- Judicial Arbitration and Mediation Services/Endispute (JAMs)
- National Academy of Arbitrators
- National Arbitration Forum
- Society of Professionals in Dispute Resolution
- World Intellectual Property Organization Arbitration and Mediation Center

> Rules for the Resolution of Employment and the Due Process Proto-
> col for the Mediation and Arbitration of Statutory Disputes Arising
> Out of the Employment Relationship have set the standard for dis-
> pute resolution in the workplace. To hear and resolve these cases,
> the AAA offers a panel of national experts—diverse in gender and
> ethnicity—who have significant employment law experience and
> have attended the Association's mandatory employment arbitrator
> training program.*

In offering its services in the area of employment disputes, the National Rules apply. In using the AAA's services, you oblige yourself to
these rules, notwithstanding agreements you may have to the contrary.

> AAA Statement on Applicable Rules of Arbitration
>
> The parties shall be deemed to have made these rules a part of
> their arbitration agreement whenever they have provided for arbi-
> tration by the American Arbitration Association . . . under its Na-
> tional Rules for the Resolution of Employment Disputes. If a party
> establishes that an adverse material inconsistency exists between
> the arbitration agreement and these rules, the arbitrator shall apply
> these rules.

You can also locate an arbitrator by contacting the Society of Professionals in Dispute Resolution, the American Bar Association's Labor and
Employment Section Membership List, the CRP Institute for Dispute Resolution, the National Academy of Arbitrators, and the Judicial Arbitration
and Mediation Services/End Dispute (JAMS). In addition, other organizations offer relevant information on arbitrating particular types of disputes,
as for example, the World Intellectual Property Organization Arbitration
and Mediation Center.

Arbitrator Qualifications

In choosing an arbitrator, you will be keenly interested in several general
as well as certain specific qualifications (see Figure 7.6). In general terms,

---

*American Arbitration Association. *1999 American Arbitration Association Annual Report.*
New York: American Arbitration Association, 2000, p.19.

Figure 7.6 Arbitrator Qualifications

General Qualifications	Specific Qualifications
• Impartiality	• Academic Background
• Integrity	• Industry Experience
• Honesty	• Technical Expertise
• Temperament	• Familiarity
• Competence	• Decision-Making Methodology
• Consistency	• Rulings
• Experience	

you want an arbitrator who is impartial, honest, of balanced temperament, analytically competent, reasonably consistent, and experienced. Review the qualifications carefully, check references, and review their recent decisions. On top of these qualifications, you may need an arbitrator with a particular background (e.g., a lawyer), a specialized competence (e.g., employment law), or familiarity with the industry or occupation connected with a dispute (e.g., a dispute between a physician and a hospital over an employment matter).

The Arbitration Process

The arbitration may be conducted in various ways. You may agree upon your own set of procedures to follow, or you may choose to follow procedures developed by provider organizations (e.g., AAA, CRP). There are several steps to follow in arbitration (see Figure 7.7).

Step 1. Agreement to Arbitrate

You need to consummate an agreement to arbitrate. The agreement may involve an existing dispute or provide for arbitration of future disputes. Sample language of predispute and existing dispute agreements developed by the AAA is shown below.

> ### 1. Arbitration of Unresolved Future Disputes
>
> Any controversy or claim arising out of or relating to this [employment application; employment ADR program; employment con-

tract] that is not resolved by the parties, shall, upon the written agreement of the parties after the dispute arises, be settled by arbitration administered by the American Arbitration Association under its National Rules for the Resolution of Employment Disputes and judgment upon the award rendered by the arbitrator(s) may be entered in any court having jurisdiction thereof.

2. Agreement to Submit an Existing Dispute to Arbitration

We, the undersigned parties, hereby agree to submit to arbitration administered by the American Arbitration Association under its National Rules for the Resolution of Employment Disputes, the following controversy: (cite briefly). We further agree that the above controversy be submitted to (one) (three) arbitrator(s). We further agree that we will faithfully observe this agreement and the rules, that we will abide by and perform any award rendered by the arbitrator(s), and that judgment of the court having jurisdiction may be entered on the award.

As revealed in the sample language, you initiate the process by submitting a written agreement to go to arbitration. The submission materials

Figure 7.7 The Arbitration Process

Step 1: Agreement to Arbitration
- Pre-Dispute
- Existing Dispute
- Arbitration Type
- Initiation

Step 2: Arbitration Management Conference
- Issues
- Date
- Evidence
- Fees

Step 3: Prepare Your Case
- Gathering Information
- Analyze Data
- Prepare Documents
- Build Case

Step 4: Hold the Hearing
- Opening
- Evidence
- Closing

Step 5: The Arbitrator's Award
- Decision
- Notification

will include a statement of the claim with a response from the accused party.

Step 2. Arbitration Management Conference

In this step, there will be a pre-hearing management conference with both parties, their counsels, and the arbitrator. The arbitrator will ask you address such matters as:

- The issues to be arbitrated
- Preferred date, time, and place of the hearing
- Rules regarding discovery of evidence
- Requisite standards of proof
- Witnesses to be called
- Briefs to be submitted
- Allocation of attorneys' fees and costs
- Form of arbitration award to be issued

If this sounds hauntingly legalistic, remember that arbitration, by design, is an adjudicatory process.

Step 3. Prepare Your Case

In the context of arbitration, you are preparing a case to win a decision. You put your best evidence forward, organize it carefully, and deliver it persuasively. You gather relevant factual evidence, review pertinent contractual language and arbitral precedents, "coach" your witnesses, and examine salient industry standards and practices germane to the case.

You want your case to be cogent, visually appealing, and commonsensical. Remember, your audience is the arbitrator. You have a limited amount of time. Specious, unruly, and impertinent arguments will only antagonize the audience.

Step 4. Hold the Hearing

The parties may specify where the arbitration hearing should be held. Alternatively, the arbitrator or administering entity may choose the location. Convenience, accessibility, cost, and the appearance of impartiality are matters to consider when making decisions about the locale of the hearing.

At the hearing, which will vary in terms of formality, you will have an opportunity to present an opening argument. You want to preview your case and make your points quickly and persuasively. After that, the parties will present the supportive evidence, including calling witnesses if needed. Last, you will make a closing statement. (More will be said about the hearing below.)

Step 5. The Arbitrator's Award

After the hearing, the arbitrator will return to his or her office to deliberate. The arbitrator will have a stipulated amount of time to render a decision. If agreed to, you may have the opportunity to file post-hearing briefs. The arbitrator will issue a written decision, condensing the facts, issues, and reasoning used to construct the award. The parties will be notified jointly of the decision.

THE ARBITRATION HEARING

To get you better acquainted with arbitration, we will walk you through an employment arbitration. In Figure 7-8, you can see the key steps of a semiformal hearing designed to handle an employment dispute. In that process, the arbitrator opens the hearing, and invites the parties to present their respective cases in an opening statement. Crisp, concise, to-the-point statements are desirable. In employment disputes, one must address relevant contractual or legal matters and how they apply to the given situation.

The opening statements are followed by presentation of the evidence.

Figure 7.8 An Employment Arbitration

- Notice of Hearing

- Arbitrator's Opening

- Parties' Opening Statement
  - √ Definition of issue(s) and statement of agreed-upon facts.
  - √ All contract clauses involved in the issue(s).
  - √ An enumeration of the important arguments that will be made in connection with the detailed presentation of the case.

- Presentation of Evidence
  - √ Relaxed rules of evidence.
  - √ Cross-examination.
  - √ Optional swearing-in of witnesses.
  - √ Types of evidence: facts; pertinent contractual provisions; past practice; industry standards; precedents; supporting documentation.

- Closing Arguments
  - √ Emphasize principal points.
  - √ Present chain-of-reasoning leading to conclusions.
  - √ Summation of relevant technical information (if needed).

- Arbitrator's Closing

Source: Adapted from: Commerce Clearing House, Inc. 1987. *Labor Law Course.* Chicago, IL: Commerce Clearing House Inc.

This is an area where the process can be expedited for speed and cost savings if all parties agree. Generally, you do not have to follow the strictures of a court proceeding. The rules of evidence are relaxed. But you are expected to be well prepared. You will focus on the facts, on past practice within the company, on industry standards, and on precedents set by similar situations. Once the evidence is displayed, your closing arguments are invited, followed by the arbitrator's closing of the hearing.

In cases involving labor disputes, arbitrators are guided by several criteria in fashioning their decisions. Among them are the literal language of the collective bargaining contract and any relevant interpretation of the parties' intent. In addition, the role of past practice or precedent is relevant, as is industry practice. In cases involving discipline or discharge, standards of fairness, equity, and just cause will be considered. Furthermore, prior arbitral rulings and industrial relations practices, perhaps across industries and certain types of cases, may be considered. Typically, the arbitrator has considerable power in conducting the hearing and afterwards in crafting the decision. Arbitrators are dealing with people's workplace lives.

Standards of Conduct

Given the power vested in arbitrators, particularly when their decisions are binding, and the increasing use of arbitration in employment matters, you have a strong interest in ensuring that they adhere to ethical standards of conduct. With this in mind, review the AAA's code as a constructive statement (see Figure 7.9). These standards not only address the requisite qualifications of an arbitrator but how the business of an arbitration should be conducted. Among a few of the items are (1) the disclosure of any potential conflict of interest; (2) the avoidance of any improper or biased communications with the parties; (3) the protection of confidentiality; (4) a willingness to rule for one or the other party equally before hearing the evidence; and (5) a willingness to withdraw from a case where

---

Figure 7.9 Standards of Conduct for Arbitrators (AAA Canons and Other Codes)

- An arbitrator should uphold the integrity and fairness of the arbitration process.

- An arbitrator should disclose any interest or relationship likely to affect impartiality or which might create an appearance of partiality or bias.

- An arbitrator in communicating with the parties should avoid impropriety or the appearance of impropriety.

- An arbitrator should conduct the proceedings fairly and diligently.

- An arbitrator should make decisions in a just, independent, and deliberate manner.

- An arbitrator should be faithful to the relationship of trust and confidentiality inherent in that office.

- An arbitrator must be as ready to rule for one party as for the other on each case.

- An arbitrator must decline appointment, withdraw, or request technical assistance when he or she decides that a case is beyond his or her competence.

Source: American Arbitration Association.

the arbitrator may lack relevant knowledge or competence. You should insist that arbitrators and the process adhere to these standards.

VARIETIES OF ARBITRATION

You can choose from among a variety of arbitral forms to resolve employment disputes. As noted earlier, you can choose whether or not arbitration is binding or advisory. Also, you may choose a panel (multiple arbitrators) or single arbitrator (see Figure 7.10). You may also decide how much freedom you want to give the arbitrator to fashion a settlement.

In conventional arbitration, you grant the arbitrator the authority to fashion a decision based on the positions and arguments provided by the parties. In other words, the arbitrator has considerable discretion to exercise. Final-offer arbitration, on the other hand, limits the authority of the arbitrator, who must choose among the options presented. Discretion beyond this point is eliminated. That is, you have restricted the arbitrator to

Figure 7.10 Arbitration Varieties

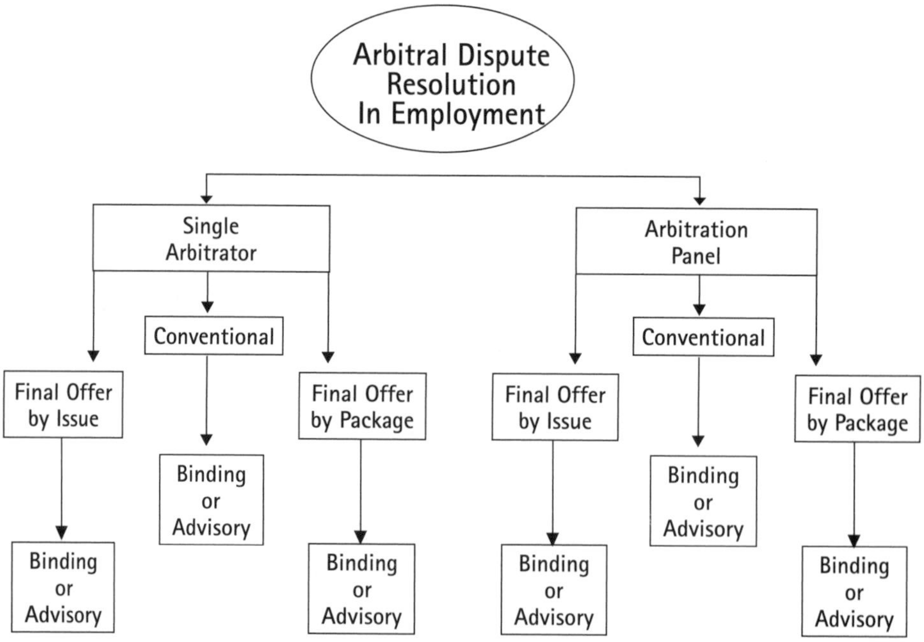

choosing your final offer or the other side's final offer. You hope the severity of the win-lose choice causes the parties to submit reasonable final offers.

You may also stipulate that the arbitrator make a choice between final offers, either by package, or by issue. In *by-package arbitration*, you lump your final offers across all outstanding issues together into one package. In *by-issue arbitration*, final offers are selected separately by issue. In that case, the arbitrator may choose your final offer on one issue and the other side's on another issue, and so on and so forth, until all issues are decided.

You will typically find final-offer arbitration used in interest-based disputes. It is the form of arbitration used to resolve salary disputes in professional baseball. You will also find it used relatively extensively to resolve public sector bargaining impasses. In this capacity, regardless of its form, arbitration is a substitute for the right to strike.

MEASURING RESULTS

How do you measure the results or effectiveness of arbitration as a dispute resolution procedure? Figure 7.11 lists five relevant criteria.

First, you are interested in speed. How long did the arbitration take compared to how long litigation would have taken to resolve the

Figure 7.11 Measuring Results

Dimension	Measure
Relative Speed	Arbitration Resolution Time/Estimated Litigation Resolution Time
Relative Cost	Arbitration Cost Calculation/Estimated Litigation Cost Calculation
Satisfaction	Claimants' Satisfaction Index Defendants' Satisfaction Index
Usage Rate	Arbitration Usage Rate/Benchmark Rate
Award	Relative to Benchmarks

dispute? The longer arbitration takes, the less advantageous it becomes.

Second, you are concerned about cost, which is correlated with speed (or delay). How much did the arbitration cost versus litigation? These cost estimates need to be realistic and comprehensive.

Third, you should take stock of how satisfied the parties were with the process. Are they satisfied that they had a chance to present their case? Are they satisfied with the arbitrator? Do they believe the outcome was produced from a fair process? Was the outcome fair?

Fourth, you will want to look at usage rates. To what extent are employment disputes going to arbitration rather than being resolved at earlier stages? Are arbitrations clustered around certain types of disputes or certain disputants? Such information can help you pinpoint problem areas in the workplace.

Fifth, you need to look at the awards. Who is winning? Why? How costly are the awards? Are you satisfied with the caliber of the reasoning behind the awards?

THE ARBITRATION CALCULATOR

An arbitration calculator provided in Figure 7.12 is one means of assessing costs. The principal cost factors are the administration fees (if, for instance, the AAA is used), the arbitrator's fees and expenses, the parties' time and expenses, the cost of the parties' legal representation, witnesses' time and expenses, an administrative overhead factor, the cost of the award, and the postsettlement costs. This formula, as was the case previously with the facilitation and mediator calculators, provides one measure to consider relative to what the estimated costs would be if the parties had litigated their disputes.

Manager's Checklist: Using Arbitration

You need to be extremely cautious in introducing arbitration because of its potential finality and quasi-judicial tone. Ensuring fairness—in ap-

Figure 7.12 The Arbitration Calculator

Cost Item	Cost Calculus
1. Administration	Fee
2. Arbitrator(s)	[Rate × Time] + Expenses
3. Parties' Representation • Pre-session • Session • Post-session	[Rate × Time] + Expenses
4. Parties' Time and Expenses	[Compensation Rate × Time] + Expenses
5. Witnesses' Time and Expenses	[Compensation Rate × Time] + Expenses
6. Administrative Overhead	[Clerical support, rental fees, etc.]
7. Award	Monetary Award
8. Post-Award Costs	Sum of Post-Award Costs
Total Cost = [1 + 2 + 3 + 4 + 5 + 6 + 7 + 8]	

pearance and fact—is critical. How the process is designed is therefore something that deserves careful attention and input from multiple perspectives. Among the issues for you to check are:

1. How shall arbitration be triggered?
2. Is it mandatory or voluntary?
3. What types of disputes will arbitration cover?
4. Will the procedure be internally or externally administered?
5. Are the parties entitled to legal representation?
6. How shall the cost of arbitration be shared, particularly when lower income employees are involved?
7. Is the procedure binding or advisory?
8. Is the procedure designed along the conventional or final-offer model?
9. What rules of evidence, including discovery, govern the process?
10. Has an expedited form of arbitration been considered for some cases?
11. Are there limits or requirements connected with arbitrator rulemaking in either interest or rights disputes?

12. Is there a backward-movement provision to allow going back to mediation or negotiation before the arbitrator renders a decision?
13. What precautions should be taken to promote confidentiality?
14. Should a panel or single arbitrator be used?
15. Shall the disputing parties have a right to challenge an arbitrator before he or she is commissioned to serve?
16. Is there provision for the enforceability of an arbitrator's awards?
17. What groups of employees are covered?
18. Have effective means been taken to ensure that affected parties are aware of and educated about arbitration as an ADR procedure?

Exercise 7.1: The Fork in the Road

You have reached the proverbial fork in the road. You have had considerable difficulty with an employee who chronically claims you mistreat him. The problems peaked last week when you denied him a vacation request for September. You and he have been at loggerheads over this and other differences in the past. He is a good performer, and works hard. He has vacation time coming, but you cannot afford to be without him in September. You have tried talking to him but he angrily says that you have violated his rights under the code of personnel. Should you mediate or arbitrate? Why?

Exercise 7.2: Should You Go to Arbitration?

You recently disciplined an employee for insubordination. She had refused to issue a memorandum informing the staff that overtime was being eliminated for the summer as a cost-saving measure (i.e., no one would be working overtime). The employee felt that it was your responsibility to deliver the bad news, not hers. You suspended her for three days with pay. She filed a grievance. According to this nonunion grievance procedure, the employee grieves to you, the supervisor (step 1), your immediate superior (step 2), and the general manager (step 3)—before going to arbitration, which is optional. The grievance was denied at steps 1 to 3, but you have received indications that your case is not that strong. You may have a hard time convincing the arbitrator. Should you settle with the employee or risk going to arbitration?

Chapter 8

Potpourri

ADR methods are not a recent find; these methods have been around since at least 1926, when the American Arbitration Association was founded. However, the growing backlog in all U.S. courts and the savings in time and money have made ADR methods more popular over the last few years. The more commonly used ADR methods include mediation and arbitration; other more-sophisticated methods include minitrials and summary jury trials. It is important to understand how to maximize the effectiveness of a particular method and to know which one makes sense for a particular type of dispute.

Maxine Lans Retsky, *Marketing News*, May 24, 1999.

Scenario

As a senior HR manager, you work in a litigation-prone company. Managers consistently take a hardline position. Employees retaliate by filing complaints and lawsuits. At present, your complaint and lawsuit files are backlogged. You get the distinct impression that people at this workplace have no appreciation of the costs of litigation. It just seems to be business as usual. You have been asked by the CEO to address this problem. What are the conflict resolution options you want to consider?

When it comes to ADR, negotiation, facilitation, mediation, and arbitration may be the first set of procedures to appear on your radar screen. But we have not completed the menu by any stretch of the imagination. You still have many more selections to make. We want to give you an idea of what's left on the menu and how a few of the selections work in practice.

CHAPTER OBJECTIVES

Metaphorically speaking, you should be sated with the ADR menu at the end of this chapter. We will survey the selections remaining and guide you through some procedures that have been used increasingly in the workplace. More specifically, the chapter presents you with:

- A survey of several ADR techniques applicable to workplace conflicts particularly, and business disputes generally
- A comparison of the techniques along core analytical dimensions
- An idea on when to use these techniques
- A guide on how factfinding, ombuds, early neutral evaluation, and peer review work

MORE ADR ALTERNATIVES

The list of remaining available options includes conciliation, dispute panels, early neutral evaluation, factfinding, minitrials, ombuds, partnering, peer review, and summary jury trial. Figure 8.1 presents the OPM definitions of these ADR techniques so that you can see in more or less precise terms how they are distinguishable. In reading these definitions, you will quickly pick up the fact that some of these procedures seem more suited to business than to employment disputes. The techniques most applicable to the workplace include conciliation, early neutral evaluation, factfinding, ombuds, and peer review.

Briefly, *conciliation* is a process that may involve elements of facilitation and mediation. One goal of the conciliator is to get the parties together: to help coordinate meeting opportunities; facilitate initial information exchanges; and to encourage the parties to test their perceptions and misperceptions. Conciliation is nonadjudicatory and nonbinding.

Dispute panels, consisting of one or more neutrals, serve somewhat of

Figure 8.1 What Are These Other ADR Techniques?

Conciliation involves building a positive relationship between the parties to a dispute. A third party or conciliator (who may or may not be totally neutral to the interests of the parties) may be used by the parties to help build such relationships.

Dispute panels use one or more neutral or impartial individuals who are available to the parties as a means to clarify misperceptions, fill in information gaps, or resolve differences over data or facts. The panel reviews conflicting data or facts and suggests ways for the parties to reconcile their differences.

Early neutral evaluation uses a neutral or impartial third party to provide a nonbinding evaluation, sometimes in writing, which gives the parties to a dispute an objective perspective on the strengths and weaknesses of their cases. Under this method, the parties will usually make informal presentations to the neutral to highlight the parties' cases or positions. The process is used in a number of courts across the country, including U.S. District Courts.

Factfinding is the use of an impartial expert (or group) selected by the parties, an agency, or by an individual with the authority to appoint a factfinder in order to determine what the "facts" are in a dispute. The rationale behind the efficacy of factfinding is the expectation that the opinion of a trusted and impartial neutral will carry weight with the parties. Factfinding was originally used in the attempt to resolve labor disputes, but variations of the procedure have been applied to a wide variety of problems in other areas as well.

Minitrials involve a structured settlement process in which each side to a dispute presents abbreviated summaries of its cases before the major decision makers for the parties who have authority to settle the dispute. The summaries contain explicit data about the legal basis and the merits of a case. The rationale behind a minitrial is that if the decision makers are fully informed as to the merits of their cases and that of the opposing parties, they will be better prepared to successfully engage in settlement discussions. The process generally follows more relaxed rules for discovery and case presentation than might be found in the court or other proceeding and usually the parties agree on specific limited periods of time for presentations and arguments.

Ombuds are individuals who rely on a number of techniques to resolve disputes. These techniques include counseling, mediating, conciliating, and factfinding. Usually, when an ombud receives a complaint, he or she interviews parties, reviews files, and makes recommendations to the disputants. Typically, ombuds do not impose solutions. The power of the ombud lies in his or her ability to persuade the parties involved to accept his or her recommendations. Generally, an individual not accepting the proposed solution of the ombudsman is free to pursue a remedy in other forums for dispute resolution.

Partnering is used to improve a variety of working relationships, primarily between the Federal Government and contractors, by seeking to prevent disputes before they occur. The method relies on an agreement in principle to share the

Figure 8.1 (Continued)

risks involved in completing a project and to establish and promote a nurturing environment. This is done through the use of team-building activities to help define common goals, improve communication, and foster a problem-solving attitude among the group of individuals who must work together throughout a contract's term.

Peer review is a problem-solving process where an employee takes a dispute to a group or panel of fellow employees and managers for a decision. The decision may or may not be binding on the employee and/or the employer, depending on the conditions of the particular process. If it is not binding on the employee, he or she would be able to seek relief in

traditional forums for dispute resolution if dissatisfied with the decision under peer review.

Summary Jury Trial. An ADR technique under court auspices aimed at promoting settlement. It has been called the jury equivalent of a mini-trial in that it involves the presentation, before a six or eight member mock jury, of counsel's opening and closing statements, as well as a narrative of each side's evidence. Typically, there is no live testimony. After brief instruction from the presiding judge or magistrate, the jury returns an advisory verdict. Thereafter, the presiding judge or magistrate will meet with the parties and their counsel to attempt to forge a settlement.

Sources: (1) U.S., Office of Personnel Management, Office of Workforce Relations. 1999. *Alternative Dispute Resolution: A Resource Guide.* Washington, DC: OPM; and (2) *http://www.pert4Law.org.*

an investigatory role, not unlike the function of an ombuds and factfinder. The panel will gather pertinent data to shed light on the situation, such as a disagreement about whether or not a party has fulfilled its obligations. The procedure is generally informal and the panel may have considerable latitude to make recommendations.

Early neutral evaluation is a different sort of conflict resolution method. Its purpose, to a certain extent, is to make the parties aware of the consequences of not settling a conflict themselves. (In the scenario above, you certainly might want to look at this option.) A neutral evaluator, whose judgment is presumably respected by the parties, hears the parties state what they would present as evidence. Based on these presentations, the evaluator will give the parties an informed evaluation of the strengths and weaknesses of their cases. This helps the parties get an objective assessment of what might happen if they pursued the conflict to a more adjudicatory forum, such as arbitration.

Factfinding is used to investigate and present the facts of the case. The procedure may be used to address interest or rights disputes. It is often associated with resolving interest-based labor disputes. But, as an investigative tool, its application is much broader. By shedding light on the "facts" of a case from a neutral, impartial perspective, factfinding is intended to dispel factual disagreements or misperceptions which may have fueled a conflict.

Minitrials blend nonadjudicative with adjudicative features, though the recommendations they produce are non-binding. The tribunal is non-judicial, typically involving business executives, perhaps from two companies in dispute. A neutral party may be appointed to fill out the tribunal. The procedure is twofold:

> First, an information exchange occurs, with the disputants presenting their evidence and arguments to the tribunal. This tribunal, by including executives from the respective parties, is presumably well qualified to assess the impact of the situation on their organizations. Second, once this information exchange has occurred, the tribunal attempts to negotiate a settlement. The neutral member may make an advisory proposal to the executives. The executives are chosen because they have the authority to settle the conflict.

The rationale for this procedure is that it involves the executives, with a stake in the outcome, before the conflict goes to litigation. A minitrial includes elements of negotiation, mediation/facilitation, and adjudication. The executives' settlement conference incorporates the negotiation phase. The third-party neutral may help facilitate and mediate the process. Finally, the presentation of cases to the tribunal resembles an adjudicatory proceeding. But the process is a nonbinding one. If a settlement is not reached, the minitrial procedure may be repeated.

An *ombuds* is used to provide a forum, outside of the normal chain of command, to investigate and attempt to resolve disputes. The ombuds may be internal or external to the organization. Typically, the ombuds does not have authority to impose a solution, but, through the process of investigation and recommendation, the ombuds can exercise considerable influence. The ombuds, by being outside formal channels, can help protect confidentiality and resolve complaints at an early stage, before more formal charges are initiated.

Partnering is a growing practice in business transactions that are complex and multi-party, thereby giving rise to many potential conflicts. The federal government in particular has promoted its use to resolve potential problems with contractors, many of which may be associated with one major project. It is also used in the construction industry, where multiparty projects and disputes are common. In a nutshell, the process is preventive, committing the parties to meet regularly or as needed to anticipate and resolve conflicts before they become problems or impediments to performance. In a sense, this is a form of multilateral interest-based problem solving.

Two other ADR types are described in Figure 8.1. One is *peer review*. This involves submitting a complaint to a group of employees and managers for a decision, which may be binding or not. Peer review involves employees directly as conflict problem-solvers or arbiters. It can serve as a powerful educational tool. However, you must be careful in creating peer review panels not to run afoul of the National Labor Relations Act's ban on the formation of company unions. Peer review boards in nonunion companies may be deemed to constitute illegal company unions.

Finally, the *summary jury trial* is a judicial appendage. It serves to save the time of the court by having the parties present a streamlined version of their cases to a mock jury. The jury renders an advisory judgment. The presiding judge then meets with the disputants to try to get them to reach a settlement. The process of generating and hearing evidence is expedited, saving the parties' legal representation costs. But the parties are nonetheless given their day in court.

In reality, these various ADR procedures differ in terms of operation, purpose, utility, and cost. They also, as noted, differ in terms of the usage in the context of workplace conflict. We distinguish, however, along these common dimensions:

- Preventive or reactive
- Decisional or advisory
- Investigative or evaluative

By *preventive*, we mean that the procedure kicks in before a conflict surfaces or a formal complaint has been filed. By *decisional*, we mean the procedure is intended to decide the matter, not advise on its resolution or attempt to negotiate one. By *investigative*, we mean that the procedure is designed primarily to gather evidence rather than render an assessment or determination of what the outcome might or should be.

Figure 8.2 presents these analytical comparisons, focusing on the four techniques most commonly used to resolve workplace or employment disputes. Three of these ADR techniques are largely reactive. Disputants activate them after their conflict has surfaced or a complaint has been lodged. The role of the ombuds, however can be largely preventive, providing employees within an opportunity to seek resolution before taking formal steps, such as going to the EEOC with a discrimination charge.

Except for the peer review system, which looks for a decision, the others are advisory rather than determinative in a final, binding sense. The factfinding and the ombuds ADR procedures are investigatory. A lot of their potential dispute resolution value rests on this dimension. By its very nature, the investigative process is intended to help the parties see the facts and issues more clearly. This exposure is intended to motivate them to be more reasonable in approaching the dispute. It also promotes dispute resolution by removing barriers associated with genuine misinterpretations of the facts. Further, it may also help to uncover attempts on the part of one or both sides to obfuscate or distort the facts. Perhaps this might mildly embarrass the parties into agreement.

Figure 8.2 Analytical Dimensions

ADR Technique	Dimension		
	Preventive or Reactive	*Decisional or Advisory*	*Investigative or Evaluative*
Early Neutral Evaluation	Reactive	Advisory	Evaluative
Factfinding	Reactive	Advisory	Investigative
Ombuds	Preventive/ Reactive	Advisory	Investigative
Peer Review	Reactive	Decisional	Evaluative

WHEN TO USE THESE ADR PROCEDURES

We provide some tips on when to use these procedures, focusing again on the procedures found more prevalently in handling workplace disputes (see Figure 8.3). *Conciliation* seems appropriate in disputes where agreement is still desired and achievable, the parties want to preserve control over the process and outcome, they want to minimize the extent of third-party intervention (a la facilitation), and finality or closure as not required immediately or desired imminently.

Early neutral evaluations, which basically provide for an expert forecast of a possible decision, not unlike a meteorologist's weather prediction for the next five days, gain favor when the disputants are on the verge of going to virtual battle. You want a neutral's early evaluation to jolt the parties back into reality. You often need an outsider to give you a convincing as-

Figure 8.3 When to Use These ADR Techniques

ADR Technique	When to Use
Conciliation	Agreement Desired and Possible Preserve Parties Control Minimize Third-Party Intrusion Finality Not Required
Early Neutral Evaluations	Parties Are Likely to Go to Litigation Parties Are Being Unrealistic Parties Have Faith in Neutral Parties Need to Air Case
Factfinding	Parties Have Reached Impasse or Stalemate Parties Do Not Agree on the Facts Parties May Save Face by Neutral Presentation of Facts
Ombudship	Parties Need an Objective Investigator Parties Want to Preserve Confidentiality Parties Want to Explore Possible Options
Peer Review	Promote Sense of Fairness and Equity Discourage Frivolous Claims Promote Employee Involvement Educate About Conflict Resolution

Sources: (1) U.S., Office of Personnel Management, Office of Workforce Relations. 1999. *Alternative Dispute Resolution: A Resource Guide.* Washington, DC: OPM; and (2) *http://www.pert4Law.org.*

sessment of what the real risks and costs of going to court will be. In order for this to work as intended, you must have confidence in the neutral's judgment. You are not going to listen to a neutral who is impeachable, a neophyte, or a charlatan. Also, you may resort to early neutral evaluation because it gives you a chance to preview your case, without risking an uncertain throw of the arbitration dice.

As an investigatory tool, you use *factfinding* when the parties, having reached a stalemate or impasse, need a clarification of the facts. Factfinding can clear the factual waters and save the face of the disputants. It is often easier to digest what a neutral observer says than to listen to the other side's rendition. You will find this type of factfinding used to resolve interest disputes, and thus it comes after an impasse. However, factfinding, in concept, is partially analogous to the role of the ombuds, and you could position this technique to serve as a preventive or certainly early-resolution form of third-party intervention.

You use an *ombuds* when you need an impartial investigation. As designed, the procedure emphasizes confidentiality. Unlike the factfinding technique, however, the role of the ombuds is broader than the resuscitation of the facts. Ombuds search for solutions. Though confidential channels, they attempt to negotiate or mediate a satisfactory conclusion to the dispute, if that is the appropriate route to take.

You use *peer review* when you not only want a decision to a dispute (assuming you invest the peer review panel with the authority to render a judgment) but also when you want to establish a procedure that promotes employee involvement and educates managers and employees about conflict resolution. Furthermore, peer review may discourage attempts to abuse the availability of a dispute resolution alternative. Employees arguably may be embarrassed to grieve frivolous claims to a body of their peers, who will undoubtedly resent the abuse and misuse of their valuable time.

How Does Factfinding Work?

You can visualize how factfinding works in an employment dispute in Figure 8.4. A factfinding procedure, aimed at the impartial collection and

Figure 8.4 How Does Factfinding Work?

Purpose:	Impartial, neutral third party, requested by disputant, gathers and reports the facts associated with an employment dispute, without conducting a hearing.
Steps:	• Employee Files Complaint • Employee's Immediate Superior Responds in Writing • Employee Relations Officer Reviews to Determine Eligibility and Sufficient Merit • Employee Request Factfinding and Agrees to Binding Decision • Employee Relations Office Appoints Factfinder • Factfinder Conducts Investigation and Issues Report to Designated Senior Manager (The report may include recommendations.) • Senior Manager Issues Binding Written Decision
Powers:	Conduct Interviews Review Documents Compile Evidence Issue Report Make Recommendations

presentation of the facts, might consist of seven steps. (This procedure is drawn from a real company's factfinding/dispute resolution program.)

Step 1. An employee files a grievance or complaint alleging a conflict over interests or a violation of workplace rights.

Step 2. The employee's immediate supervisor, or whoever is the target of an allegation, issues a response to the claim in writing.

Step 3. The complaint and response are reviewed by an employee relations officer or other appropriate official to determine if the conflict merits pursuance or is either too impertinent or ineligible for further consideration.

Step 4. The grievant requests factfinding and agrees to be bound to the final decision of this procedure if it reaches that stage.

Step 5. The employee relations officer assigned to the case appoints an investigator. While the factfinder may not be organizationally independent, the person will be removed from the conflict and perceived, to the extent possible, as impartial.

Step 6. The factfinder conducts an investigation, writes a report on the facts, and releases it to the employee relations officer and the senior manager of the workplace area in which the dispute arose. The report may include recommendations.

Step 7. If the disputants cannot settle themselves, with the assistance of the employee relations officer, then the senior manager, at the request of the grievant, will render a decision, after reviewing the factfinder's report.

As you can see, the factfinder possesses the power to investigate the facts (i.e., conduct interviews and review documents), to issue a report, and to make non-binding recommendations. In such a position, the factfinder can exert great influence over the outcome of a dispute, especially if he or she carries a strong reputation for fairness and thoroughness.

How Does an Ombuds Program Work?

You might find a few background words about ombuds useful. According to the University and College Ombuds Association (*www.colorado.edu/ombuds*): "The position of ombudsman was originally created in Sweden in 1809. . . . Ombud, a common word in the Swedish language, means the people's representative, agent, attorney, solicitor, deputy, proxy, or delegate." In the United States and Canada, ombuds have been created to serve the interests of citizens, consumers, and employees "who wish to address concerns about administrative actions or lack of action."

The University of California at Berkeley's Staff Ombuds office (*http://stfombuds.berkeley.edu*) includes a useful description of the function of an ombuds:

Q. What is the Staff Ombuds Office, and what does an ombuds do anyway?
A. The Staff Ombuds Office is a confidential, informal, impartial, and nonadversarial alternative for the resolution of work-related problems and conflicts. We are a designated neutral in the handling of these types of issues.

Q. What do you mean by conflict and what kinds of issues can you help with?
A. The Staff Ombuds Office can informally help with many issues involving many kinds of conflict in the workplace. We can provide an outside perspective on a work-related problem, or just a confidential and informal sounding board to discuss options for handling a particular dilemma. Conflicts between co-workers, between manager and employee, or between managers involving communication problems, treatment issues, job status worries, organizational difficulties and many, many other issues of concern in the UCB work environment can be confidentially discussed in this office.

Q. What kinds of employees can use your office?
A. ANY person working in a staff position, certain non-Senate academics, supervisors, managers and executives, including deans, department chairs and directors can use our services.

Q. What else does the Staff Ombuds Office do?
A. We offer a variety of services. In addition to individual consultation, assessment, and referral, we provide group conflict resolution services, mediation services, facilitation services for both individuals and groups, communication skills training, conflict management training, special workshops by arrangement, and informal investigations or unit reviews.

Q. What if I want to take formal action on my situation?
A. You should try to resolve your concerns informally through available channels before resorting to the formal. Talking to us, however, does not preclude your using formal complaint and grievance procedures if your attempts at informal resolution don't succeed. Talking to us does not extend the time lines for filing a formal complaint.

Clearly, the University's ombuds program has broad jurisdiction, covering an array of possible conflicts. It operates impartially, confidentially, collaboratively, and informally. The ombuds is a problem-solver, like a mediator, but does not conduct a formal mediation session. The emphasis is on early settlement.

In practical terms, you might view the ombuds procedures as being a rather straightforward three-step process (see Figure 8.5).

First, the employee contacts the ombuds officer, with a concern or complaint. Generally, this precedes the filing of a formal complaint

Figure 8.5 How Does an Ombuds Program Work?

Purpose: Impartial, neutral third party, helps resolve employee grievances and complaints through nonbinding procedures.

Steps:
- Employee Contacts Ombuds
- Employee's Immediate Superior Responds in Writing
- Ombuds Hears Complaint and Conducts Informal Investigation
- Ombuds Attempts to Resolve Dispute Through Counseling, Negotiation, and Mediation

Powers: Hear Complaints
Conduct Investigations
Counsel/Mediate/Negotiate Resolution
Meet with Senior Managers
Makes Recommendations to Change Employment Policies and Practices
Influence Concurrent Decision-Making Procedures

Scope: Conflicts Between Co-Workers
Interpersonal Conflicts
Cultural Conflicts
Performance Appraisal
Discipline
Promotion/Demotion
Discrimination
Harassment
Benefits/Compensation
Whistle-blowing

or grievance, when the conflict enters another dispute resolution venue (e.g., the grievance procedure or EEOC office).

In Step 2, the ombuds hears the concern or complaint and initiates an investigation. The investigation may entail interviewing involved parties and others with a bearing on the case. It may also include obtaining and reviewing relevant documents, such as internal memoranda, reports, and policy manuals. The investigation is informal and confidential, but serious and potentially extensive.

In Step 3, when the investigation has been completed and the relevant facts have been gathered, the ombuds shifts roles from a factfinder to a negotiator or mediator. One of the principal functions of the ombuds is to attempt a collaborative resolution, if that is appropriate under the circumstances. Also, the ombuds may counsel the complainant and other parties if they need to adjust their behaviors or a fuller explanation as to what "the problem" is. In addition, the ombuds may make broader policy recommendations to the organization based on concerns or problems with existing policy or practice in the workplace.

In a nutshell, the ombuds' powers include hearing complaints, conducting investigations, mediating disputes, meeting with senior managers to discuss specific or more general concerns, and making recommendations to change policy and practice to handle workplace conflict more effectively or address underlying concerns that give rise to disputes.

Generally speaking, the ombuds' jurisdiction over workplace conflict is broad. You may define that jurisdiction in establishing the ombuds office. As an example, you may include conflicts between co-workers, interpersonal conflicts, cultural conflicts, performance appraisals, disciplinary actions, discrimination allegations, harassment, disputes over benefits or compensation, and whistle-blowing.

How Does Early Neutral Evaluation Work?

A seven-step guide is presented in Figure 8.6. This illustration is adapted from a real-world company's procedure. As you can see, the objective is to forewarn: to give the parties a realistic assessment of what might happen if they proceed to a more adversarial adjudicative venue, such as arbitration or litigation. This assessment will hopefully induce the parties to settle without such recourse.

Step 1: The employee files a complaint under the existing grievance procedure, be it union or nonunion.

Step 2: The employee's immediate supervisor, or whoever is the target of the grievance, files a written response.

Step 3: The employee requests the employee relations officer to appoint a grievance mediator, an independent third-party neutral selected from an outside provider's roster.

Figure 8.6 How Does Early Neutral Evaluation Work?

Purpose:	Impartial neutral hears and evaluates employment disputants' respective cases and evaluates their relative merits.
Steps:	• Employee Files Complaint • Employee's Immediate Superior Responds in Writing • Employee Requests Grievance Mediation • Grievance Mediator Conducts Informal Hearing to View the Disputants' Respective Sides • Grievance Mediator Offers Evaluation of What An Arbitrator Would Decide • Parties Attempt to Negotiate Settlement • Arbitration
Powers:	Hear Evidence Issue Early Advisory

Step 4: The mediator conducts an informal, expedited hearing. The parties present abbreviated versions of their cases to the mediator.

Step 5: The mediator offers an informed judgment as to what would be ruled in an arbitration. This judgment is given orally.

Step 6: After providing this evaluation, the mediator attempts to get the parties to reach an agreement.

Step 7: If an agreement is not obtained, the grievant may request arbitration. In that event, another neutral is obtained to conduct a formal hearing de novo.

The power of the neutral evaluator is based on hearing the evidence and rendering an assessment or prediction. Early neutral evaluation has been referred to as a "peek-a-boo" arbitration (Feuille, 1999). It could just as easily be referred to as "peek-a-boo" litigation if a neutral with judicial experience were to be used.

HOW DOES A PEER REVIEW PROCEDURE WORK?

Figure 8.7 provides a slightly modified peer review procedure, which is currently in place at a major manufacturing company. In peer reviews, you

Figure 8.7 How Does a Peer Review Procedure Work?

Purpose: Panel of peers (managers and employees) conducts hearing on employment dispute and renders a decision. Intended to avoid litigation and to encourage parties to settle early before hearing of panel is necessary.

Steps: • Employee Files Complaint
    • Employee's Immediate Superior Responds in Writing
    • Senior Manager Responds in Writing
    • Senior Vice President Responds in Writing
    • Panel of Peers Conducts Hearing and Renders Decision. Decision is Binding Unless Appealed
    • Senior Management Court of Appeals Reviews Case and Renders Final Decision

Powers: Holds Hearing
    Renders Decision

convene a panel or board of reviewers to hear a dispute and render a decision. You can see its similarity to panel arbitration. The reviewers are presumed impartial, although they are not independent of the company.

In this example, the peer review ADR procedure consists of six steps. In Step 1, the employee files a grievance (this is a nonunion grievance procedure). In Step 2, the supervisor or other designated target of the complaint files a written response. In Step 3, a designated senior manager reviews the complaint and written response. He or she then issues a decision in writing. If dissatisfied, the grievant may push the complaint to Step 4, where an even more senior person hears the case.

Once again, a written decision is given. Should that decision be objectionable to the grievant, the complaint goes to Step 5, which is a formal hearing of the case by a standing peer review panel consisting of managers and employees. This panel is empowered to render a written decision by majority vote. Should the grievant object to the panel's ruling, then the claim may be taken to Step 6, the Court of Appeals. This court includes the very highest executives of the company, a body of three. The court will review the evidence and various written decisions. Its majority-vote decision is binding on the parties to the dispute.

Manager's Checklist: Criteria for Decision Making

With this myriad of options available, what should you consider in making a decision as to which to choose? Here is a checklist to guide your decision making:

1. What is the central objective desired: prevention or resolution?
2. What kinds of conflicts (interests or rights) are to be addressed?
3. What is the nature of the relationship among and between managers and employees? Is it prone to conflict?
4. How complicated are the conflicts?
5. Is it important to give employees or others a broader voice?
6. Is it important to ensure due process?
7. Are there often conflicts over the facts or interpretation of relevant standards and policies?
8. Is it important to give the parties the option of having their day in court?
9. Is confidentiality important?
10. Is it often necessary to give the parties a reality check about the consequences of the pursuit of further action?
11. Do conflicts have a tendency to spread and spin out of control?
12. Do employees or others have a sense of being treated unfairly under a current system?

Answers to these questions may not guide you to one solution or an easy course of action, but they should help inform you of what the problems are, or what the needs are, and how these alternatives may serve those needs. Redundant, early-warning alternatives are probably the best answer.

Exercise 8.1: The Passionate Disputants

An employee and her supervisor have been entangled in a disagreement over a promotion that he denied her. The merits of the case are complex, and do not point clearly to who is right or wrong. But the employee is quite disgruntled, feels mistreated, and believes she is the victim of sexual discrimination in what is a "hostile" workplace environment. The parties have vowed to go to the mat on this one. You, as the HR manager, fear a lawsuit. Is this a case ripe for early neutral evaluation? Or, would you recommend another dispute resolution procedure?

Exercise 8.2: Clustering Conflicts

As a senior HR officer of the company, you have noticed a pattern in workplace conflicts and employee problems. They tend to be clustered around a handful of managers. You are not really sure who is at fault. Under your nonunion grievance procedure, however, you have had very few formal complaints. You suspect that employees are afraid to complain because the second step of the complaint procedure involves informing the supervisor of the complainant and asking for her or his response. How would you go about revising your dispute resolution system to deal with this problem? Is this a case where an ombuds program would be appropriate?

PART 3

SPECIAL TOPICS

Several relatively recent developments have propelled a cluster of topics to the forefront of workplace conflict and conflict resolution. These topics include workplace violence, resolving equal employment opportunity disputes, dealing with unions, and international perspectives on dispute resolution. In Part 3, four chapters are devoted to these respective topics.

First, violence has become a serious workplace concern. A series of mass killings at work sites has provoked outrage and instilled fear. Employers are increasingly interested in securing a safe workplace for their employees. Companies are motivated to take appropriate protective measures not only to promote an environment conducive to safe performance but also to avert lawsuits for negligence.

Second, managing EEO disputes has become a big business in and of itself. Since the early 1960s, the federal government has adopted a host of policies to prohibit discrimination in the workplace. Laws exist to protect workers from discrimination on the basis of race, gender, religion, color, national origin, age, and disability. These protections extend to prohibitions on racial and sexual harassment in the workplace. An increasing number of citizens have exercised their rights under the law. EEO complaints have been encouraged by a confluence of factors, including the liberalization of damages and remedies, intensified enforcement efforts, downsizings that have adversely affected certain groups, and heightened worker awareness. The growth in EEO claims, combined with the increased penalties employers may suffer, have prompted greater interest in ways to streamline the process of handling claims while balancing the interests of employers and protected classes.

Third, to compete effectively on a global scale, companies have had to become more strategic and proactive in their approach toward unions. For nonunion companies, this means adopting those measures needed to remain union-free. Managing conflict effectively is an indispensable union-prevention strategy. For partially or wholly unionized companies, negotiating with unions more effectively is essential.

Fourth, the globalization of business has generated growing interest in how to resolve conflict crossnationally. Hence, there is a need to know more about how workplace disputes are handled on a multinational basis. How do dispute resolution procedures vary across nations? To what extent is ADR practiced globally? There are also mounting pressures to internationalize certain labor standards, which will have direct and indirect implications for managing workplace conflict.

Chapter 9, "Confronting Workplace Violence," addresses the nature and scope of the problem and how companies can deal with it preventively and strategically. Chapter 10, "Resolving EEO Disputes," surveys the EEO terrain and discusses the traditional approach to handling disputes under EEOC procedures vis-a-vis the alternative—expedited machinery available under the agency's National Mediation Program. It also provides a guide on how to handle sexual harassment complaints.

Chapter 11, "Dealing with the Unions," examines the current state of unions in the United States. It provides guidance to employers who want to remain union-free. And it offers tips on how to negotiate more effectively if you do have a union.

Chapter 12, "International Perspectives on Workplace Conflict," presents a conceptual framework for analyzing the breadth of alternative means of resolving workplace conflict on a multinational basis. It examines the nature of certain international labor standards, including those promulgated by the International Labour Organization (ILO). Finally, the chapter surveys the availability of ADR in selected countries to resolve employment disputes.

Chapter 9

Confronting Workplace Violence

"One out of four workers is attacked, threatened, or harassed each
year. Most harassers are co-workers. Desk rage joins road, air, express line, sports, parking lot, and pedestrian rages."
"Fortune 1000 corporate managers rank workplace violence as the
top security threat."
"A 1999 survey of human resource professionals showed that 57 percent have had at least one incidence of workplace violence in the
recent past."
"According to the Workplace Violence Headquarters, warning signs
are evident in 85 percent of the incidents of workplace violence."

Workplace violence is one of the most serious problems facing companies and managers today. It takes a toll that extends far beyond those
who are its unfortunate immediate victims. Incidents and threats of violence at work create immeasurable psychological hardships, disrupt normal work operations, and force employers to take costly preventive and
responsive measures. Every company and manager has the responsibility
to be on alert and prepared to deal with the possibility of workplace violence. The scope of related managerial responsibility is extensive. According to a March 23, 2001, *Newsday* report on "Addressing Violence in the
Workplace" by Carrie Mason-Draffen, "Companies concerned about preventing workplace violence should tackle the issue at every level of the
employer-employee relationship—hiring, managing, and firing."

Workplace violence is a complex, wide-ranging problem. It is inextri-
cably linked to broader societal problems that trigger violence. Violence at

work comes in many forms, occurs for numerous reasons, and requires a combined corporate-community response to deal with effectively.

In this chapter, we do not attempt a complete treatment of this difficult subject. Our focus is on what managers can do to prevent violence at work and to respond to it should it occur. We are especially concerned about violence that may be perpetrated by those with a connection to work or the workplace, as opposed to those incidents committed by outsiders in the course of criminal or terroristic acts. However, in order for companies to protect their workforce, it is necessary to take steps to secure the periphery, the effect of which may also be reduced vulnerability to acts of violence committed by outsiders.

CHAPTER OBJECTIVES

Our overarching objective is to show you how to confront the problem of workplace violence proactively and strategically. More specifically, the chapter discusses:

- What you need to know about the nature and scope of the problem of workplace violence
- What signs you should be on the alert for at work
- How to protect your workforce
- Steps you can take to protect managers when terminating employees
- How to indemnify your company

WHAT MANAGERS NEED TO KNOW

What do you need to know about workplace violence in order to be a responsible, effective manager? There are six basic things.

> *First*, you must recognize that this is a serious problem, even though your company may not have encountered any noticeable incidents.

Workplace violence is linked to the violent nature of society at large. It affects more workers than we realize. Its effects on these workers are more corrosive than we comprehend. Tragically brutal incidents make headlines, and their broader import cannot be denied. But the more ominous reality is the chilling climate of fear workplace violence introduces into the collective psyche of a workforce.

Second, workplace violence occurs in many forms, which vary in terms of the direct threat they pose to a person's physical well-being. According to Kinney (1995), violence manifests itself at three levels. One is the extreme form that inflicts physical harm. Assaults (fatal and nonfatal), theft, sabotage, and vandalism fall into this category. Another intermediate-type form occurs when threats are made to do physical or psychological harm. Such threats may be overt or subtle. A third level involves violence in the form of verbal abuse, attacks, or other acts of harassment. Examples include vulgarities, taunts, shouting, staring, stalking, or intruding upon one's physical space—anything that intimidates a worker or causes that person to worry or be fearful. All three forms of violence may be perpetrated in the workplace by someone who is connected to the work, either presently or formerly. The most common type of violence that you are likely to have to deal with managerially involves acts of verbal abuse or harassment, most of which are perpetrated by co-workers. Unfortunately, many of these may go unreported, creating the false impression that a workplace is relatively violence free.

Third, workplace violence occurs for many reasons. Three of the principal causes are emotional disturbance, personality clashes, and work-related stress. Alcohol and substance abuse is a significant contributor. Practically speaking, you must be prepared to address those aspects of work that may trigger violence as well as the psychological stability of the workforce.

Fourth, to a considerable extent, workplace violence is preventable. You should be on the alert for warning signs that employees may show, such as changes in working habits or personal hygiene. You can intervene before verbal onslaughts escalate into physical confrontations. You can take concrete steps to screen out prospective employees who may have a propensity to be violent. You can remove employees or others who pose a threat. And, you can secure the perimeters of your workplace to prevent unwanted intruders, such as vengeful ex-workers, who might pose a threat to your workforce.

Fifth, you must approach the problem of workplace violence from as much a cultural as a programmatic perspective. Your company must convey, by word and deed, the unmistakable message that violence will not be tolerated (some advocate propounding a zero-tolerance policy), regardless of how minor it may seem. Harassment, intimidation, and incivility become unacceptable, requiring a disciplinary if not more organizationally severe (e.g., termination) response. ADR can help you address these behaviors effectively and fairly.

Sixth, you must recognize that workplace violence requires a community-wide effort as much as an organizational response. Managers and employees must be trained by professionals to recognize the early warning signs of violent behavior coworkers may exhibit. They must be informed on how to alert law enforcement to respond quickly to ongoing incidents at work. They need to refer substance abusers to treatment programs before violence occurs. To invoke an overused phrase, it takes a village to confront the problem of workplace violence.

WHAT YOU SHOULD WATCH FOR AMONG CO-WORKERS

If you are to deal with the possibility of workplace violence, particularly among co-workers (or others who are working at the sites, such as contractors or leased employees), you need to recognize the behavioral signs. Obviously, you do not want to over-react, but you should look for key behaviors that may portend violence or reveal emotional disturbances.

Figure 9.1 identifies several signs to watch for. First, focus on behaviors that depart from the normal or expected. Notice such things as increased tardiness or absences, reduced productivity, significant swings in

Figure 9.1 What to Notice

Job Performance Changes:
- Excessive tardiness or absences, especially if this was not the case in the past.
- Reduced productivity, especially of a previously efficient and productive colleague.
- Significant changes in work habits, including alternating high and low productivity or quality.
- Violation of safety or security procedures, including a sudden increase in accidents.

Personal Characteristics:
- Changes in health or hygiene, a colleague suddenly disregards personal health or grooming.
- Strained relationships at work, including disruptive or isolating behavior different from the past.
- Apparent signs of drug or alcohol abuse.
- Stress, which may be indicated by excessive phone calls, yelling, crying, or personal difficulties.
- Inability to concentrate when that was not a problem before.
- Unshakeable depression often having low energy; little enthusiasm; making despairing remarks.
- Unusual behavior for that individual, different from the past.
- Unusual fascination with weapons or stories of violence in the media.
- Threatening, intimidating, or harassing behavior.

Immediately Pending Threat:
- Direct or veiled threats of harm.
- Intimidating, belligerent, harassing, bullying, or other inappropriate and aggressive behavior.
- Numerous conflicts with supervisors and other employees.
- Bringing a weapon to the workplace; brandishing a weapon in the workplace; making inappropriate references to guns; or fascination with weapons.
- Statements showing fascination with incidents of workplace violence; statements indicating approval of the use of violence to resolve a problem; or statements indicating identification with perpetrators of workplace homicides.
- Statements indicating depression (over family, financial, and other personal problems) to the point of contemplating suicide.
- Drug/alcohol abuse.
- Extreme changes in behavior.

Source: U.S. Office of Personnel Management. 1998. *Dealing with Workplace Violence: A Guide for Agency Planners.* Washington, DC: OPM.

work habits, and violations of safety or security precautions (e.g., improper entry; failure to secure company property; unauthorized use of equipment).

On top of this, look for signs of deteriorating health or hygiene, strained relationships, drug or alcohol abuse, stress, lack of concentration, withdrawal or depression, or unusual swearing, shouting, or intruding upon one's physical space. Early and proper intervention can help avert violence down the road, even when it may initially appear a remote possibility. At the least, you should provide accessible and nonthreatening ways for people to get help. EAPs or in-house medical facilities are possible avenues.

In addition, be on high alert for signs that portend immediate danger. Direct threats, belligerence, persistent and escalating conflicts, carrying weapons, and extreme behavioral changes may require your immediate intervention, including discipline or removal from the work site. While intervening, you may require assistance, and it is therefore important for you to develop threat response plans and train employee-manager teams to execute them.

You need to set clear limits on tolerable behaviors—what is acceptable and what is unacceptable. To some extent, these standards will need to be calibrated with industry or organizational norms. For example, what is acceptable conduct in a football team's locker room may not be permissible in a hospital's reception area. If your company is serious about ridding itself of workplace violence, then it must set the tone, from the top down. If your top executives, middle managers, and first-line supervisors blatantly violate such a policy with seeming impunity, then they are clearly signaling that your company is not serious about workplace violence.

HOW TO PROTECT YOUR WORKFORCE

What measures can you take to protect your workforce from violence? Figure 9.2 presents a nine-step program. You may introduce each step separately, but all steps are essential to developing a comprehensive effort.

Figure 9.2 Step-by-Step Guide to Protect Your Workforce

Step 1:   Assess Risk of Workplace Violence
Step 2:   Encourage Reporting and Maintain Records
Step 3:   Establish Clear Workplace Violence Policy
Step 4:   Educate and Train at All Levels
Step 5:   Emphasize Pre-Employment Screening
Step 6:   Use ADR
Step 7:   Deal with Substance Abuse and Abusers
Step 8:   Secure Periphery
Step 9:   Provide Post-Incident Counseling

Step 1: *Assess risk.* You must first assess your workforce's vulnerability to violence. The prevalence of illegal drugs, substance abuse, cultural tensions, stressful work, and dangerous weapons raise the risk of violence. So does exposure to violent-prone populations (e.g., emotionally disturbed, substance-abuse treatment patients), interaction with the general public, late working hours, and isolated working habitats. You should look carefully at the record of past incidents in your company and the levels of violence in the areas surrounding your work sites.

Step 2: *Encourage reporting.* Your company needs to encourage the reporting of all incidents of workplace violence. Employees at all levels must have the ability to report incidents without fear of reprisal. Multiple reporting channels should be made available, some of which depart from the normal chain of command.

From these reports, your company should compile and maintain careful records on incidents of workplace violence. What types are occurring? Where are they occurring? Who is involved? These data will help you pinpoint problem areas and take appropriate corrective measures.

Step 3: *Establish a policy.* You need to establish a comprehensive policy statement. The policy should unambiguously convey the following points:

• Maintaining a safe work environment is everyone's responsibility.
• Prohibited acts of violence include harassment, intimidation, and other disruptive behaviors as well as direct physical attacks.

- Employees are protected from violence perpetrated not only by co-workers but also by customers, suppliers, clients, and others who may invade the work site.
- The company will respond appropriately to all reported incidents.
- The company will intervene to stop inappropriate activities or behaviors that suggest the potential for violence.
- The company will support managers and employees in their efforts to prevent and respond to workplace violence

The following is a modified policy statement drafted by the U.S. Office of Personnel Management (1998). You may adapt it to your corporate needs.

Memorandum for Employees of the Company _____

From: Company Head
Subject: Workplace Violence

It is the Company's policy to promote a safe environment for its employees. The Company is committed to working with its employees to maintain a work environment free from violence, threats of violence, harassment, intimidation, and other disruptive behavior. While this kind of conduct is not pervasive at our Company, no company is immune. Every company will be affected by disruptive behavior at one time or another.

Violence, threats, harassment, intimidation, and other disruptive behavior in our workplace will not be tolerated; that is, all reports of incidents will be taken seriously and will be dealt with appropriately. Such behavior can include oral or written statements, gestures, or expressions that communicate a direct or indirect threat of physical harm. Individuals who commit such acts may be removed from the premises and may be subject to disciplinary action, criminal penalties, or both.

We need your cooperation to implement this policy effectively and maintain a safe working environment. Do not ignore violent, threatening, harassing, intimidating, or other disruptive behavior. If you observe or experience such behavior by anyone on Company premises, whether he or she is a Company employee or not, report it immediately to a supervisor or manager.

> I will support all efforts made by supervisors and Company special-
> ists in dealing with violent, threatening, harassing, intimidating, or
> other disruptive behavior in our workplace and will monitor
> whether this policy is being implemented effectively.

Step 4: *Educate and train.* Education and training constitute a critical
step on the road to promoting workforce security. You have an obligation to educate all employees about what workplace violence
means and that it encompasses far more than a direct physical assault. You also need to educate workers about how to report incidents of violence.

In addition, your company should train workers on how to recognize signs that portend violence. Employees need to be able to
recognize coworkers who are showing signs of emotional instability, disturbance, or substance abuse, each of which may foretell violence. They also need to be trained on appropriate intervention
steps, how to contact law enforcement, and how to alert others so
as to secure as much of the workforce as possible. Your company
should establish and train workplace violence response teams that
can be deployed at a moment's notice.

Step 5: *Pre-employment screening.* Pre-employment screening is your
first line of defense to prevent violence perpetrated by coworkers.
You should exercise this responsibility seriously, taking advantage
of the opportunity it affords to screen out problematic individuals.
We recommend, to the extent permissible and practical, a three-
pronged process (see Figure 9.3). First, you should conduct a comprehensive and careful review of each applicant's background. You
should check and verify application data. You should conduct criminal record searches. You should check references even when you
get the standard name, rank, and serial number response. Credit
and motor vehicle record checks may also be advisable.

Second, you should require job-related and valid pre-employment testing. Drug tests are appropriate for many jobs. Finally, you
should conduct behaviorally-based interviews. You should probe
how prospective hires have behaved in various situations in which
they may have been challenged or stressed.

Figure 9.3 Pre-Employment Screening

Background	Criminal Record Check
	Employment/Education Verification
	Employment Record: Spotty, Interrupted
	Address Verification
	References: Furnished and Blind
	Credit Check
	Motor Vehicle Record Cheek
Testing	Ability
	Personality
	Honesty
	Drug
Interview	Behaviorally-Based
	Panel

Step 6: *Use ADR.* You should incorporate alternative dispute resolution (ADR) as part of a violence-prevention strategy. ADR, if properly designed, can offer a means for releasing tensions and addressing employee concerns, before matters are allowed to boil to unacceptable levels. In addition, ADR can reveal where there are organizational or work site stressors that can trigger violence among those who are prone or among those whose emotional stability has been broken. Also, ADR can be coupled with conflict management skill development to help your employees and supervisors cope in difficult situations, such as performance reviews, disciplinary actions, or other necessary but potentially explosive personnel interactions.

Step 7: *Deal with substance abuse and abusers.* Alcohol and other substance abuse among employees is one of the most significant risk factors associated with workplace violence. Such abuse manifests and exacerbates emotional instability, which may precipitate violence in the course of day-to-day workplace interactions. This societal malady is a workplace problem irrespective of its relationship to workplace violence (which certainly magnifies its import). Alcohol and substance abuse creates safety hazards, reduces productivity, broadens legal vulnerability, and raises healthcare and workers compensation costs. One study reveals that alcohol and drugs in the workplace are among the very top security concerns among companies, especially in the manufacturing sector.

You must respond to this problem by:

1. Recognizing the signs of abuse (e.g., tardiness, absenteeism, emotional outbursts, reclusiveness, and lax personal hygiene)
2. Making treatment through EAPs available and accessible
3. Periodically testing current workers for drugs
4. Removing workers who cannot cope with this disease until they can be safely brought back to the workplace
5. Establishing a clear and consistently enforced policy that bans alcohol and drug use on the job

Also be mindful of the extent to which workplace conditions themselves may be exacerbating these problems. Work stress and personality clashes between coworkers can contribute to alcohol and drug abuse. They can trigger a host of inappropriate behaviors.

Step 8: *Secure periphery*. We read all too frequently about incidents in which a vengeful ex-worker returns to work and proceeds to commit senseless acts of violence, which often cost lives. In fact, being fired, laid off, or suspended may be triggering events. You need to secure the perimeters of your workplace to prevent ex-workers from entering without proper authorization or an escort. Such a step, needless to say, must be taken in the broader context of introducing security measures that restrict access to the workplace to authorized personnel only or to those who have a demonstrably legitimate reason for being there. In organizations that operate openly and are highly accessible, such as retail establishments, you need to inform security and other employees to be on the alert for ex-workers who may return unannounced to the premises.

We should note that this step may not only mitigate violence perpetrated by vengeful or otherwise disturbed ex-workers but reduce the likelihood of violence committed by customers, vendors, or strangers with a criminal motivation. This step, if accompanied by other measures, such as metal detectors, identification systems, electronic surveillance, and beefed up security personnel, can further protect the workforce from acts of violence that may emanate from various types of perpetrators.

Step 9: *Post-incident counseling*. To deal effectively with workplace violence, you must address the needs of victims after the incidents. Your company should provide opportunities for counseling, take measures to reassure victims that they will not be victimized further or retaliated against for coming forward, and make whatever transitional adjustments are necessary to reintroduce victims who may have been away from work due to the incident.

Post-incident counseling should address not only victims of physical assault or threat but also victims of harassment and psychological intimidation, the more common sorts of workplace violence. To be effective, post-incident counseling must occur in the context of a company that aggressively seeks to cleanse itself of coworkers who commit acts of violence, from physical assault to psychological intimidation. It is essential that you create a workplace climate in which people feel safe and do not fear recurring victimization.

TAKING PRECAUTIONS WHEN TERMINATING EMPLOYEES

You know that certain employment situations are bound to be emotionally charged and prone to escalated conflict. Termination is one. Unfortunately, due to competitive pressures, it has become increasingly necessary to terminate workers for economic and performance-related reasons. Mindful of the tensions likely to be provoked in such delicate situations, you can help structure the termination process itself to mitigate the potential for escalating conflict and violent response. Figure 9.4 lists several precautionary steps. Among other things, if the dismissal is for performance-based reasons, you want to focus on the facts—that is, the straight-

Figure 9.4 Precautionary Steps in Termination

- Terminate at the beginning or end of a shift.
- Do not allow the employee to return to his/her work area.
- Make the firing a statement of fact, not a discussion or debate.
- The act of termination and all associated paperwork and other activities, including counseling and/or out-placement, should take place in the same locale.
- The terminated employee's dignity must be preserved.
- The post-terminated employee's dignity must be preserved.
- If a violent reaction can be reasonably anticipated, brief the security department and ask them to stand by.

Source: Illinois State Police. *Safety Messages and Programs—Combating Workplace Violence.*

forward and concise presentation of the facts, not a long-winded, rambling, guilt-ridden discussion. The terminated employee, except in unusual circumstances that may require forced removal, should be treated with dignity. If a violent response is anticipated or feared, you should alert security to be ready to assist.

INDEMNIFYING YOUR COMPANY

As a manager or HR professional, you have an obligation to help your company indemnify itself. Failing to address the problem of workplace violence not only exposes your workforce to risk but also raises your company's legal vulnerability. Some recent awards to workplace violence victims (or their families) reveal a company's potential legal hazard:

- $7.9 million awarded to families of two North Carolina workers killed by an ex-employee
- $5.2 million awarded to a supervisor who was permanently disabled after being shot by a disgruntled former employee
- $5.49 million awarded to family of shooting victim from temporary employment agency that did not take adequate screening measures

Figure 9.5 Corporate Security and Indemnifying Steps

- Policy Statement: Coherent, Comprehensive, Publicized

- Program Development and Implementation: Analysis, Reporting, Education and Training, Prevention, Response, Evaluation

- Enforcement: Consistent, Rigorous, Timely

- Commitment: Personnel, Resources, Climate

- Involvement: Employees, Vendors, Providers, Community, Law Enforcement

- Current: Review, Correct, Update

- Integration: Pre-Employment Screening, Adequate Supervision, Current Employee Review

What can you do to promote indemnification? Figure 9.5 provides several steps your company can take. They include issuing a comprehensive policy, committing the necessary resources, keeping a workplace violence program current, and integrating workplace violence prevention into the managerial function as part of pre-employment screening, supervision, and employee performance reviews.

Manager's Checklist: Workplace Security Hazards

To begin the process of developing or reviewing a workplace violence program, we recommend that you take the following "True or False" test developed by the Occupational Safety and Health Administration.

Please use the following checklist to identify and evaluate workplace security hazards. *TRUE* **notations indicate a potential risk for serious security hazards:**

___ T ___ F This industry frequently confronts violent behavior and assaults of staff.

___ T ___ F Violence occurs regularly where this facility is located.

___ T ___ F Violence has occurred on the premises or in conducting business.

___ T ___ F Customers, clients, or coworkers assault, threaten, yell, push, or verbally abuse employees or use racial or sexual remarks.

___ T ___ F Employees are NOT required to report incidents or threats of violence, regardless of injury or severity, to employer.

___ T ___ F Employees have NOT been trained by the employer to recognize and handle threatening, aggressive, or violent behavior.

___ T ___ F Violence is accepted as "part of the job" by some managers, supervisors, and/or employees.

___ T ___ F Access and freedom of movement within the workplace are NOT restricted to those persons who have a legitimate reason for being there.

___ T ___ F Employees or staff members have been assaulted, threatened, or verbally abused by clients and patients.

___ T ___ F Medical and counseling services have NOT been offered to employees who have been assaulted.

___ T ___ F Alarm systems such as panic alarm buttons, silent alarms, or personal electronic alarm systems are NOT being used for prompt security assistance.

___ T ___ F There is no regular training provided on correct response to alarm sounding.

___ T ___ F Security guards are NOT employed at the workplace.

___ T ___ F Employees have NOT been trained to recognize and control hostile and escalating aggressive behaviors, and to manage assaultive behavior.

___ T ___ F Cellular phones or other communication devices are NOT made available to field staff to enable them to request aid.

___ T ___ F Employees work where assistance is NOT quickly available.

Exercise 9.1: Responding to Portending Behaviors

As a manager, you supervise a group of telemarketers. In the past couple of weeks, you have noticed a change in the work habits and behaviors of one of your senior telemarketers. She has been with your firm for six years, and has been a more than satisfactory employee. She never causes a problem, is generally quiet, and concentrates on her job. Recently, however, you have noticed that she has become a bit moody. She has shouted at co-workers, using profanities. She has let her personal hygiene slide somewhat. She does not appear to concentrate as well. How would you handle this situation? Do you foresee a potential for violence?

Exercise 9.2: Terminating the Employee

As the HR manager, it is your job to notify employees when they are being terminated for cause. In this case, you are terminating a ten-year custodial employee for consistent failure to perform adequately. You know that he has a tendency to bully co-workers. He has had a couple of DUI violations that you know about, but drinking on the job has not been a problem. You fear that he might explode when confronted with the news. How would you handle this situation? What precautions would you take during the meeting? What precautions would you take to avoid problems should this person unexpectedly return to work after being terminated?

Chapter 10

Resolving EEO Disputes

"TWA Pays $2.6 Million to Settle Sexual Harassment Lawsuit." (*AP News*, May 25, 2001)

"EEOC Files Sexual Harassment Lawsuit Against Ford Motor Co." (*Washington Post*, April 14, 2001)

"Ford Pledges to Spend $27 Million on Sexual Harassment Sensitivity Training." (*Washington Post*, April 14, 2001)

"FBI Settles Ten-Year-Old Antidiscrimination Lawsuit Filed by 500 Current and Former African-American Agents." (*Los Angeles Times*, May 1, 2001)

In the past few decades, workplace disputes over discrimination have mushroomed. Lawmakers have extended employees' antidiscrimination rights, increased the damages employees can receive, and widened companies' liabilities. Employers have been penalized for intentional and unintentional acts of discrimination. The magnitudes of penalties have skyrocketed. According to the management consultant group, Zero Tolerance, *"Workplace discrimination is the single most important liability exposure issue to hit the American workplace in decades"* [italics added]. As a result, companies have become increasingly interested in finding alternative ways of dealing with equal employment opportunity (EEO) or discrimination disputes.

CHAPTER OBJECTIVES

In this chapter, we examine several things you need to know to resolve EEO disputes. We look at the scope of EEO protections. We review the traditional EEOC approach to resolving disputes, which can be very litigious. Then we examine the EEOC's innovative mediation program, which is available to companies under certain circumstances. Finally, we look at internal approaches that companies can use, with particular emphasis on the growing problem of sexual harassment in the workplace.

EEO PROTECTIONS

To comprehend your scope of responsibility for complying with EEO law, you should look at the EEOC's enforcement jurisdiction. As you can see in Figure 10.1, the EEOC administers a sizable set of statutes. Title VII of the Civil Rights Act of 1964, as amended, prohibits discrimination based on race, gender, religion, and selected other characteristics. It covers employers with fifteen or more workers in the private sector. The Equal Pay Act requires employers to pay men and women equally if they are doing similar work, other things being equal (e.g., seniority, performance).

The EEOC also enforces the Age Discrimination in Employment Act, the Americans with Disabilities Act, and the Vocational Rehabilitation Act. In addition, the EEOC, under its authority derived from Title VII of the Civil Rights Act of 1964, has also issued guidelines prohibiting sexual harassment. According to the EEOC, sexual harassment is a form of sex discrimination. Employees may file charges against an employer if they are the victims of unwelcome sexual advances or requests for sexual favors. Recent court rulings have significantly extended employers' liabilities under this important area of EEO law.

Together, these statutes and guidelines make it illegal for you to discriminate against an employee on account of:

- Race
- National origin
- Gender
- Religion
- Color

Figure 10.1 Laws Enforced by the U.S. Equal Employment Opportunity Commission (EEOC)

Law	Central Purpose(s)	Jurisdiction
Title VII of the Civil Rights Act of 1964	Prohibits discrimination in employment on account of race, religion, gender, color, or national origin.	Private employers with 15 or more employees, state and local governments, educational institutions, employment agencies, and labor organizations.
Equal Pay Act of 1963	Prohibits discrimination on the basis of gender in the payment of wages and benefits where men and women perform substantially equal work.	Employers covered by the Fair Labor Standards Act (Federal Wage and Hour Law).
Age Discrimination in Employment Act of 1967 (ADEA)	Prohibits discrimination in employment against persons 40 years of age or older because of their age, unless age is a *bona fide* occupational qualification.	Private employers with 20 or more employees, state and local governments, employment agencies, and labor organizations.
Title I and Title V of the Americans with Disabilities Act of 1990 (ADA)	Prohibits discrimination in employment against qualified persons with disabilities.	Private employers with 15 or more employees, state and local governments, educational institutions, employment agencies, and labor organizations.
Section 501 and 505 of the Rehabilitation Act of 1973	Prohibits discrimination in employment against qualified persons with disabilities.	The federal government.
Civil Rights Act of 1991	Authorizes compensatory and punitive damages in cases of intentional discrimination.	Same as Civil Rights Act of 1964.

Source: U.S., Equal Employment Opportunity Commission. *http://www.EEOC.gov*

- Age (forty and above)
- Disability (if otherwise qualified)

Further, these laws make it illegal for you to discriminate in any aspect of employment, including:

- Hiring and firing
- Compensation, assignment, or classification of employees
- Transfer, promotion, layoff, or recall
- Job advertisements
- Recruitment
- Testing
- Use of company facilities
- Training and apprenticeship programs
- Fringe benefits
- Pay, retirement plans, and disability leave
- Other terms and conditions of employment

To extend matters further, you may be legally liable for practices that involve:

- Harassment on the basis of race, color, religion, sex, national origin, disability, or age.
- Retaliation against an individual for filing a charge of discrimination, participating in an investigation, or opposing discriminatory practices.
- Employment decisions based on stereotypes or assumptions about the abilities, traits, or performance of individuals of a certain sex, race, age, religion, or ethnic group, or of individuals with disabilities.
- Denying employment opportunities to a person because of marriage to, or association with, an individual of a particular race, religion, national origin, or an individual with a disability. Title VII also prohibits discrimination because of participation in schools or

places of worship associated with a particular racial, ethnic, or religious group.

What this means is that EEO laws provide a broad array of protection and cover an extensive span of employment practices. You could be charged with discrimination for literally any employment decision made or action taken. In addition, as an employer, you do not necessarily have to have intended to discriminate or even been aware of the discriminatory conduct to be held liable for the acts in dispute.

THE TRADITIONAL EEOC COMPLAINT RESOLUTION PROCEDURE

As an enforcement agency, the EEOC has established formal procedures for addressing employees' complaints alleging violations of one or more of the above-mentioned antidiscrimination laws. Generally speaking, employee complaints set in motion a chain of actions which, if sufficient evidence of wrongdoing is accumulated, may result in costly litigation and awards against employers. In fact, the EEOC's caseload has grown considerably in recent years. In fiscal year 2000, over 91,000 complaints were filed with the agency. On average, it took the EEOC 216 days in that same year to resolve a complaint, which is considerably reduced from the 379-day average it took in fiscal year 1996.

The typical complaint-handling procedure works this way. First, an employee who believes he or she has been the victim of employment discrimination files a complaint with the EEOC or state agency counterpart. Employees have 180 days after the alleged act of discrimination to file a charge. Upon receipt of the charge, the EEOC will conduct an investigation. If the complaint lacks merit, it will be dismissed. Upon dismissal, the EEOC will notify the employee that there is a 90-day period in which to file a private lawsuit. If the EEOC finds that there is sufficient merit to the complaint to warrant proceeding, it will initiate steps to conciliate a settlement between the employee and the employer. Should that process yield a settlement, there is no need for further action. If conciliation does not result in a settlement, then the agency will either dismiss the case or pursue litigation on behalf of the employee. Again, upon dismissal, the EEOC will notify the employee of the option to pursue a lawsuit privately.

Clearly, under this procedure, your company *reacts* to an employee complaint that is being examined under procedures beyond its direct control. Whether or not you end up in litigation depends on the EEOC's investigation, your willingness to reach a conciliated disposition, and the intent of the alleged victim to pursue recourse. EEOC investigations in and of themselves can be enormously costly, challenging, and stressful. Formal complaints also expose your company to public scrutiny and bad publicity.

EEOC's National Mediation Program

Faced with a growing case load and mounting criticism from employers, employees, and lawmakers about the protracted length of time it took to resolve discrimination complaints, the EEOC began exploring ways to expedite the complaint-handling process. It focused on reducing the need for extensive investigations and introducing ADR procedures to resolve disputes at an early stage. Your company may benefit from considering this option if faced with an EEO complaint.

Specifically, in 1991, the EEOC initiated a one-year pilot mediation program in field offices in Philadelphia, New Orleans, Houston, and Washington. Receiving a positive response, the EEOC took the program national a few years later. By the end of fiscal year 1997, each EEOC district office had a mediation program.

In simple terms, the EEOC mediation program "is a pre-investigation dispute resolution procedure" (McDermott, 2000). It works this way:

1. An employee files a charge.
2. The EEOC advises the employee that voluntary mediation is available.
3. If the employee agrees and the charge is eligible for mediation, then the company is informed and asked if it wants to participate in mediation.

4. If the company agrees to mediation, the EEOC will assign a mediator, who will schedule a mediation.

The mediation session precedes a full-scale EEOC investigation. A mediated settlement is binding, precluding further legal action against the employer. If mediation does not yield a settlement, the EEOC will commence a formal investigation.

A recent evaluation of the National Mediation Program conducted on behalf of the agency by McDermott and colleagues (2000) revealed positive results. Company use of the program has grown in volume. Settlements have occurred in a sizable majority of the cases in which the parties agreed to mediation. Moreover, the parties are generally satisfied with the process and outcome. Importantly, the program has significantly reduced the typical amount of time it takes to resolve an EEOC charge.

Figure 10.2 summarizes the principal features of the National Mediation Program. Importantly, the program is voluntary, allows legal representation, relies on EEOC and external mediators, erects confidentiality firewalls, is targeted to early resolution, results in enforceable settlements (if they are reached), imposes no administrative charges, and holds mediation sessions that typically last between one and five hours.

INTERNAL COMPANY PROCEDURES

To mitigate formal EEOC complaints and the attendant pursuit of litigation, your company may want to establish its own internal ADR procedure

Figure 10.2 EEOC's National Mediation Program: Key Features

- Voluntary
- Internal/External EEO Mediators
- Pre-Investigation Stage
- Confidential: "Firewall" Between Mediation/Investigation and Litigation
- Legal Representation Permitted at Mediation Session
- No Administrative Fees
- Enforceable Agreements
- Unresolved Reverts to Investigation
- One–Five Hour Typical Mediation Session

to handle EEO-type disputes. Various studies show increasing use of ADR among companies for precisely this purpose. Further accelerating this trend is the U.S. Supreme Court's recent Circuit City ruling that employers may require the mandatory arbitration of EEO-type employment disputes as a condition of employment and continued employment. In effect, you may require employees to relinquish their right to pursue litigation in exchange for having their dispute taken to arbitration. Figure 10.3 gives you an idea of what such an internal procedure might look like.

HANDLING SEXUAL HARASSMENT COMPLAINTS

Sexual harassment is one of the most vexing types of workplace conflict that you can encounter. Since 1994, the number of sexual harassment complaints has risen by more than 250 percent. The average federal jury

Figure 10.3 A Prototypical Procedure

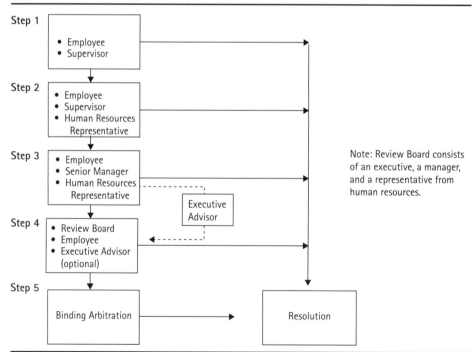

Source: U.S., General Accounting Office. 1995. *Employment Discrimination: Most Private Sector Employers Use Alternative Dispute Resolution.* Washington, DC. GAO.

award exceeds $250,000, with associated legal fees exceeding $200,000 per case. Because it is such a sensitive and costly matter, you probably want to establish a dispute resolution procedure with special provisions for sexual harassment claims. Also, you have special obligations to prevent acts of harassment from occurring.

In this section we provide some practical steps you can take to address this important concern. After discussing briefly the basic antiharassment law, we identify the principal elements you want to include in a comprehensive sexual harassment policy and program. Then we give you an example of what a grievance procedure modified for harassment might look like. Finally, we identify the key steps you want to take to prevent incidents and to minimize your liability.

EEOC Guidelines on Sexual Harassment

The 1980 EEOC guidelines define sexual harassment in the following terms:

> Unwelcome sexual advances, requests for sexual favors, and other verbal or physical conduct of a sexual nature constitutes sexual harassment when:
>
> 1. Submission to such conduct is made either explicitly or implicitly a term or condition of an individual's employment;
> 2. Submission to or rejection of such conduct by an individual is used as a basis for employment decisions affecting such individual; or
> 3. Such conduct has the purpose or effect of unreasonably interfering with an individual's work performance or creating an intimidating, hostile, or offensive working environment.

Thus, you are potentially liable for two basic types of harassment. First, there is the quid pro quo type, in which a person's refusal to submit to an unwelcome act results in an adverse employment decision. Second, there is the hostile work environment type, in which a person is forced to work in an environment which is perceived by her (or him) to be hostile, offensive, or intimidating, irrespective of whether or not an adverse action has been taken.

The EEOC guidelines cover three sets of employment relationships or interactions:

1. Superior and subordinate
2. Co-workers or peers
3. Employee and customer or client

Thus, you are potentially liable for acts of harassment that occur outside the traditional supervisor-employee relationship.

Employer Liability

As the law currently stands, you want to be able to assert an "affirmative defense" to avoid liability in the area of sexual harassment. Such a defense requires that you (1) take steps to prevent harassment, (2) institute an accessible grievance or complaint procedure to handle sexual harassment claims, and (3) take prompt and corrective measures to respond to harassment, including appropriate disciplinary action.

Thus, your sexual harassment policy and program should include elements that address:

- Prevention
- Complaint-processing
- Corrective response

Sexual Harassment Policy

According to Roberts and Mann (1996), authors of "Sexual Harassment in the Workplace: A Primer," you should develop an antiharassment policy around these core features: (1) understanding sexual harassment, (2) communicating the policy, (3) organizational procedures, and (4) enforcement. More specifically, your policy should include:

1. *Understanding Sexual Harassment*
   - Definition of sexual harassment, in its quid pro quo and hostile environment types
   - Specification of your company's liability for actions in the types of employment relationships covered (i.e., supervisor-employee, co-worker, and employee-customer)
   - Statement of intent to enforce seriously and promptly
   - Coverage of both men and women
2. *Organizational Procedures*
   - Appointment of top corporate officer to oversee policy and its enforcement
   - Organization-wide training and education programs on sexual harassment
   - Establishment of a complaint procedure outside the normal chain of command to hear, investigate, and evaluate complaints
   - Allowance for more than one venue to file complaints (e.g., an ombuds and a special sexual harassment complaint procedure)
   - Establishment of safeguards to promote confidentiality
3. *Enforcement*
   - Clear specification of the penalties for violation of harassment policy
   - Accurate and current reporting
   - Prompt investigation and corrective response
   - Prompt discipline
   - Protection of complaint filers from retaliation

Hypothetical Complaint Procedure

Based on what you know so far, you may be able to construct a sexual harassment complaint procedure along the following lines:

Step 1: File Complaint. Employee files confidential complaint with ombuds or employee relations officer.

Step 2: Investigation. Ombuds or employee relations officer conducts confidential investigation.

Step 3: Informal Resolution. Employee relations officer or ombuds attempts informal resolution or mediation of dispute. (Employee may
proceed to Step 4 or 5.)

Step 4: Mediation. Employee may request independent, neutral mediator to hold a session (employee is entitled to legal representation).

Step 5: Binding Arbitration. Employee may request binding arbitration
with independent, neutral arbitrator. Employee is entitled to legal
representation.

Indemnifying Steps

Simply put, you should take the following steps to protect your employees
and mitigate your corporation's liability:

1. Establish a clear, comprehensive antiharassment policy.
2. Educate, train, communicate.
3. Establish a fair, accessible, confidential, and timely complaint-
   resolution procedure outside the chain of command.
4. Take prompt corrective and disciplinary actions.
5. Appoint a senior officer to oversee policy and its appropriate implementation and enforcement.
6. Keep accurate and comprehensive statistics on complaints.

Manager's Checklist: Is ADR Appropriate?

We recommend that you go through the following checklist to determine whether or not ADR is appropriate for EEO claims in your company:

1. What is the nature and scope of EEO claims in your organization?
2. Has your organization had prior experience with ADR, especially
   in the employment area?
3. Is the primary purpose to avert litigation or resolve issues and
   build relationships?
4. Is the ADR procedure to be voluntary or mandatory?

5. What types of due process protections will be embedded in the procedure?
6. To what extent is there a sense that your company tries to handle EEO complaints fairly?
7. Is your company willing to enter into enforceable settlements of such complaints through mediation or arbitration?
8. Is your company willing to retain outside, professional neutrals?
9. To what extent should EEO-type complaints be treated differently from other conflicts or grievances?
10. Does your company need to establish special procedures for any particular type of EEO complaint, e.g., sexual harassment?

Exercise 10.1: Handling the Chronic Disputant

You are an employee relations officer. You spend much of your time processing employee complaints under your company's dispute resolution procedure. You have encountered an employee in particular who grieves chronically. He averages more than one a month, alleging racial discrimination or harassment. You have dismissed most of his complaints for lacking sufficient merit. Some, however, have gone to mediation (the traditional form), but do not result in agreement or settlement. Although the employee often threatens to sue, he has never done so. How would you handle this situation? Is transformative mediation appropriate? Are there other factors causing the problem that are unlikely to be addressed through mediation of any sort?

Exercise 10.2: Dealing with Sexual Harassment

You are a senior corporate officer in charge of the company's sexual harassment prevention and response program. You have held that position for three years. You have noticed a pattern in complaints. A lot of complaints come from women who interact with suppliers, vendors, and customers. They complain generally about a hostile work environment. Vulgarities. Profanities. Tasteless jokes. Obscene gestures. Glaring. Occasional "accidental" touching. How would you handle this situation?

Chapter 11

Dealing with the Unions

"Union organizers target dot.coms, capitalizing on company failures, long hours, and layoffs." (*Investor's Business Daily*, February 5, 2001)

"Las Vegas dealers, with low pay and fragile job security, try to unionize." (*The Wall Street Journal*, March 7, 2001)

"Mechanics at Northwest Airlines threaten to strike. Flight Attendants at United Airlines alert members that it may strike." (Reuters, March 2, 2001)

Do unions pose a threat to your company? How can you keep unions at bay? If you have a union, how can you negotiate with it more effectively? We address these questions in this chapter. We emphasize that how you deal with conflict has implications for your vulnerability to a union threat and your relationship with an already present labor organization in the workplace.

Unions feed off workplace conflict. They exploit it to organize new workers. And they leverage it at the bargaining table. Unions succeed where management fails. Whether you want to keep a union at bay or negotiate with it effectively when it has representational rights, you have to be able to manage workplace conflict.

By managing conflict effectively, you can benefit in several ways in dealing with the unions. First, you can reduce employee demand for a union and keep a union-free environment, but one that also addresses the legitimate needs and grievances of employees. Second, you can prevent acrimonious negotiations and strikes. Third, you can create ongoing partnerships to involve employees, improve the labor relations climate, and reduce formal grievances and other employee complaints that can burden your personnel/employee relations system.

CHAPTER OBJECTIVES

This chapter will help you to deal with unions more effectively and to manage conflict so as to achieve your objectives related to unions. More specifically, the chapter will give you a better understanding of:

- The declining union threat
- How to keep unions at bay
- How you can use dispute resolution to prevent unions from penetrating your workforce
- How to negotiate with unions

THE DECLINING UNION THREAT

Unions are in a seemingly irreversible state of serious decline. Union membership, as a percentage of the total U.S. workforce, has shrunk continually since the 1950s (see Figure 11.1). Today, it has fallen to less than 14 percent of the workforce. In fact, just 9 percent of the private sector workforce is unionized. In the manufacturing sector, widely considered a labor stronghold, less than 15 percent is unionized. Compare this to the situation just twenty years ago, when over 32 percent of the manufacturing sector wore the union label.

In today's environment, with continually decreasing union membership, your biggest danger is complacency. First, you may neglect to meet the basic needs of your workforce because you do not have a union knocking at your door. Second, you may be caught off guard, not realizing that new entrants into the workforce may have stronger preferences for unions, especially if they are culturally diverse and economically disadvantaged. Finally, if you do have to confront a union, especially if it is for the first

Figure 11.1 U.S. Union Membership Trends, 1950–2000

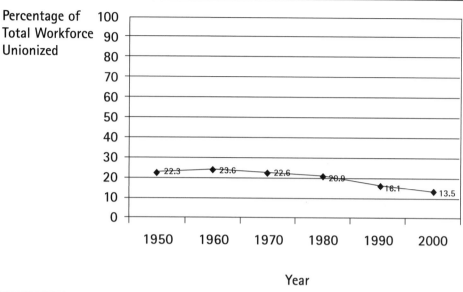

Sources: Masters (1997); U.S. Bureau of Labor Statistics.

time, you may have no reservoir of union-experienced managers to tap for help. A sophisticated union may take advantage of your inexperience in an organizing drive.

OPERATING UNION-FREE

If you operate union-free, you probably want to keep it that way. How can you do so? Consider three strategies: avoidance, substitution, and resistance (see Figure 11.2). You should link the first two strategies to keep unions at bay. Resort to the third strategy when they are at your doorstep, leaflets in hand.

Union Avoidance

There are three things to do if you want to avoid unions. First, recruit a workforce that fits into a collaborative, team-oriented culture. Second, select site locations away from areas where unions are densely populated.

Figure 11.2 Union–Free Strategies

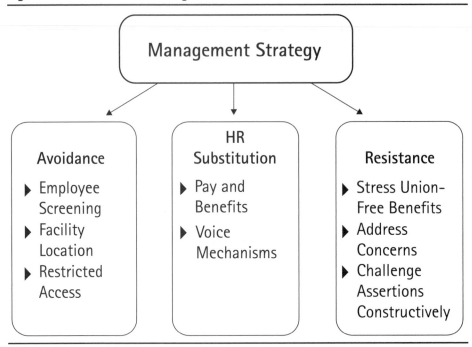

Third, pay as much if not more attention to selecting a management team—including supervisors—that is employee oriented, team oriented, and problem-solving oriented. One of the biggest predictors of union-organizing success is a poor, or conflictual, relationship between employees and their supervisors.

Union Substitution

You want to link union avoidance to direct union substitution. Reinforce a collaborative workplace culture with employment policies and practices that will reduce employees' need and demand for a union. Use economic and noneconomic substitutes. Pay the union wage or better. Offer union-equivalent benefits or better. And give employees a voice, a means of expressing their concerns and interests. In this vein, providing accessible conflict resolution procedures to address employee grievances can be a particularly effective preemptive strategy. As mentioned, unions exploit workplace conflicts and grievances, especially those that are mishandled or left to fester. A dispute resolution procedure can take the wind out of the union sail.

Union Resistance

When confronted with a direct union-organizing drive, you should not be passive. But you need not be overly confrontational. We urge a three-pronged *positive* union resistance strategy.

> *First,* stress the benefits of a union-free environment. Do so in a factual but compelling manner. Do not distort or mislead.
>
> *Second,* address real concerns that surface. Admit mistakes. Express your genuine interest in listening and bettering the quality of work life. Open rather than close the doors of communication at this delicate stage. Avoid dividing your workforce into "we" versus "they" camps.
>
> *Third,* challenge debatable or false assertions made by union organizers. Question their logic and factual basis. Do not dismiss them cavalierly or resort to ad hominem attacks.

DISPUTE RESOLUTION AS A UNION–PREVENTION STRATEGY

One of the principal benefits that unions arguably offer employees is a negotiated grievance procedure. The overwhelming majority of collective bargaining agreements in the United States include a formal grievance procedure culminating in binding arbitration (with an impartial, neutral, independent arbitrator agreed upon by the parties). These grievance procedures protect the rights of employees derived from the negotiated labor-management contract. Employees may grieve alleged violations of the contract. A typical contract, for example, would forbid discharging or disciplining an employee except for just cause, which is a fundamental restriction on managerial prerogative under the employment at-will doctrine. In protecting these rights, grievance procedures give employees an important voice to serve their interests as manifested in a collective bargaining agreement.

Without question, negotiated grievance procedures constitute one of the most powerful organizing weapons that unions have. If your firm is plagued with conflict that cannot be ventilated or that is going unaddressed, you raise your vulnerability to a union-organizing drive by a considerable measure.

In fact, instituting a formal dispute resolution procedure is one of your most potent union-prevention weapons. Ewing makes this point crystal clear:

> . . . corporate due process [i.e., a formal grievance procedure] is a good way to hold unions at bay. At every company where I interviewed, managers cited it as a valuable and proven defense. In fact, in some companies studied, the concept was not seriously supported until after a union scare.*

A cornerstone of your union-prevention strategy, therefore, is to institute a dispute resolution procedure. For this strategy to work effectively, you must design a nonunion procedure that includes some of the core features of a unionized grievance procedure. To guide you in this design process, we list some of the main features of a unionized grievance procedure in the context of a dispute resolution system:

First, the procedure is accessible and affordable. Unions represent grievants and incur the representational costs in the process.

Second, a multistep procedure is provided in which several steps allow the parties to try to work things out collaboratively before an arbitration.

Third, binding arbitration is offered as the last step of the procedure. An independent, neutral, impartial arbitrator is chosen jointly by labor and management, often through an administered process.

*Ewing, David W. *Justice on the Job: Resolving Grievances in the Nonunion Workplace*. Boston: Harvard Business School Press, 1989, p.7.

Fourth, the arbitrator's authority is found within the "four corners" of the collective bargaining agreement. This agreement stipulates the respective rights of the parties. Combined with personnel rules and a body of workplace practice, it determines what is expected of employees and managers.

An increasing number of nonunion employers have heeded Ewing's admonition and developed their own grievance procedures. According to a study by the U.S. General Accounting Office (1995), most employers surveyed by the GAO used one or more ADR procedures to handle employment disputes. According to Rowe, nonunion employers are not only acting to prevent unions but also to reduce the expense of not having an alternative to litigation:

> Thousands of employers are reacting to the fact that the obvious tip of the iceberg of nonunion dispute resolution is handled slowly and expensively by government agencies and the courts.*

One of the most widely publicized nonunion grievance procedures is the Halliburton four-level dispute resolution program (DRP). This program began in 1993 in one of the subsidiaries of Halliburton, a global energy services, engineering, and construction company. It provides a multistep procedure that culminates in binding arbitration (see Figure 11.3). The DRP relies on external neutrals when a grievant selects formal, binding arbitration, which covers rights-based disputes. Your company may want to consider it as a model for dealing effectively with workplace conflict and minimizing a union threat.

Under the DRP, arbitration is mandatory "for disputes that might otherwise go to court" (Stallworth, 1997). That is, as a condition of employment, employees agree to arbitrate rights-based disputes rather than

*Rowe, Mary. "Dispute Resolution in the Non-Union Environment: An Evolution Toward Integrated Systems for Conflict Management." In Gleason, Sandra E., ed. *Workplace Dispute Resolution: Directions for the 21st Century*. East Lansing: Michigan State University Press, 1997, p.80.

Figure 11.3 Halliburton Four-Level Dispute Resolution Program (DRP)

Stage	Option	Coverage	DR Source
1	Open Door	Interests and Rights	Internal
Loop Backward			
2	Conference	Interests and Rights	Internal
	Informal Mediation	Interests and Rights	Internal
Loop Forward			
3	Formal Mediation	Rights	External
4	Formal Arbitration (Final, Binding)	Rights	External

Source: Adapted from Chorda Conflict Management, *http://www.chorda.com* and from Karl A. Slaikeu and Ralph H. Hasson. 1998. *Controlling the Costs of Conflict,* San Francisco: Jossey-Bass.

to litigate. Another interesting feature of the DRP is that the company will reimburse employees (up to $2,500) for legal fees.

HOW TO NEGOTIATE WITH UNIONS

Negotiating with a union, as an exclusively recognized bargaining representative of a unit of employees, is different in several respects from negotiating with employees on an individual basis.

> *First,* you are legally obligated, under labor law, to negotiate in good faith. If you fail to do so, you may be charged with an unfair labor practice (ULP).
> *Second,* under this obligation, the courts have established certain items as mandatory. That is, if you or the union raises them, you must negotiate them in good faith. Mandatory items include rates

of pay, wages, hours, overtime, benefits (e.g., healthcare, pensions, vacation), employment security, job performance, and grievance procedures.

Third, unions may strike, or effectively withhold their labor, if an impasse is reached over these mandatory items. Labor law establishes a legally protected right to strike under these circumstances. To a certain extent, the right to strike, and thus disrupt your business operations, is what gives unions bargaining leverage over you that individuals do not have acting on their own. You may not fire employees who are legally on strike, but you may temporarily or permanently replace them in order to maintain your business operations. Resorting to replacements, however, can turn a peaceful work stoppage into an ugly or violent one. Unions despise those who replace them, referring to the replacements pejoratively as "scabs."

Fourth, when you negotiate with a union, you must keep in mind that it is a distinctive institution with its own organizational dynamics and politics (just as a corporation is a distinctive organization with its own culture). A union is more than a collection of individuals. The group you negotiate with may belong to a national union (e.g., the United Auto Workers, Communications Workers, or Service Employees International Union), where decision-making power is more or less concentrated or centralized away from the negotiating site.

With these distinctions in mind, here are nine tips on how to negotiate effectively with unions (see Figure 11.4). In offering these tips, we recognize that you or the union may choose an adversarial strategy. More generally, there are certain issues, such as wages, benefits, hours, and job-performance requirements, that are often quite divisive, leading to a competitive (win-lose) exchange. However, even within this context, it is still possible to pursue collaboration. At the same time, even when you are collaborating, it is important for you to assert your interests and needs from a business and managerial standpoint.

Figure 11.4 Nine Tips on Negotiating With Unions

- Do Your Research
- Prepare a Strategy
- Establish a Rapport
- Share Information Early and Consistently
- Exhibit a Collaborative Style
- Hold the Line
- Be Willing to Walk Away
- Open Multiple Channels of Communication
- Listen to the Pavement

1. *Do your research.* Know the union institutionally. Know how it is structured, governed, and administered. Where does the decision-making power lie? Are union leaders under pressure to be militant? Also, know the union's finances (which unions are required to report annually to the U.S. Department of Labor under the 1959 Labor-Management Reporting and Disclosure Act, LMRDA), and their ability to take a strike. Many unions pay strikers benefits from their treasuries. And, know the personalities of the local, regional, and national union leaders who may have influence over your negotiations.

2. *Prepare a strategy.* Determine what your bargaining goals are. Know the issues on which you are willing to be flexible and those on which you will be more insistent. Also, know the relationships between issues so that you do not make unwise trade-offs.

3. *Establish a rapport.* Get to know your union negotiating counterparts—and other relevant leaders—before you start negotiating. Open a dialogue. Hold get-acquainted meetings. Socialize. Play golf. Go to picnics. Doing this is especially important if you have a new union leadership or if you are facing a union that has just been recognized as a bargaining representative.

4. *Share information early and consistently.* Let the union know, before you arrive at the bargaining table, your company's financial condition, its business strategy, and the changes it may be considering to position itself better in the marketplace. Do this early and regularly.

5. *Exhibit a collaborative style*. Even when negotiations involve divisive or contentious issues (e.g., health insurance, pensions, wages, or job security), do not let the union rattle your chain. Act collaboratively. Think of mutual interests. Reframe issues so that they are more palatable.

6. *Hold the line*. This may seem contradictory to the point made just above, but it is not. On certain issues in negotiation, you may need to take a firm stand. You do not, however, have to advertise that you are taking a firm, unbending stance. As a rule, try to avoid declaring things non-negotiable or putting things in "take-it-or-leave-it" terms. But you are entitled to and should assert and advocate your interests, though you should do so in a civil tongue and with a collaborative demeanor.

7. *Be willing to walk away from the table without an agreement*. In negotiation and conflict resolution, you want to avoid the temptation to just get things settled. The temptation grows as a deadline approaches or if you are feeling pressure (from the boss) to resolve the disagreement or dispute. But bad settlements will come back to haunt you. If your counterpart union is really not satisfied, it will probably have difficulty living up to the agreement. The same applies to you. And no one really respects someone who gives something for nothing in return (at least in negotiating).

8. *Establish multiple channels of communication*. Although you must be careful not to bypass union representatives, give those representatives access to a broad array of management, not just the labor relations or HR managers. Also, offer to hold joint union-management meetings so that you can reach a wider audience.

9. *Listen to the pavement*. What do we mean by this? Be observant. Is the union holding more meetings? Are employees clustering for prolonged discussions about an upcoming negotiation or a contemplated strike? Is the union taking steps to prepare for a strike? Are union meetings well or poorly attended? Is there a lot of union-related activity going on, whether it is informal or formal?

It has been reported that the Teamsters strike against United Parcel Service (UPS) in the summer of 1997 took the company by surprise. It would not have, if the company had been listening to the pavement. For in the cold months of winter in that year, union members were holding meetings in the wee hours of the morning to rehearse how to behave on the picket lines. If only someone had listened to the songs they were being taught to sing when out on strike in the summer.

Manager's Checklist: Employee Interest in Unionization

Irrespective of whether you have an antiunion bias, you should not be oblivious to interest in unionization among employee groups. Each manager should go through this checklist of signals of collective discontent or embryonic unionization efforts. Note that these signals can be found even among employees who are technically not able to join a union with legal protection.

As a manager, have you observed any of the following signs present in the workplace? These signs may suggest the stirrings of a unionization drive or interest in unionizing.

	Recent Signals Present		
Indicator	Yes	No	Don't Know
Terminated employees or strangers talking with your employees after work.	☐	☐	☐
Union leaflets in trash cans or littering the parking lot.	☐	☐	☐
Groups of employees act nervous or stop talking when supervisors approach.	☐	☐	☐
Employees suddenly begin asking questions about company policies, wages, fringe benefits, and working conditions, and how the company feels about unions.	☐	☐	☐

Indicator	Recent Signals Present		
	Yes	No	Don't Know
Increased trips to the restrooms during work.	☐	☐	☐
Increased complaints to governmental regulators.	☐	☐	☐
An effort by employees to get names or addresses of other workers.	☐	☐	☐
Increased unrest and outspokenness from workers regarding major changes.	☐	☐	☐

Source: Used with permission of Gene Levine Associates: *www.genelevine.com.*

Exercise 11.1: Keeping the Union at a Distance

You are the manager of a telecommunications company's regional site. Your employees maintain equipment, service customers, and market new products. Recently, you have noticed a lot of tension at work. You do not have a union nor do you have a formal grievance procedure, but you sense and hear a lot of complaining. You are experiencing more performance problems: absenteeism, tardiness, turnover, and customer complaints. You suspect that poor supervisor-employee relations are contributing to this problem. How would you deal with this situation? What practical steps would be taken? What steps are important to keeping a union at bay?

Exercise 11.2: Negotiating with a Difficult Union

You have had a history of difficult labor-management relations. Three years ago, your last contract negotiations resulted in a strike. Four years before that, the union worked without a contract for six months as your negotiations proceeded at a snail's pace. You are preparing for next year's negotiation. The firm's financial situation is still problematic. The union has the same old guard militants on the negotiating team. What steps would you take to improve the prospects for a negotiation that would enable you to realize your objectives while not provoking a disruptive work stoppage?

Chapter 12

International Perspectives on Workplace Conflict

"81,000 Zambian Civil Servants on Strike Since May 28, 2001, Demanding 100% Pay Hike."

"3,000 Airline Employees on Strike at Paris' Orly Airport on June 13, 2001."

"International Court of Arbitration Rules in Favor of Andersen Consulting Split from Andersen Worldwide on August 7, 2000."

Economic globalization has several significant implications for your company's dispute resolution interests and practices.

First, as your company expands its international operations, the potential for workplace and business-related conflicts rises. In expanding globally, you broaden the scope of operations and the complexities of employment and business interactions, both of which invite more conflict at work. Indeed, the demarcation between business and workplace conflict becomes increasingly blurred. A globe-trotting company's workplace is about opening new markets, recruiting in new labor markets, lining up new suppliers, and negotiating myriad agreements so that you can do the work of your business. According to the American Arbitration Association (AAA), which just recently opened its first office outside the United States (i.e., the International Center for Dispute Resolution-Dublin), about two-thirds of the Fortune 500 companies have arbitration clauses in their cross-national contracts.

Second, economic globalization makes it increasingly necessary for your company to understand the existing conflict resolution machinery across different countries. To a certain extent, the machinery will vary depending upon the degree of unionization, labor laws and enforcement procedures, and the prevalence of ADR. In general, there has been an international decline in unionization and a decentralization or deregulation of employment affairs. As a result, dispute resolution machinery may become more uncertain and heterogeneous. This development could lead to a counter-push toward more universal labor and dispute resolution standards, or uniform international ADR forums.

Third, the liberalization of trade agreements has often been directly or indirectly tied to promoting (and presumably elevating) labor standards. Recent trade agreements, such as the North American Free Trade Agreement (NAFTA), have included collateral labor agreements. Various international labor standards address the rights of workers to exercise a voice and to have their rights under negotiated workplace agreements decided fairly.

Fourth, globalization diversifies the profile of your company's workforce. At the time of their arbitrated split, Arthur Anderson had 78,000 employees in eighty-four countries, and Anderson Consulting had 65,000 employees in forty-eight countries. The sheer breadth of such operations—combined with diversity in nationality, language, legal systems, race, religion, culture, and business customs—is bound to generate a high potential for workplace conflict.

CHAPTER OBJECTIVES

At the end of this chapter you will have a better appreciation of the variety of workplace dispute resolution machinery across countries, the role that international labor standards play in establishing general conflict resolution principles, and the extent to which selected countries practice ADR. Specifically, this chapter examines:

- The range of workplace dispute resolution machinery across countries
- Selected international labor standards relevant to workplace conflict
- Cross-national comparisons in industrial relations systems
- The availability of ADR in selected countries

CROSS-NATIONAL DISPUTE RESOLUTION MACHINERY

In the United States, companies have a wide array of methodologies to handle conflicts in the workplace. Along with making more concerted efforts to promote collaborative conflict resolution and interest-based or win-win negotiating in the workplace, companies are showing greater interest in ADR procedures. Their interest is motivated by a desire to avoid litigation, reduce conflict, control costs, and improve organizational performance.

The complexity and variety of dispute resolution machinery widens as the comparisons become more international in scope. In the employment or workplace arena, cross-national comparisons can be aided by distinguishing the nature of conflict along two dimensions. The first dimension is whether or not the conflict involves an interest, such as the pay raise one should get next year, or a right, such as whether or not a company followed procedure in disciplining an employee. The second dimension pertains to the collective or individual nature of a dispute. Is the conflict one that affects groups of workers or workers as individuals? The availability of dispute resolution machinery, under law and in practice, may vary depending upon these distinctions.

Apart from these distinctions, there is the question of what types of dispute resolution methodologies can be found. Figure 12.1 presents a partial listing of available venues in the United States and in—as a comparative example—Germany. The array of methodologies or venues, at least

Figure 12.1 International Comparative Conceptual Framework on Conflict Resolution Venues (A U.S. Illustration)

	Union Representation (Collective Bargaining/ Grievance) Procedures	*Labor Courts or Tribunals*	*General Courts*	*Specialized Agencies*	*Alternative Dispute Resolution*
U.S.	Interests and Rights Collective	—	Rights Collective and Individual	Rights Collective and Individual	Interests and Rights Collective
Germany	Interests Collective	Rights Collective and Individual	—	—	—

on a conceptual basis, includes union representation (collective bargaining and grievance procedures), labor courts or tribunals, general courts, specialized governmental agencies (e.g., the EEOC, NLRB, OSHA), and private or public-mandated ADR procedures.

Thus, your company may confront considerable diversity in the approaches taken to resolve disputes in the workplace across nations. In some countries, your company may handle certain workplace conflicts within labor courts or industrial tribunals. In others, your company may resolve disputes in specialized governmental agencies or in general courts. Across countries, the level of conflict will depend upon the degree of unionization and the propensity for work stoppages. Also, you will find varying degrees of commitment to international labor standards and the acceptability of ADR.

INTERNATIONAL LABOR STANDARDS

Your company's dispute resolution interests and practices may be directly or indirectly influenced by international labor standards. As part of their trade agreements, countries may attempt to promote certain workplace practices with conflict resolution implications. In addition, selected regional and international bodies, such as the European Council and the International Labour Organization (ILO), have promulgated standards relevant to this area. These standards, although often of limited practical effect or enforceability, nonetheless serve as guideposts by which you can assess your conflict resolution and other workplace-related policies and practices. They also serve as ethical benchmarks, recognizing that there are certain moral and political values associated with workplace conflict and conflict resolution that may transcend the immediate interests of your company.

The ILO, in particular, has promulgated several noteworthy labor standards relevant to workplace dispute resolution. The ILO is a tripartite (i.e., government, labor, and employer) specialized agency of the United Nations. Its UN mandate illustrates its role relative to developing policy to guide practice on matters relevant to workplace conflict:

> The International Labour Organization is the UN specialized agency which seeks the promotion of social justice and internationally recognized human and labour rights. . . . The ILO formulates international labour standards in the form of Conventions and Recommendations setting minimum standards of basic labour rights: freedom of association, the right to organize, collective bargaining, abolition of forced labour, equality of opportunity and treatment, and other standards regulating conditions across the entire spectrum of work related issues.

Among the ILO's articulated strategic objectives are to:

- Promote and realize standards and fundamental principles and rights at work
- Create greater opportunities for women and men to secure decent employment and income
- Enhance the coverage and effectiveness of social protection for all

Figure 12.2 identifies several ILO policies pertaining to the kindred areas of workplace conflict and dispute resolution. The ILO recognizes

Figure 12.2 Selected International Labor Standards

Source	Content Area	Selected Provisions
International Labour Organization (ILO)	Freedom of Association and Protection of the Right to Organize Convention, 1949 (C87)	Article 2: Workers and employers, without distinction whatsoever, shall have the right to establish and, subject only to the rules of the organization concerned, to join organizations of their own choosing without previous authorization.
ILO	Right to Organize and Collective Bargaining Convention, 1949 (C98)	Article 1: Workers shall enjoy adequate protection against acts of anti-union discrimination in respect of their employment.
ILO	Collective Bargaining Convention, 1981 (C154)	Article 5: Measures adapted to national conditions shall be taken to promote collective bargaining . . . [C]ollective bargaining should be made possible for all employers and all groups of workers in the branches of activity covered by this Convention.
ILO	Collective Bargaining Recommendation, 1981 (R163)	Part II: In so far as necessary, measures adapted to national conditions should be taken to facilitate the establishment and growth on a voluntary basis, of free, independent, and representative employers' and workers' organizations.
ILO	Collective Agreements Recommendation, 1951 (R91)	Part I: Machinery appropriate to the conditions existing in each country should be established, by means of agreement or laws or regulations as may be appropriate under national conditions, to negotiate, conclude, revise, and renew collective agreements, or to be available to assist the parties in the negotiation, conclusion, revision, and renewal of collective agreements.

Source	Content Area	Selected Provisions
ILO	Termination of Employment Recommendation; 1963 (R119)	Part II: Termination of employment should not take place unless there is a valid reason for such termination connected with the capacity or conduct of the worker or based on the operational requirements of the undertaking, establishment, or service. . . . A worker who feels that his employment has been unjustifiably terminated should be entitled . . . to appeal, within a reasonable time, against that termination with the assistance, where the worker so requests, of a person representing him to a body established under a collective agreement or to a neutral body, such as a court, an arbitrator, an arbitration committee, or a similar body.
ILO	Termination of Employment Convention, 1982 (C158)	Article 4: The employment of a worker shall not be terminated unless there is a valid reason for such termination connected with the capacity or conduct of the worker or based on the operational requirements of the undertaking, establishment, or service. . . .
		Article 8: A worker who considers that his employment has been unjustifiably terminated shall be entitled to appeal against that termination to an impartial body, such as a court, labour tribunal, arbitration committee, or arbitrator.

Figure 12.2 (Continued)

Source	Content Area	Selected Provisions
ILO	Examination of Grievances Recommendation, 1967 (R130)	Part II: Any worker who, acting individually or jointly with other workers, considers that he has grounds for a grievance should have the right—(a) to submit such grievance without suffering any prejudice whatsoever as a result; and (b) to have such grievance examined pursuant to an appropriate procedure.
ILO	Voluntary Conciliation and Arbitration Recommendation, 1951 (R92)	Part I: Voluntary conciliation machinery, appropriate to national conditions, should be made available to assist in the prevention and settlement of industrial disputes between employers and workers.
European Social Charter (Revised) 1996	General Principles	Part I: 5. All workers and employers shall have the right to freedom of association in national or international organizations for the protection of their economic and social interests. 6. All workers and employers have the right to bargain collectively. . . . 20. All workers have the right to equal opportunities and equal treatment in matters of employment and occupation without discrimination on the grounds of sex. . . . 24. All workers have the right to protection in cases of termination of employment. . . . 25. All workers have the right to dignity at work.

Sources: International Labour Organization; Council of Europe.

the right to form organizations of employees to acquire a voice through collective bargaining. In addition, workers should enjoy antidiscrimination protections for exercising their organizing and bargaining rights.

The ILO has also issued standards that support the use of third-party dispute resolution to resolve grievances, including those over matters of termination. Impartial appeal and review is considered an important labor standard that countries, and companies operating therein, should adopt. Further, the ILO has recommended voluntary conciliation and arbitration, where appropriate, to "assist in the prevention and settlement of industrial disputes between employers and workers." Thus, the ILO has endorsed third-party dispute resolution machinery to resolve both rights-based and interest-based conflicts at work.

INDUSTRIAL RELATIONS SYSTEMS

As a global company, your company will be dealing with countries with vastly different industrial relations systems. The differences will involve your rights as employers vis-a-vis your employees, the rate of unionization and bargaining representation in the workforce, the machinery developed to resolve interest and rights disputes, and the degree of acceptability of and familiarity with alternative dispute resolution procedures. This chapter reviews selected data and policies to give you a feel for the degree of inter-country variation you can expect. Also, you should anticipate considerable intra-country variation, much like what is encountered in the United States, with fifty different states and thousands of municipalities.

Unionization Rates

The rate of unionization differs greatly across countries. Although data in this area are neither complete nor consistent, they nonetheless reflect the wide disparities in union strength among nations. For example, unionization rates in the early-to-mid 1990s varied from 6 percent for France to over 32 percent for Brazil. Most countries had unionization rates higher than the United States.

Notwithstanding these disparities, the overarching international trend is one of union decline (Masters 1997). For example, the unionization rate in Japan has fallen to less than 19 percent. In Australia, the rate has dropped to 28.6 percent. In the United Kingdom, it has fallen to just above 26 percent. Across the globe, countries have faced keen economic pressures to deregulate and decentralize. Companies have faced similar pressures to reduce costs, encouraging investments in union-free locations. Operating globally, you can expect to find the influence of unions to be receding.

Labor Courts

Another distinguishing feature of a country's industrial relations system is the judicial venue for resolving disputes. In the United States, conflicts that involve statutorily protected rights in the workplace may go to general courts. In contrast, "[n]owhere in Europe are ordinary courts of law used to any appreciable extent to resolve labor disputes, but judicial-style labor courts or tribunals are widespread" (Clarke 1997). These courts, however, may differ in terms of whether they handle interest- or rights-based disputes and individual or collective disputes. They may also differ to the extent to which they encourage parallel tracks of alternative dispute resolution methods, such as conciliation.

Figure 12.3 presents a summary of the roles played by labor courts in selected countries. It shows, for example, that the labor courts of Belgium cover disputes over such matters as employment contracts and social assistance. In so doing, they deal with disputes over both rights and interests. Germany's labor courts, however, deal with rights-based disputes, as do the Israeli labor courts.

The use of specialized labor courts not only affects the venues within which disputes may be settled but also the incentives that multinational companies have to homogenize labor standards and enforcement procedures and to seek international forums for resolving disputes. As work becomes increasingly cross-national, both in terms of content

Figure 12.3 Disputes Covered by Labor Courts or Tribunals in Selected Countries

Country	Categories of Disputes	Distinguishing Conflicts of Rights and Conflicts of Interest
Belgium	Employment contracts; accidents and illnesses; health and safety; social assistance	Covers rights and interests
Denmark	Breach and interpretation of general agreement between Danish Employers' Confederation and the Danish Federation of Trade Unions; breach of collective agreements	Covers disputes of rights/ breaches of collective agreements. Disputes concerning interpretation of collective agreements are dealt with before an arbitration panel or the general courts.
Germany	Private law only: Notice of termination, wages, collective agreements and other labor matters; social security issues.	Covers rights disputes. Conflicts of interests in work council affairs are dealt with in an ad hoc settlement committee.
Israel	Private law and social security issues. Jurisdiction includes: collective labor disputes; prevention of discrimination in the workplace; pension cases; social security cases; national medical insurance and care.	Covers only rights conflicts and does not hear economic disputes.
Italy	Private law disputes. Social insurance and social security issues. Civil service disputes.	Yes. Distinction is less important in labor issues.
Norway	Collective disputes of rights: disputes concerning the interpretation, application, and validity of collective agreements. No jurisdiction in individual rights related to an employment contract, dismissal disputes, social security, administrative, or criminal matters. All such disputes pertain to the ordinary courts.	Yes. Covers collective rights disputes. Interest disputes are a matter for collective bargaining, possibly mediation, and recourse to industrial action.

Figure 12.3 (Continued)

Country	Categories of Disputes	Distinguishing Conflicts of Rights and Conflicts of Interest
Spain	Related to contract of employment: individual disputes between an employer and one or more employees (over, e.g., wages, dismissals, holidays); collective disputes between an employer or an employers' association and employee representatives in the undertaking, or trade unions, for interpretation of a legal rule or a collective agreement, or to challenge a collective agreement clause (unlawful or detrimental to a third party's interests or rights).	No.
United Kingdom	Individual employment disputes involving rights over unfair dismissals including unfair dismissal, redundancy entitlement, unauthorized deductions from wages, wrongful dismissals, race, sex, and disability discrimination. Social security issues are covered by a Separate Social Security Tribunal System.	No.
Venezuela	Labor law: individual and collective disputes. Social security.	Yes. Tribunals deal only with rights disputes.

Source: International Labour Organization, Government and Labour Law and Administration. 2000. *Eighth Meeting of European Labour Court Judges,* Jerusalem, September 3, 2000.

and location, resolving disputes according to the peculiarities of a particular country's legal system may lose favor. In that case, international arbitral forums may gain popularity for resolving employment disputes, just as they have in the area of commercial transactions.

AVAILABILITY OF ADR IN SELECTED COUNTRIES

Limited data exists on the status of alternative dispute resolution across nations, especially as that term is used in a nonunion context. It seems fair to say, however, that interest is growing, sparked in part by the use of ADR in unionized settings (much like what has transpired in the United States). As the ADR movement gains more exposure, through the proliferation of services offered by such entities as the AAA, usage will probably increase within countries. In this vein, the widespread decline of unionization may kindle support for ADR procedures. With union decline comes a loss in employee voice. This can lead to counter-pressures to restore voice, regarded as important to promoting company performance. As Locke (1995) comments: "It is ironic that just as unions in many countries around the world have been declining in influence and membership, the need for a strong role for employee voice in corporate decision making, industry-level interactions, and national policy making is growing."

Figure 12.4 sketches the availability of ADR in an employment context in selected countries. It reveals that, to a certain extent, ADR is available in Belgium, Denmark, Finland, Israel, Italy, and the United Kingdom. Generally speaking, it is less available in Germany and Norway. Interestingly, the reason cited for its uncommon use in Norway is its relative expense.

Figure 12.4 Availability of Alternative Dispute Resolution Machinery in Employment, Selected Countries

Country	Availability
Belgium	It exists in diverse forms, including conciliation mediation and arbitration. The judicial code establishes arbitration as a private machinery.
Denmark	According to the General Agreement between the Danish Employer's Confederation and the Danish Federation of Trade Unions . . . an effort

Figure 12.4 (Continued)

Country	Availability
	must be made to settle any dispute of an industrial nature, whether it is a matter of disputes of interest or right, by conciliation. As a rule, disputes on interpretation of agreements on wages and working conditions are brought before arbitration tribunals set up for the purpose.
Finland	A collective agreement, both for private sector employees and civil servants, may provide that disputes falling under the jurisdiction of the Labour Court are to be settled by arbitration. There is also a private mediation system arranged by the Finish Bar Association. The settlements reached in private mediation are binding. The decisions of arbitrators are final and binding in the same way as the decisions of courts of law.
Germany	In general, alternative dispute resolution machinery does not exist. Sometimes it exists on the basis of internal company rules without obligation—not binding.
Israel	Alternative dispute resolution is voluntary and non-binding, except where the parties have agreed in advance that the arbitrator's decision is binding. Parties are not compelled to mediate, but Labour Courts request that the parties mediate prior to the pretrial hearing and hearing. In addition, there is an experimental alternative dispute resolution program with social welfare cases.
Italy	The government, to resolve the old crisis of the judiciary, is pushing towards alternative dispute resolution (private mediation and arbitration in civil issues). Recent laws have introduced arbitration changes within the chambers of commerce, representatives bodies of the nonprofessional self-employed, and small enterprises.
Norway	In the field of labor law, alternative dispute resolution is uncommon. This is true for collective labor rights disputes and employment law issues. With minor exceptions, there is no set machinery for alternative dispute resolution. Generally, parties may submit rights disputes to arbitration, pursuant to provisions set out in the Civil Procedure Act, in which case the decision by the arbitration panel is binding and final. Cost is a reason why this procedure is not more commonly used.

Country	Availability
United Kingdom	Parties are encouraged to seek conciliation through the offices of ACAS (Advisory, Conciliation, and Arbitration Service) but are not required to do so before embarking upon employment Tribunal proceedings.
	There is now a separate pilot scheme for alternative dispute resolution before a single arbitrator. The decision of the arbitrator is binding. Note: It is not thought likely that this scheme will have much effect on the volume of claims handled by employment tribunals.

Source: International Labour Organization, Government and Labour Law and Administration. 2000. *Eighth Meeting of European Labour Court Judges,* Jerusalem, September 3, 2000.

Manager's Checklist: International Dispute Resolution Options

A useful exercise for you is to assess the range of possible international disputes and dispute resolution options available to your company. Use the following checklist, focusing on the employment area:

Non-U.S. business establishments where you have union-management contracts

_____

_____

Countries that have labor courts

_____

_____

Jurisdictions of labor courts

_____

_____

Non-U.S. machinery for settling industrial disputes or interest-based work stoppages

_____

_____

Grievance procedure machinery in non-U.S. unionized locations

_____

_____

Grievance procedure machinery in non-U.S. nonunion locations

_____

_____

Legal status of ADR in non-U.S. countries

_____

_____

Availability of ADR services in non-U.S. countries.

_____

_____

International venues for handling cross-national disputes

_____

_____

(Note: If you are interested in pursuing further the topic of international ADR, we encourage you to visit the Web sites of the American Arbitration Association, the International Labour Organization, the International Academy of Mediators, the International Chamber of Commerce, and the International Court of Arbitration.)

Exercise 12.1: Managing Cross–National Workplace Conflict

You are the company's senior HR officer. Your jurisdiction covers North and South America. Your company has an office and plant in Sao Paulo, Brazil. In Sao Paulo, you have a large U.S. management contingent. Unfortunately, the U.S. managers and their Brazilian counterparts have not gotten along too well. They are constantly complaining to you about the others' unwillingness to listen or to look at things from different perspectives. You have also had complaints from the Brazilians that the U.S. managers are confrontational, combative, hostile, and disrespectful. How would you handle this situation before it gets out of hand?

Exercise 12.2: Negotiating Cross-Culturally

Your company has a large, multinational workforce. Your managers continually negotiate projects, assignments, and other transactions across your multinational sites. You, as the senior director of training and development, have noticed that these transactions do not go very smoothly. They often take a seemingly inordinate amount of time and consume a lot of money in the form of travel and travel-related expenses. How would you propose to address this concern?

PART 4

DESIGN, IMPLEMENTATION, AND DEVELOPMENT

This part is divided into two chapters. Chapter 13, "Establishing an Integrated Conflict Resolution System," presents a five-phase model on design and implementation. We approach this from the perspective that designing a comprehensive, integrated system offers advantages to a piecemeal approach. However, one size does not fit all, and piloting, experimenting, and altering are certainly appropriate. Our model, in fact, recognizes the importance of continual review and modification.

In Chapter 13, we pay special attention to practical design and implementation issues. In this vein, the methodology you choose for design is important, for it can speak volumes about the way your company feels about employee involvement and conflict resolution. The chapter also examines the relative advantages of administered versus self-administered ADR.

Chapter 14 presents an approach to building your organization's conflict resolution human capital. It reviews the skills required to manage conflict and the special education and training needed to handle an integrated conflict resolution system effectively. The needs of diverse stakeholders are addressed and education-and-training curricula are calibrated accordingly.

Chapter 13

Establishing an Integrated Conflict Resolution System

Companies have diverse conflict resolution interests and needs. Some may face urgent needs to control costs. Others may seek to avert potentially disastrous industrial disputes. Yet others may have a genuine concern about treating people fairly and equitably. Whatever the pressing need or motivation, we urge you to think expansively about designing a conflict resolution system. View it as an opportunity to acquire organizational knowledge, to release untapped human capital and energy, and to prevent disagreements from escalating beyond manageability. Dealing with conflict effectively not only vitiates problems but also stimulates creativity and personal or organizational development.

In this chapter, we present a five-phase methodology for designing an integrated system. We examine the various elements that might be part of each phase. The phases range from establishing the process itself to modifying the original design: the methodology goes full circle, recognizing that the machinery of conflict resolution should be viewed as of a dynamic or a static quality. Although we do present an integrated-system prototype, we do not offer it as the be all. Your company must take measures appropriate and proportionate to its interests, needs, and capabilities. Stretching and increasing capability may certainly be desirable, but it can be pushed beyond acceptable tolerance.

THE FIVE-PHASE METHODOLOGY

Figure 13.1 identifies the five phases and their core elements. The methodology is intended to be participatory, comprehensive, and self-correct-

Figure 13.1 Establishing a Conflict Resolution System: A Five-Phase Process

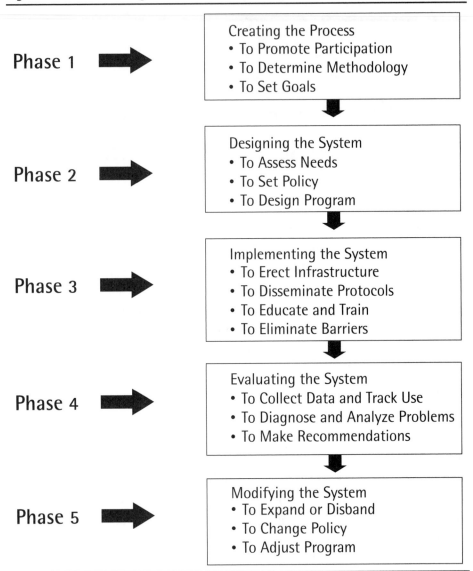

Phase 1

Creating the Process
• To Promote Participation
• To Determine Methodology
• To Set Goals

Phase 2

Designing the System
• To Assess Needs
• To Set Policy
• To Design Program

Phase 3

Implementing the System
• To Erect Infrastructure
• To Disseminate Protocols
• To Educate and Train
• To Eliminate Barriers

Phase 4

Evaluating the System
• To Collect Data and Track Use
• To Diagnose and Analyze Problems
• To Make Recommendations

Phase 5

Modifying the System
• To Expand or Disband
• To Change Policy
• To Adjust Program

ing. Although it focuses on conflict resolution, the process may yield information beneficial to other areas, including personnel policies and practices that may be damaging the organization without offering sufficient countervailing benefits.

The specific phases are:

1. Creating the process, which is participative and collaborative
2. Designing the system, which requires addressing major policy questions
3. Implementing the system, which involves anticipating and surmounting barriers
4. Evaluating the system
5. Modifying the system to meet needs or correct problems revealed in the evaluation.

These phases are discussed in detail below. Before doing so, however, we want to acknowledge that our thinking in the area has been informed by practical experience and by the thoughtful works of others, including Costantino and Merchant (1996), Dunlop and Zack (1997), Ewing (1989), and Mayer (2000), as well as the interagency contributors to the *Federal ADR Program Manager's Resource Manual* (U.S. Interagency ADR Working Group, 2000), a marvelously comprehensive treatment of the subject.

Creating the Process

To some, this first phase may sound unnecessary or inconsequential, a step that delays real action. But nothing could be further from the truth. This phase is perhaps the most important stage. It focuses your company on the issue, produces a sense of purposeful momentum, and lays the foundation for lasting acceptance of effective conflict resolution.

In this phase, you should develop a procedure for designing, drafting, and implementing a conflict resolution system. As Figure 13.2 shows, your efforts should address three questions:

1. Who should participate?
2. How should the process unfold?
3. What should the goals be?

We urge the policymakers, at this stage, to think in participatory, open, and balanced terms.

Figure 13.2 Creating the Process

Who Should Participate?	• Policy Makers • Specialists • Internal Customers • External Customers • Consultants
How Should the Process Unfold?	• Scope of Design • Information Sharing • Drafting • Review Steps • Final Approval
What Should the Goals Be?	• Reduce Disputes • Avoid Litigation • Expand Involvement • Address Problems • Build Relationships • Creative Thinking

More specifically, we urge your company's policy makers (i.e., senior managers) to establish a multiparty Design Task Force. Such a task force would be composed of a set of top policy makers; human resource, labor, and employee relations specialists; potential internal and external customers or users of the system-in-design; and, perhaps, outside consultants who can bring an unbiased assessment of the company and introduce knowledge and understanding from other companies' experiences and from the realm of academic research.

We also recommend that your policy makers think clearly in terms of how the process should unfold. Guidelines should be drawn on the scope of the Design Task Force's mission: Is it a comprehensive conflict resolution system or something narrower in scope? How should information be collected and shared within and outside the organization on the design process? We urge open sharing and the solicitation of diverse perspectives about the issues, problems, and proposed organizational responses.

You should also establish a process for circulating, commenting upon, reviewing, and approving a draft conflict resolution system. It is important for you to share the draft, to get feedback, and to respond thoughtfully to feedback. This can aid immeasurably in building support for the eventual product.

Finally, your policy makers need to be clear about what their goals are. It is both too simplistic and lackadaisical to say that the goal is to resolve conflict. The policy makers should enumerate what they really want to achieve, such as, for example, a reduction in formal complaints, avoiding litigation, or expanding involvement. From the perspective of developing a comprehensive, integrated conflict resolution system, we urge you to think in terms of a balanced approach. This requires specifying a combination of cost-saving, creative-thinking, and relationship-building goals.

Designing the System

When it has been formally charged, your Design Task Force must go about designing a system. The design phase consists of three parts: assessments, policy decisions, and programmatic choices. It is important that your designers understand the context within which a new system will operate. Metaphorically speaking, if they recommend transplanting a foreign organ, then they must take steps to ensure that the host body does not reject it. And they must realize that the system involves many critical policy questions, each of which has programmatic implications.

More specifically, the assessments may consist of an organizational audit, a conflict audit, and goal clarification (see Figure 13.3). The organizational audit should assess employees' attitudes about work and management and the industrial relations climate (if unionized). It is also important to get a handle on the dominating organizational approach to conflict: Is it avoidance, collaboration, accommodation, competition, or compromise? Also, an audit should be conducted on the competency level of your company in the area of conflict resolution, its prior experiences with conflict resolution machinery, and its capacity (attitudinally and resource-wise) to change.

A conflict audit takes stock of the type and frequency of conflicts and disputes (e.g., grievances, EEO complaints, work stoppages). You look for patterns in the parties or units involved, the issues that might recur, and

Figure 13.3 Assessment for Design Task Force

Type	Dimension
Organizational Audit	Organizational Climate
	Industrial/Labor Relations Climate
	Organizational Structure
	Conflict Resolution Infrastructure
	Management Philosophy and Style
	Capacity to Change
	State of Turbulence
	Resource Availability
Conflict Audit	Types and Frequencies of Conflict
	Parties Involved in Conflict
	Amount of Litigation
	Direct and Indirect Costs of Disputes
	Conflict Management Style
	Conflict Resolution Machinery
Goals	Economic—Cost Savings
	Equity—Fairness
	Legal—Compliance
	Voice—Involvement

the degree to which successful resolution has occurred or not. In addition, you look at the mechanics of the existing conflict resolution machinery, the amount of litigation your company has been involved with as a result of workplace conflicts, and the estimated direct and indirect costs of the conflicts found.

Finally, your Design Task Force should begin to assess more precisely the goals you want to achieve. Look at these goals in terms of which should be given greater weight, which should be emphasized in the short term, and which will require a lengthier period to achieve.

Policy Decisions

The design committee should address a variety of policy questions and be prepared to make recommendations on each. Among the issues to decide are those enumerated in Figure 13.4. They include the organizational scope of the system (unit, divisional, company-wide), the type of disputes

Figure 13.4 Policy Issues for Design Task Force

- Organizational Scope
- Types of Disputes Covered
- Employees Eligible
- Dispute Resolution Methodology and Sequence
- Backward-and-Forward Loops
- Due Process Guarantees
- Neutral Sources
- Final Authority
- Pilot Phase-In
- Sunset and Renewal
- Resource Commitments

to be covered (e.g., interests or rights or both), the employee populations eligible to use the system, and the dispute resolution options to be made available (e.g., mediation and/or arbitration).

As the list goes on, your Design Task Force will need to address the extent the parties can move forward and backward among the dispute resolution technologies. Another important issue, especially as it pertains to handling disputes involving statutorily protected rights, is the degree to which the system offers due process protections, ranging from the right to legal representation and the ability to gather evidence to the neutrality of the ultimate decision makers.

If mediators and arbitrators are to be used, you need to consider whether internal or external sources will be used. Also, you need to stipulate the award powers of an arbitrator, if arbitration is to made available. Furthermore, your Design Task Force should decide whether to introduce the system on a pilot basis, whether there should be a mandatory review or sunset provision—terminating the system unless renewal is explicitly authorized—and the extent to which your company will have to commit resources—time, personnel, and money—to make any proposed system work.

At this stage, your Design Task Force should address the multitude of related programmatic considerations (see Figure 13.5). You need to determine where the conflict resolution system will be housed within the company structure. Will it have separate status or be an appendage of

Figure 13.5 Programmatic Considerations for Design Task Force

- Administrative Location
- Program Manager(s)
- Case Activation Criteria
- Information Management
- Delineation of Roles and Responsibilities
- Cost Allocations
- Case Management and Review
- Settlement Enforcement

human resources or employee relations? Another issue is whether specific conflict resolution program managers will be assigned. This need not entail hiring new personnel or raising head count but instead may involve reassigning and training existing personnel. Having program managers can help promote appropriate system advocacy, professionalism in the delivery of available services under the new system, and consistency in the way situations and employees are treated.

In addition, you have to decide how the conflict resolution system will be triggered. What venues exist for making complaints? How will these complaints be evaluated initially to see if they are deserving of further investigation or if they should be dismissed for lack of merit?

Other relevant considerations include how information will be collected, stored, and managed. This is vital to ensure that cases are being managed properly and that data are available for appropriate tracking, reporting, and evaluating. Your Design Task Force will also want to clarify any changes in the roles of existing personnel required to accommodate the new system. For example, are human resource specialists expected to inform new hires of their rights under the new system? Are managers expected to respond formally to employee complaints within a specified period of time? Are employees generally expected or required to be forthcoming in the course of an investigation into a dispute?

We urge your Design Task Force to pay careful attention to matters involving cost allocations, case management, and settlement enforcement. First, the system should not create perverse incentives or disincentives because of the way costs are allocated. Consider this scenario: A company offers disputants an early opportunity to settle through voluntary mediation. However, the unit in which the disputants are employed must pay for the mediator out of its own budget. This could effectively encourage management to put not-so-subtle pressure on the parties to avoid mediation. You may want to address this possibility by establishing a separate conflict resolution fund from which neutrals would be paid.

We further recommend, where possible, to have conflict resolution specialists assigned to specific cases to ensure that they are being managed appropriately and in a timely manner. The specialists would also be charged with the responsibility of ensuring that settlements reached as part of the conflict resolution process are actually being abided by and enforced.

Implementing the System

Your Design Task Force should also address the implementation process. The rubber hits the road at this point. Your Task Force should spell out the implementation process and develop the materials that are necessary for start-up and execution (see Figure 13.6). Thus, it will need to address issues associated with how the new policy will be announced and how relevant information will be disseminated. It will also need to ensure, to the extent desirable and practicable, that appropriate administrative of-

Figure 13.6 Implementing the System

- Policy Announcement and Dissemination
- Administrative Offices and Personnel Assignments
- Procedural Forms
- Neutral Selection
- Reporting Forms
- Database Management
- Training and Education: Awareness
                           Policies and Procedures
                           Administration and Use
                           Conflict Resolution
                           Advanced Skill Development
- Report Generation
- Management Support and Resource Commitment

fices, personnel assignments, and information technologies are made available. Further, you should:

- Specify criteria for neutral selection.
- Make sure that necessary reporting forms (submission requests for neutrals; initial complaints; complaint responses; settlement agreements) are produced.
- Make sure that data management and reporting requirements are set.

Finally, you must commit the financial resources needed to administer the system effectively. And your Design Task Force should develop education-and-training curricula for the various stakeholder populations (we address this topic more fully in Chapter 14).

Evaluating the System

Your Design Task Force should also pay careful attention to how the system is to be evaluated, although it probably should not be given the task of doing the actual evaluation when the time comes. We recommend creating a new evaluation committee because the design group may be vested in sharing the success of the system it created. But your Design Task Force should set the evaluation perimeters (see Figure 13.7)

Obviously, data collection feeds measurement. Possible evaluative metrics include volume or rate of use, the direct and indirect costs of the system, users' satisfaction, program specialists' satisfaction, observable reductions in litigation, and improvements in performance (e.g., increased productivity or reduced lost time). Data-collection methodologies will depend on the metrics, but we urge that they include efforts to obtain hard data (i.e., rates of settlement or costs), attitudinal measures, and focus group responses. Ultimately, based on appropriate analysis of whether the system is meeting its goals, your evaluation should yield recommendations for change, or for outright abandonment if the system is found to be fundamentally flawed.

Figure 13.7 Evaluating the System

Metrics:	Volume
	Outcomes
	Costs
	Displacement
	Satisfaction
	Performance
Data Collection:	Record Tracking
	Case Report Reviews
	Interviews
	Surveys
	Cost Compilations and Estimates
Program Analysis:	Cost–Benefit
	Effectiveness
	Efficiency
	Impact
	Benchmark
	Recommendations

Modifying the System

We encourage the group evaluating your company's system to think critically and expansively, adopting a zero-based budgeting mind-set. Based on the analysis, the group may decide that your organization should reassess its conflict resolution needs. It may recommend taking the program organization-wide if a pilot test has gone well. Disbanding the system altogether is an option if it is not going well for incurable reasons. Your group could recommend policy changes regarding the selection of neutrals, the eligibility of employees, and the availability of particular dispute resolution procedures. In essence, the evaluation and modifications proposed should involve extensive critical thought. Your evaluation group should not rubber-stamp a new system, however appealing it may be to some with a vested interest in its continuance.

A PROPOSED CONFLICT RESOLUTION INTEGRATED SYSTEM

To crystallize thinking about design, we offer a prototype. We begin by identifying a set of features associated with a comprehensive, integrated system. As shown in Figure 13.8, the system is open to a wide array of workplace concerns. It is comprehensive in its availability to employees. It includes multiple dispute resolution venues. In addition, the system is nondiscriminatory; it prohibits reprisals; and it promotes appropriate education, training, and staff support.

In terms of the specific components of a possible design, Figure 13.9 provides a sketch. First, your prototypical integrated conflict resolution system includes an array of voice mechanisms to handle individual and collective concerns on matters involving both interests and rights. These mechanisms are intended to tap the creative juices of employees at all levels and to provide a safety valve for the release of tensions before they are allowed to boil over beyond control.

However, to the extent not inconsistent with law or a collective bargaining agreement, interest and rights claims may be filed with an ADR office, which will conduct an initial review and determine whether they merit further pursuit. If the ADR's initial investigation determines that the case should be selected for dispute resolution, a two-track process is delineated. One track covers cases that are rights-based, in this situation

---

Figure 13.8 Key Features for an Integrated Workplace Dispute Resolution System

- Deal with a very wide spectrum of workplace concerns.
- Be open to all categories of personnel.
- Handle group issues as well as individual complaints.
- Have multiple options or mechanisms including encouraging person-to-person or group-to-group negotiations and problem resolution; informal or formal mediation; fact finding and peer review; and arbitration.
- Allow "looping backward and forward" to the informal and formal procedures at various stages in the resolution process.
- Provide a variety of helping resources such as training, advising, and representation not only to the complainant but also to the respondent and the supervisors and coworkers affected by the dispute.
- Include people of color, women, and men in the various roles in the system.
- Be taught to all participants in the organization.
- Proscribe reprisal and provide for monitoring and evaluation.
- Include a wide cross section of employees and managers in the design of the system.

Source: Testimony of Professor Mary Rowe, April 6, 1994, Commission on the Future of Worker-Management Relations. *Fact Finding Report.* June 2, 1994.

Figure 13.9 An Integrated System Design

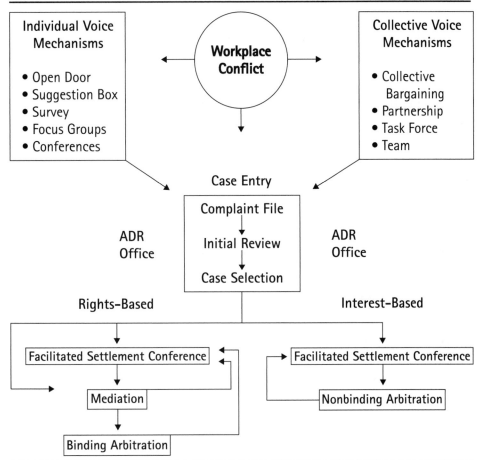

involving the interpretation of specific contractual rights (e.g., terms of an individual employment contract) or statutorily protected rights (e.g., antidiscrimination claims). The aggrieved party may request a facilitated settlement conference, or go directly to mediation. If neither step results in a settlement, then the aggrieved party may pursue binding arbitration. At mediation and arbitration, the parties, by mutual consent, may revert back to a facilitated settlement conference without forfeiting the right to return to mediation or arbitration.

Interest-based conflicts—such as those over a performance appraisal, promotion, pay raise, or assignment—are handled in a different way. The aggrieved party may request a facilitated settlement conference. If that fails to produce a satisfactory settlement, then she may proceed to nonbinding arbitration.

Under this prototypical process, the parties would be entitled to legal representation, neutrals would be selected from outside panels, employees would not be required to commit to this system as a condition of employment, and other due process protections, including affordability, would be provided.

ADMINISTERED VS. NONADMINISTERED ADR PROCEDURES

In drafting a conflict resolution system, your Design Task Force will need to consider whether to use an administered or nonadministered arrangement if it offers ADR procedures such as mediation and arbitration. The AAA is a preeminent provider and advocate of administered arrangements. In a fully administered arrangement, the provider would, for a specified or negotiated fee, do the following:

- Arrange for the selection of an arbitrator or mediator from its pre-approved roster
- Coordinate arrangements for the arbitration or mediation, including time, place, and location
- Conduct a pre-hearing conference if needed
- Establish time limits for resolution
- Ensure that arbitrators/mediators adhere to certain standards of conduct and pertinent rules

In contrast, under a self-administered or nonadministered ADR arrangement, the parties retain greater control of these particulars. The CPR Institute for Dispute Resolution is one of the major advocates of self-administered ADR. In a nutshell, in a self-administered procedure, the parties select the neutral, agree to a resolution procedure, and let the neutral handle matters from that point.

There are advantages and disadvantages to each. According the AAA, the administered form offers these advantages to the parties.

- Self-executing rules, which do not have to be invented or reinvented on an ad hoc basis
- Experience and professionalism, which novice parties may lack
- A mechanism for handling procedural objections
- A ready-made roster of qualified neutrals
- Administrative assistance is setting up the ADR session
- Consistent procedural rules
- A buffer between the parties and the neutrals over potentially sticky matters

The self- or nonadministered arrangement is argued to offer its own advantages. According to James F. Henry (1997), president emeritus of the CPR Institute for Dispute Resolution, self-administration is preferable because:

- It gives the parties greater control over the process.
- It is less expensive, more cost-effective.
- It is more flexible.
- It is quicker and more efficient.

We do not attempt to resolve this debate here. Which arrangement is advisable will depend somewhat on the experience level and sophistication of the parties. However, we would strongly encourage inexperienced parties to consult providers of administered services. Also, ensuring consistency and the appearance of neutrality and impartiality are important goals that administered arrangement can help promote.

SOLUTION AT ABC

We conclude this chapter by describing the feature of a real-world company's conflict resolution system (see Figure 13.10). (The names of the company and program, however, are fictitious.) Under company ABC's SOLUTION program, all nonunion employees (union employees are cov-

Figure 13.10 Corporate Conflict Resolution (CR) Illustration

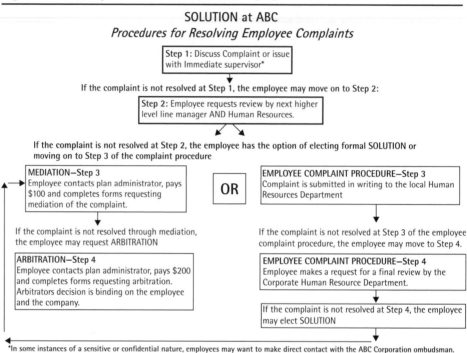

SOLUTION at ABC
Procedures for Resolving Employee Complaints

Step 1: Discuss Complaint or issue with Immediate supervisor*

If the complaint is not resolved at Step 1, the employee may move on to Step 2:

Step 2: Employee requests review by next higher level line manager AND Human Resources.

If the complaint is not resolved at Step 2, the employee has the option of electing formal SOLUTION or moving on to Step 3 of the complaint procedure

MEDIATION—Step 3
Employee contacts plan administrator, pays $100 and completes forms requesting mediation of the complaint.

OR

EMPLOYEE COMPLAINT PROCEDURE—Step 3
Complaint is submitted in writing to the local Human Resources Department

If the complaint is not resolved through mediation, the employee may request ARBITRATION

If the complaint is not resolved at Step 3 of the employee complaint procedure, the employee may move to Step 4.

ARBITRATION—Step 4
Employee contacts plan administrator, pays $200 and completes forms requesting arbitration. Arbitrators decision is binding on the employee and the company.

EMPLOYEE COMPLAINT PROCEDURE—Step 4
Employee makes a request for a final review by the Corporate Human Resource Department.

If the complaint is not resolved at Step 4, the employee may elect SOLUTION

*In some instances of a sensitive or confidential nature, employees may want to make direct contact with the ABC Corporation ombudsman.

ered by a duly negotiated grievance procedure that culminates in binding arbitration) may register a complaint over any of the following concerns:

- Disagreements over ABC policies or practices at work
- Discriminatory treatment based on age, gender, race, religion, or disability
- Disciplinary actions
- Inappropriate working conditions
- Wrongful discharge or layoff

The complaint procedure is divided into several steps and is a bifurcated one. The first step involves an attempt at informal reconciliation among the parties. If this is unsuccessful, then the employee may go to the next step, which involves an informal review with the parties, a higher level manager, and a human resources representative. If resolution is not reached at Step 2, the complainant reaches a proverbial fork-in-the-road decision: go the traditional route, requesting review by local and then corporate human resources, or alternatively, go to the SOLUTION program.

SOLUTION, at Step 3, involves voluntary mediation. An aggrieved employee, if unsatisfied after Step 2, may request mediation. A small processing fee is required. If the complaint is not satisfactorily resolved at mediation, the employee may request binding arbitration (Step 4). A $200 processing fee is charged. We should note that, under SOLUTION, outside neutrals from AAA rosters are used. Also, complainants are entitled to legal representation at both mediation and arbitration—at their own expense, however. Finally, reprisals for using SOLUTION are strictly prohibited.

Manager's Checklist:
Considering an Integrated Conflict Resolution System

When considering the development of a comprehensive, integrated conflict resolution system, you should walk through the following checklist:

1. *Creating the Process*
   - Who should be involved?
     Policy makers
     Specialists
     Internal customers
     External customers
     Consultants
   - How should the process unfold?
     Scope of design
     Information exchange
     Drafting
     Review
     Approval

- What are the goals?
  Efficiency
  Equity
  Performance
  Growth
  Involvement
2. *Designing the System*
   - Assessments
     Organizational audit
     Conflict audit
     Goal clarification
   - Policy issues
     Organizational scope
     Coverage: issue/employee
     Dispute resolution methods
     Neutral sources
     Due process protections
     Pilot
     Sunset and renewal
     Resource commitments
     Neutral authority
   - Program considerations
     Administrative location
     Program manager
     Case activation criteria
     Information management
     Role clarification
     Cost allocations
     Case management
     Enforcement
3. *Implementing the System*
   - Policy announcement
   - Administrative offices and equipment
   - Forms
   - Neutral selection

- Database management
- Reporting
- Budgets
- Training and education

4. *Evaluating the System*
   - Objective evaluation committee
   - Metrics
   - Data-collection methods
   - Program analysis
   - Recommendations

5. *Modifying the System (Zero-Based)*
   - Reassessing needs
   - Altering policy
   - Adjusting program
   - Changing scope
   - Disbanding

Chapter 14

Education and Training

Handling conflict isn't so difficult. All you do is confront the employee with the issue and tell him what to do. If he doesn't do it, it's an act of insubordination and the guy's out. It's that simple.

Conflict Resolution class participant, October 2000

Many more people *think* they are adept at managing conflict than actually are. Admitting ignorance in this regard can be embarrassing to some. Your company may shun developing a conflict resolution system for fear of uncovering problems or opening old wounds. The reality of the current situation is that, across the gamut of organizations, most provide little or no systemic education or training in conflict resolution. For those companies that have, the exposure has probably been limited and sporadic.

Such an approach will simply not work if the company is serious about introducing an integrated conflict resolution system. A more systematic education and training effort is required. No doubt, this undertaking can be expensive. To earn a good return on this investment, your company must know what it is looking for and how to measure it. A properly conceived and administered conflict resolution system, one that emphasizes resolution and personal/organizational growth, can yield enormous benefits while simultaneously avoiding crippling costs.

In this chapter we develop a multi-audience education-and-training program in conflict resolution. Your company, obviously, will want to adapt a program to its specific needs and interests. But one feature should be relatively common across companies: the curriculum must fit the audience. Not all employees, including managers and executives, need the same type or level of development, though a basic level may be appropriate for most. Parenthetically, by focusing on employees, we do not mean to exclude others with a less direct or indirect working relationship with the company. Your company may wisely choose to expand its education-and-training program beyond its core employment base.

CONFLICT RESOLUTION STAKEHOLDER COMMUNITY

The first step in curriculum development is to contemplate your relevant audiences. Figure 14.1 illustrates partitioning your potential conflict resolution stakeholder community into distinguishable but not mutually exclusive audiences. Specifically, you have the *general audience*, the internal (and, if so desired, external) customers who will directly or indirectly benefit from effective conflict resolution. It includes executives, managers,

Figure 14.1 CR Stakeholder Community

• **General Audience**
    Executives
    Staff Specialists (HR, LR, ER, ADR)
        Human Resources   Labor Relations   Employee Relations   Alternative Dispute Resolution

    Manager
    Employer

• **Potential Users and Points of Contact**

• **Users**

• **ADR Program Managers and Specialists**

• **External or Internal Third-Parties**

staff specialists, and employees. Getting people on the same page in terms of their ability to manage conflict effectively is a laudatory goal. One of the purposes of the design of an integrated system is to enable and empower your workforce to resolve its own differences without having to resort to costly and adversarial venues that sap your company's talent and reserve.

Another audience is the potential (and ultimately actual) *users* of the system. This group also includes those managers, professionals, and employees (e.g., team leaders and union representatives) who may be expected to refer people to system specialists or inform them as to how the process works. In addition, there is the audience of *ADR or conflict resolution program administrators and staff specialists*, who may need to work closely with disputants before, during, and after the conflict. Finally, your company may need to offer education and training to build an external or internal pool of *qualified neutrals*: facilitators, mediators, and arbitrators. This need will grow commensurately with the amount of subject matter and organizational system knowledge the neutral needs in order to perform effectively. Education and training in conflict resolution, as previously mentioned, will need to be calibrated to your different audiences. We propose a building-block approach to achieve this purpose.

CORE COMPETENCIES

To tailor a curriculum to the needs of such diverse stakeholders, you should map out the competencies associated with conflict management and conflict resolution systems, much like was shown in Chapter 3. Figure 14.2 lists the relevant knowledge, ability, and skill requirements. In the area of knowledge, your developmental needs may vary from an understanding of alternative conflict resolution styles to the specifics of ADR methodologies.

You also look for certain core abilities in this area. Not everyone needs to be at the same ability level. But your company will want to ensure that, within its ranks, it has sufficient capacity. Recruiting personnel with such abilities in the first place is a good approach to use in promoting effective conflict resolution. These desirable abilities include communications (ver-

Figure 14.2 Conflict Resolution Core Competencies

Knowledge	Abilities	Skills
• Conflict Resolution System	• Communication	• Listen
• ADR Methodologies	• Comprehension	• Facilitation
• System Procedures	• Analysis	• Mediation
• Organizational Goals	• Decision-Making	• Arbitration
• System Goals	• Problem-Solving	• Negotiation
• Organizational Culture	• Empathy	• Conflict Management
• Conflict Resolution Styles	• Relate	

bal and nonverbal), analytical thinking, decision making and problem solving, and comprehension. In addition, your company will want people who are able to relate to the needs of others (recognize) and to empathize with (understand and feel) those interests.

Finally, you will want to develop the skill-base of your workforce. The development needs will vary across hierarchical level and occupation. Overall, however, you should develop your employees' (at all levels) skills with regard to conflict management, listening, and negotiating. Also, make certain that the talent pool is available to fulfill your need for facilitators, mediators, and arbitrators. Specialized instruction may have to be offered for this purpose.

GENERAL AUDIENCE CURRICULUM

Figure 14.3 specifies the elements of a conflict resolution curriculum for your general audience. The curriculum may be viewed as offering the basics that your company's employees need, regardless of their prospective connection with the conflict resolution machinery itself.

The basics include making the audience aware of your company's approach to conflict resolution, the need for and purpose of its conflict resolution system, and the operational components of the system—i.e., who can use it, how it can be used, etc. At a very basic skill level, the curriculum emphasizes listening skills, conflict management skills, negotiating skills, and communications. One might add managing time and meetings, plus

Figure 14.3 General Conflict Resolution (CR) Curriculum

- Organizational CR Needs and Interests
- Philosophy and Structure of CR System
- CR Contact Information
- Listening Skills
- Conflict Management Skills
- Negotiating (Interest-Based) Skills
- Communications
- Relevant Specialized Topics (e.g., Workplace Violence Prevention and Response Program)

teambuilding. These components reflect values as well as skills. Last, you may have a need to cover certain specialized topics, such as workplace violence, or conflict resolution/negotiating styles from international perspectives.

POTENTIAL AND ACTUAL USERS

Your curriculum for potential and actual users of the conflict resolution system builds on the general-audience program. To these basics, you would add more detailed information about the procedures and mechanisms of the conflict resolution system, from neutral selection criteria and mediation request forms to criteria for case selection. On top of this, you may also help this group develop its knowledge base in the field of conflict resolution by identifying sources of expert assistance (see Figure 14.4). Potential users, and those who may refer others to system specialists, should have some appreciation of how the ADR components work and their relative advantages and disadvantages. The importance of providing meaningful informal counsel cannot be overstated.

Figure 14.4 Potential and Actual User Curriculum

- General Conflict Resolution Curriculum
                    Plus
- Procedures and Mechanics of CR System
- Sources of Expert Assistance

ADR Program Managers and Selected Staff Specialists

For those individuals charged with managing a conflict resolution or ADR system, as well as those who will work closely with users in their capacities as human resources, employee relations, or EEO specialists, you will need to provide advanced education and training. In step with the building-block approach, Figure 14.5 identifies those curricular elements that would address this need. Specifically, this group will need development in the area of ADR procedures (how do they work, what are they intended to do, what should one expect, etc.). The group may also benefit from education in program evaluation methodologies and also certain legal issues or trends, such as the implications of the Circuit City decision by the U.S. Supreme Court.

External Development

Finally, your company may need to develop a cadre of qualified neutrals (see Figure 14.6). You may, for example, offer training in new mediation techniques, such as the Postal Service has done in the area of transformative mediation. You may also offer education and training on how a new program works, such as the EEOC has done in connection with its National Mediation Program. Or, you may need to offer specialized education in key subject areas where expertise is required: employment law, such as construction industry disputes or intellectual property rights.

Your company need not do this kind of training alone. You may part-

Figure 14.5 Program Managers and Selected Staff Specialists Conflict Resolution Curriculum

- General Conflict Resolution Curriculum
- Potential and Actual User Curriculum
          Plus
- ADR Procedures
- Program Evaluation
- Legal Issues

Figure 14.6 External Development

- Educating Outside Neutral
  CR System Design
  CR System Mechanics

- Training Outside Neutral
  Mediation
  Arbitration
  Subject Expertise (e.g., commercial transactions, employment law, intellectual property)

ner with entities such as AAA or you may retain consultant/trainers. In addition, you may go to universities to develop customized education in areas such as employment law or environmental regulation. As the use of mediation and arbitration increases in various areas, such as the employment field, your need for such training is inescapable:

> There is a manifest need for mediators and arbitrators with expertise in statutory requirements in the employment field who may, without special training, lack experience in the employment area and in the conduct of arbitration and mediation sessions. . . . Training in the statutory issues should be provided by the government agencies, bar associations, academic institutions, etc. . . . *

Manager's Checklist: Education and Training Programs

We recommend that you focus on developing a comprehensive and coordinated education-and-training program. To do so, you should refer to the following checklist:

- *Who is in the conflict resolution stakeholder community?*
  General audience
  Potential users
  Actual users

*This protocol was developed by a privately created Task Force on Alternative Dispute Resolution in Employment, which issued the *Due Process Protocol for Mediation and Arbitration of Statutory Disputes Arising out of the Employment Relationship* report (May 9, 1995).

ADR/CR program managers and other staff specialists

External or internal neutral pool

- *What are the core conflict resolution competencies?*

Knowledge

Abilities

Skills

- *Who is the audience for the curriculum?*

The general audience?

The potential and actual users?

Staff specialists?

Outside neutrals?

- *What should such education and training accomplish for each group?*

Impart knowledge

Change behavior

Reduce conflict

Improve relationships

PART 5

CONCLUSION

We have constructed this book to give you an appreciation of the breadth and complexity of the topic of workplace conflict. In so doing, we have addressed a variety of the so-called alternative dispute resolution techniques, including negotiating, mediation, facilitation, and arbitration. In addition, we have explored the special topics of EEO and conflict resolution/ADR, workplace violence, and ADR in international contexts. Finally, we have shown how to go about designing and implementing a comprehensive conflict resolution system, one that seeks to realize the benefits while mitigating the costs of conflict. Throughout, we have attempted to offer tips, practical information, and informative data.

We conclude not with a summary, since we offered the chapters as much as possible as stand alone units. Instead, we want to present a conceptual map of workplace conflict and dispute resolution, and offer ten guideposts for you to follow in developing a conflict resolution policy and program for your company.

Chapter 15

Workplace Conflict Resolution Map and Guideposts

"Class-Action Suit Alleging Sex Discrimination Filed on Behalf of up to 750,000 Against Nation's Largest Private Employer, Wal-Mart." (*AP News*, June 20, 2001)

"In 1994, 18 Million Cases Were Filed in U.S. Federal Courts." (Stewart Levine, 1998)

"Fortune 500 Executives Spend 20 Percent of Time on Litigation." (Stewart Levine, 1998)

"Atlanta-Based Coca-Cola Pays $192 Million to Settle Race-Bias Suit." (*USA Today*, March 27, 2001)

"50 Percent of Employers Report Having Been Sued by Workers in a Survey by Jackson Lewis Law Firm and Society for Human Resource Management." (*USA Today*, March 27, 2001)

These recent headlines and troubling data are prime reasons why your company is exploring ways of handling conflict more effectively. Conflict management and negotiation are increasingly popular topics in educational curricula and business training. In academe, these fields, plus ADR and specialized topics, are gaining stature and distinctiveness.

With this rising attention, however, comes a potential pitfall for you and your company. You can get lost in the trees. Drowned in technique. Blinded by the arcane. Overwhelmed with legalisms. We offer this final chapter in the hope of averting this pitfall. You should keep focused on why you have conflicts, how you—personally—can handle conflict, and how your company can equip itself to deal constructively with this workplace reality.

WORKPLACE CONFLICT RESOLUTION MAP

To keep it simple, Figure 15.1 presents a Workplace Conflict Resolution (WCR) Map. Its central points can be summarized as follows:

- Workplace conflict occurs between and among a variety of internal and external customers over interests, rights, and powers.
- Workplace conflict can be caused, exacerbated, or escalated by a confluence of organizational, work site, and environmental factors,

Figure 15.1 WCR Map

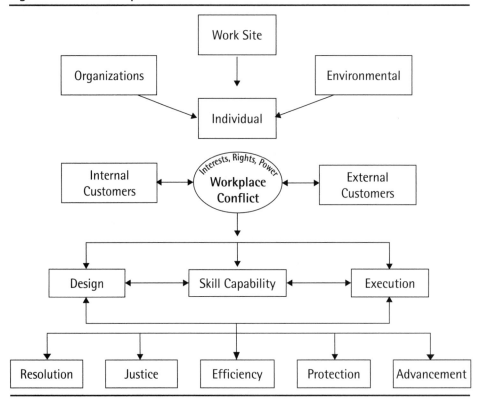

which impinge on individuals with varying capacities to handle disagreement or conflict.

- Companies can attempt to deal with workplace conflict effectively by designing comprehensive dispute resolution systems, investing in collaborative conflict management and conflict resolution skill-building, and administering a program effectively.
- Workplace conflict resolution systems should focus on a balanced set of goals, including resolution, justice/fairness, efficiency, advancement of the organization, and protection of the employee from psychological and physical harm.

THE TEN GUIDEPOSTS

In developing and administering a workplace conflict resolution program—or, as we have previously called it, an integrated conflict resolution system—you should follow these guideposts:

Guidepost 1: Keep it simple.
All those affected by it should be able to understand how it works.

Guidepost 2: Keep it positive.
Make certain the stakeholders know why the program is being adopted—that it is to give people a chance to change the status quo, to resolve disagreements, and to promote and protect interests without fear of reprisal.

Guidepost 3: Set balanced goals.
Keep it about promoting personal growth and opportunity as much as keeping the company out of court.

Guidepost 4: Promote accessibility.
Ensure that the system is accessible (and affordable) to employees across diverse income, occupational, and hierarchical ranks.

Guidepost 5: Allow multiple venues.
Create multiple points to raise concerns, and allow the parties maximum opportunity to resolve disagreements themselves.

Guidepost 6: Encourage early intervention.

Allow the parties to arrange opportunities to address and resolve issues early in the stages of disagreement. Encourage the parties to deal with issues before they fester. Don't sweep concerns under the rug.

Guidepost 7: Get leadership commitment.

Ensure that leaders are committed to the program, understand what it is about, and are willing to make the investments necessary to make it work.

Guidepost 8: Cover interests and rights.

Construct the system so that employees or users can address interest- and rights-based concerns. Create voice mechanisms for both to be raised in nonadversarial forums.

Guidepost 9: Give due process protection.

Maximize the parties' due process protections, especially in matters dealing with statutorily protected rights.

Guidepost 10: Build a collaborative culture.

Emphasize collaboration in internal and external relations. Educate. Train. Preach. Practice.

Appendix A

Solutions to Exercises

In this section, we recommend brief solutions to the end-of-chapter exercises. We offer these recommendations not as *the* solutions but rather as approaches to help stimulate your thinking. Each of the exercises is based on real events in which we have been involved as consultants or managers/administrators.

EXERCISE 3.2: RESOLVING A COMPLEX CONFLICT

Recommended Solution

We recommend starting off with an openly collaborative approach. You need to ascertain the underlying interests of the senior manager, which could range from the need to be heard, to vent, to be recognized, to the need to be valued. Also, you need to be open to the possibility that your restructuring plan, with its attendant productivity indicators, is at least somewhat off target. Likewise, your performance appraisal could be off the mark.

Listen actively and empathetically. Be prepared to assert your interests in moving forward, and look for a constructive way to involve the senior manager. Litigation is a real possibility, heightened if the senior manager feels shut out, slighted, or punished.

If a collaborative approach does not at first succeed, try again. But state your case that you intend to move forward. Offer to have another senior executive review the performance evaluation. But create clear performance expectations for the senior manager. However, you must be prepared to reevaluate the situation if the senior manager's arguments are persuasive.

EXERCISE 4.1: NEGOTIATING A SALARY RAISE

Recommended Solution

We recommend preparing by identifying the various ways in which you can value an employee through recognition and reward. Opportunities for early promotion, new assignments, paid vacations, and extra training are among them. Do not go on the defensive if the direct report challenges your judgment. Merit pay is only one form of recognition. Ask her what other kinds she might find appropriate. Ask how her interests are not being served. Explain your decision-making process. This is an opportunity for you to listen. Be prepared to couch your decision in reference to market-based salary decisions as well as legitimate internal standards of performance. Be open-minded. Emphasizing the rationality of your decision-making and the opportunities for the person is essential.

EXERCISE 4.2: NEGOTIATING A REASSIGNMENT

Recommended Solution

We recommend that you prepare by listing the important reasons why you have made this decision. You are extending the performer extra recognition. The stellar performer is needed in areas that have underperformed. Look for ways to ensure that the person's sacrifice will be an opportunity for greater reward and recognition in the near and more removed future. Discuss the interests or needs of the person regarding the reassignment or move in terms of housing, family support, etc. Your main effort needs to be focused on impressing how valuable the person's talents are and how he can contribute to the bottom-line, the overall welfare of the company, and his future status/position by making this move. Obviously, it is important to listen and be open-minded. There may be things that you have not considered or issues that make this an unwise move. Make sure you address these issues (e.g., parent-care, spouse's career) before proceeding.

EXERCISE 4.3: NEGOTIATING A JOB REDUCTION

Recommended Solution

We recommend that you approach this individual confidentially about the need to address some concerns. Without being disingenuous, you want to put as positive a spin on the proposed change as possible. The decision you have reached has been made in the best interest of the person and the company. A failure to take some action to enable the person to handle the work situation poses serious difficulties. The real issue you want to address is the HR manager's performance and the need to get important work done. If the person is overburdened, the failure to perform adequately will only exacerbate his situation and harm the company. You need to listen carefully to the HR manager and find out what is really going on and what you can do to help. Invite him to advise you on how to present the change to the broader corporate community. His esteem (self- and in the eyes of colleagues) is important.

EXERCISE 5.1: FACILITATING AN EXECUTIVES' MEETING

Recommended Solution

We recommend inviting an outsider to facilitate the meeting. (The outsider might be a consultant with whom the direct reports are familiar and in whom they have trust.) This act conveys the message that you are intensely interested in listening. Also, rather than your having to referee the meeting, that burden falls on the facilitator. You do not have to interject yourself authoritatively and risk promoting group-think or a chilling discussion because of your superior position. You want a facilitator respected for his or her independence and completeness. You want the facilitation to result in a plan of action that assimilates the best ideas generated from the group. You do not want the session to be a protracted, blame-the-other-person meeting. You do not expect miracles, and more than one meeting may be necessary.

EXERCISE 5.2: FACILITATING A MEETING WITH A GROUP OF PROFESSIONALS

Recommended Solution

We recommend conducting a facilitated session. This is important because there may be an element of suspicion or distrust. Also, the parties involved speak different professional languages. There may be cultural barriers, professional norms, or working contexts that cause these parties to have difficulty seeing each other's perspective. A facilitator can help clarify the perspectives, frame issues, and generate possible solutions or understandings to serve the parties' respective interests. We would expect the session, which may need to be repeated more than once, to establish an ongoing dialogue. You are interested in building trust, promoting a common language, and sharing feelings and data.

EXERCISE 6.1: MEDIATING A PROMOTION DISPUTE

Recommended Solution

We recommend that you prepare for this meeting by reviewing carefully the thinking process used to make your recommendation against promotion. Many times, the aggrieved parties do not understand the process.

They do not fully appreciate the reasoning and range of considerations involved. You need to explain it objectively, focusing on the facts as you understood them.

However, you should also be open to the possibility you erred. But be prepared to explain that your thinking process (if this is true) yields consistent results. Present your case with an understanding that this decision is difficult for the adversely affected person. Propose ways in which the person might amend performance so as to secure promotion. Continually stress the value of the relationship and that this is a *temporary, correctible* outcome. A settlement might focus on how performance can be improved to yield promotion opportunities in the foreseeable future.

EXERCISE 6.2: MEDIATING A WORKPLACE CONFLICT

Recommended Solution

This exercise asks you to think about a situation at work. It is designed to guide you through the process of preparing for a mediation. By addressing the questions posed, you will have, in the context of your own situation, gone a long way toward preparing thoroughly for a mediation. You need to make certain you know the facts, know what is fact versus opinion; know what the various interests are; know what your options are; and know how to present these options in a way that commands respect.

EXERCISE 7.1: THE FORK IN THE ROAD

Recommended Solution

We recommend trying mediation. Going directly to arbitration might rigidify your respective positions and encourage adversarialism. A mediated session offers an opportunity for you calmly to present your views in the presence of a neutral third-party. Mediation is less threatening and less costly. You (and the other party) retain control over the outcome. You will think more in terms of reaching a mutually agreeable solution than persuading an arbitrator to rule in your favor. You might be able to build trust, look for solutions, and emphasize the long-term importance of having a good relationship at work. You have the option of arbitration after mediation.

EXERCISE 7.2: SHOULD YOU GO TO ARBITRATION?

Recommended Solution

We recommend finding a way to "settle" with the employee. This suggests your interest in solving a problem rather than making a point, grinding an ax, or trying to intimidate her into submission. You also do not want to waste the resources of the company for problematic purposes. A mediated or negotiated session that explores options is desirable. You need to explore underlying difficulties that may exist in the relationship, ambiguities in the parties' roles, and the need to clarify responsibilities.

EXERCISE 8.1: THE PASSIONATE DISPUTANTS

Recommended Solution

We recommend coupling a mediated session with a neutral evaluation. The mediator would be called upon to help arrive at a settlement. If this did not occur, then the mediator would offer an assessment of how she or he would rule in an arbitration. Also, she or he might be asked to evaluate what might happen in a litigated case. The mediator would have had experience arbitrating EEO-type cases, be familiar with EEO law, and have litigated EEO cases. The mediator's evaluation must be credible to both parties. It is important that the mediator have no conflict of interest and that both parties feel confident about her credentials.

EXERCISE 8.2: CLUSTERING CONFLICTS

Recommended Solution

We recommend that you seriously consider establishing an ombuds as long as proper assurances are given to employees that they will not suffer retaliation. You might also consider offering the employee relations or HR offices as the first step in a revised complaint procedure. More broadly, you have a serious cultural problem to address. You may have supervisors who need training or who need to be replaced. Are there serious personality clashes? Are there chronic malcontents present? Are there troublesome working conditions that give rise to conflict? These are the kinds of questions an ombuds, given appropriate investigative charter and authority, can address.

EXERCISE 9.1: RESPONDING TO PORTENDING BEHAVIORS

Recommended Solution

We recommend that you act cautiously but promptly. Approach the employee discretely and confidentially. Ask her if there is a problem that the company can help her with. Shift the burden on her to explain the situation. Do not be confrontational or threatening. Suggest that she take some time off (paid), and refer her to an EAP. The signs that portend violence or other destructive (particularly self-destructive) behaviors are present. You need to impress that conduct that threatens others will not be tolerated by suggesting you want to avoid any situation that might cause anyone to be harmed or feel threatened. You may want to have a counselor or other supervisor present with you when discussing this matter.

EXERCISE 9.2: TERMINATING THE EMPLOYEE

Recommended Solution

We recommend that you make certain that your case has been carefully documented and approved. You do not want to be fumbling during your termination session. This is time for brevity and specificity. Make certain that progressive discipline has been followed. Confront the employee at the start of the workday (or end); inform him of the decision and that he is expected to leave at once and not return without proper authorization. Offer whatever exit services are customary. Have someone present with you, and alert security to be nearby to escort the person off the premises. Make certain that the dismissed employee relinquishes keys or ID badges that might give him access to the premises.

EXERCISE 10.1: HANDLING THE CHRONIC DISPUTANT

Recommended Solution

We recommend that you consider a transformative type of approach at least once. The traditional model has not worked. However, it may well be that a complaining-mediating cycle dependency exists. The employee may need counseling to reveal underlying personal difficulties. Or it may be that his work assignment needs to be changed. Perhaps some more general management-employee team-building training would be helpful.

EXERCISE 10.2: DEALING WITH SEXUAL HARASSMENT

Recommended Solution

We recommend that you recognize this as *your* company's problem. You should convene a series of meetings to identify who is perpetrating these acts. Second, you should emphasize that antiharassment laws require your company to protect your employees from such conduct. Third, inform others that such conduct will not be tolerated. Fourth, offer to hold joint training sessions with company employees and vendors/suppliers on the requirements of an antiharassment policy.

EXERCISE 11.1: KEEPING THE UNION AT A DISTANCE

Recommended Solution

We recommend that you meet this situation head-on. Develop a plan to train or retrain supervisors. Hold joint training with employees and supervisors on team-building, problem-solving, and interpersonal skills. Set clear expectations for performance in supervisory-employee relations. Ensure that your other personnel policies value employees. Consider establishing a formal dispute resolution procedure and one that allows complaints to be made outside the normal chain of command.

EXERCISE 11.2: NEGOTIATING WITH A DIFFICULT UNION

Recommended Solution

We recommend that you avoid the temptation to blame the union. You want to open a dialogue with union leaders, long before the negotiations start. Hold joint labor-management conferences to share information about the business, its strategy, its financial outlook, and the resulting labor-relations implications. Be assertive of your interests, but do not attempt to remain blameless. Assume a fair share of responsibility. Be up front about your desire to change the negotiating psychology for the betterment of all parties' interests.

EXERCISE 12.1: MANAGING CROSS-NATIONAL WORKPLACE CONFLICT

Recommended Solution

We recommend that you convene a facilitated meeting of the managers to discuss their respective issues. The focus should be on empowering them to identify what the problems are and how they can best be addressed.

You have a serious problem that requires a systemic solution. Are there feelings of differential status, treatment, opportunity, and reward?

EXERCISE 12.2: NEGOTIATING CROSS-CULTURALLY

Recommended Solution

We recommend that you conduct an in-house cross-cultural negotiating program. The focus should be on how to use interest-based problem-solving to promote mutually beneficial solutions. Problems of communications, cultural differences, and uncooperative behaviors should be addressed in the process.

Appendix B

EEO Mediation Simulation

In this simulation, a woman vice president of research has filed a charge against her employer, Telit, alleging sex discrimination and harassment. She was not considered for promotion to chief operating officer (COO), which prompted the charge.

Rather than investigate the charge, the EEOC has referred the parties to voluntary mediation. The parties, represented by counsel, have agreed to this procedure, which does not commit them to settle. If a settlement is not reached, the complainant may pursue formal charges.

The mediator's objective is to help the parties reach a mutually satisfactory agreement. Through role-playing (see background information for the use of participants at the end of the case) or discussion, this case can stimulate thinking about the nature of mediation, the role of the mediator, and the value of mediation vis-a-vis litigation.

Case Study and Simulation
Redressing an EEOC Complaint at Telit

BACKGROUND

Telit is a high-profile dot.com business headquartered in Cranberry, Pennsylvania. It recently went public in a highly successful IPO. Its major business line is to help clients prospect for donors. Its major clients include universities, corporate foundations, hospitals, and cultural enterprises. In

2000, its total revenues exceeded $40 million and its net profits were $1 million. It employs 250 people in five main areas: information technology, research, customer service, marketing, and human resources. The research area consists of ten employees, whose job it is to gather and analyze data regarding donor markets. Each area is headed by a corporate vice president, each of whom reports to the CEO and president, Jack Webb, Jr. (son of the star of the popular 1950s TV series "Dragnet"). The vice president of research is Ms. Janet Wilcox, a 35-year-old M.B.A. graduate of the University of Pittsburgh, class of 1994.

Telit has grown rapidly over the past two years, with employment climbing from 100 to 250. It projects to double employment in the next two years. In 1999 it broke even financially; an impressive feat, given that it was founded in 1997.

Table B-1. Breakdown of Telit Workforce

Occupation	Total	Gender	Race	Age	Terms
CEO/President	1	M	W	45 years	4 years
COO	1	—	—	—	—
VPs	5	75% M	100% W	39 years	2 years
Managers	25	80% M	95% W	36 years	2 years
Professionals	25	60% M	95% W	34 years	2 years
Technicians	25	70% M	95% W	38 years	1 year
Clerical	25	10% M	85% W	36 years	1 year
Production/ Maintenance	25	95% M	90% W	40 years	1.5 yrs.
Temps (full-time)	20	50% M	80% W	33 years	1 year

Situation

On April 15, 2001, the COO, Mr. Ramsey Clark, departed suddenly. His departure (he was "pirated" by another company) created an important vacancy.

Telit's implicit policy for filling executive/managerial positions is to recruit from within. Telit is interested in building and retaining talent, especially in today's highly competitive labor markets. It subsidizes formal and continuing education, and promotes employee development as part of its formal performance review process.

Immediately after Mr. Clark's departure, Ms. Wilcox approached Mr. Webb about being considered for the position of COO. She felt strongly that she was the most qualified and capable among the senior executive team (excluding Webb). Mr. Wilcox indicated that he would consider the application.

Over the course of several weeks, Mr. Wilcox considered replacing the departed COO with internal candidates. Each of the VPs had expressed an interest in the position. Each of the VPs had strong records of performance, had been evaluated highly, and had comparable experience levels and education backgrounds.

After mulling over selecting an internal person for the chief operating officer opening, Mr. Webb decided to look for an external candidate. He retained the services of a headhunting firm, ITEX, and announced this decision in a meeting with the VPs on May 15, 2001.

Understandably, Mr. Webb's decision disappointed the VPs, especially Ms. Wilcox. The decision to look externally triggered a whole range of negative thoughts.

"This is what is wrong with TELIT."
"TELIT is a male-dominated bastion of socially insensitive techies."
"This is the last straw. I've been put down long enough."

Ms. Wilcox did not verbalize these thoughts immediately. However, she did begin to chronicle a set of "critical incidents" that she felt reflected the discriminatory atmosphere at TELIT. Specifically, her list of critical incidents included:

- Too few women managers and executives at TELIT
- A "boy's club" mentality among managers and executives: football, baseball, basketball games; golfing; after-hours bar-hopping
- Sexually explicit jokes told at staff meetings, in the hallways, and at the mail/coffee room

- Inappropriate pictures on display in executives' and managers' offices
- Downloading of pornographic material
- A general recruitment and hiring practice of relying heavily on referrals, reinforcing the exclusivity of the "club"

The mere act of chronicling these matters added fuel to a burning fire. Ms. Wilcox felt excluded; she was a single parent who struggled to balance family and work with little opportunity to partake in the social "amenities" of work. The situation had grown intolerable. The time for decisive action had come. Ms. Wilcox consulted her attorney, Mr. Walter Bailey.

FILING A CHARGE

Based on Mr. Bailey's advice, Ms. Wilcox filed an informal complaint with the Equal Employment Opportunity Commission (EEOC) field office in a letter drafted by Mr. Bailey and delivered to the EEOC office via certified mail on June 2, 2001. She alleged both sex discrimination and sexual harassment. She charged Telit, the CEO (Mr. Webb), and the HR vice president (Mr. Jack Johnson) with violating her civil rights as protected under Title VII of the Civil Rights Act. In the informal complaint, she sought promotion to the position of COO and punitive and compensatory damages in the amount of $200,000.

The written complaint stated in relevant part:

Telit, its CEO, Mr. Webb, and its H.R. vice president, Mr. Johnson, have violated my rights under Title VII of the Civil Rights Act. I was denied consideration for promotion COO because of gender, a clear case of disparate treatment. Telit did not want to promote a woman to COO, so it opted to conduct an external search. This perpetuates a practice of denying equal opportunity to women, as reflected in the systematic underrepresentation of women in the workplace, especially among executive, managerial, and professional ranks.

Furthermore Telit, its CEO, and HR vice president, have encouraged and tolerated an intimidating and hostile atmosphere. On more than one occasion, I have suffered unwelcome sexual advances from male colleagues. In addition, the roguish male-dominated atmosphere reinforces this sense that women should occupy a subservient position, especially in a high-tech environment. On more than one work-related occasion I have heard the refrain "she probably doesn't have the tech background or ability" even though the person has an IT degree.

All in all, Telit is unfit for women. It is a throwback to what we would hope is a bygone era of work.

Relevant Legal Language

1. Title VII of the 1964 Civil Rights Act, as amended, states in part:

   Section 703. (a) It shall be an unlawful employment practice for an employer—
   (1) to fail or refuse to hire or to discharge any individual, or otherwise to discriminate against any individual with respect to his compensation, terms, conditions, or privileges of employment, because of such individual's race, color, religion, sex, or national origin; or
   (2) to limit, segregate, or classify his employees or applicants for employment in any way which would deprive or tent to deprive any individual of employment opportunities or otherwise adversely affect his status as an employee, because of such individual's race, color, religion, sex, or national origin.

2. The 1980 Guidelines on Sexual Harassment promulgated by the EEOC pursuant to Title VII defines sexual harassment as:

   Unwelcome sexual advances, requests for sexual favors, and other verbal or physical conduct of a sexual nature constitute sexual harassment when:

   1. Submission to such conduct is made either explicitly or

implicitly a term or condition of an individual's employment;

2. Submission to or rejection of such conduct by an individual is used as a basis for employment decisions affecting such individual; or

3. Such conduct has the purpose or effect of unreasonably interfering with an individual's work performance or creating an intimidating, hostile, or offensive working environment.

3. The EEOC's "Enforcement Guidance: Compensatory and Punitive Damages" states in part:

The limitation on the amount of [compensatory and punitive] damages is based on the size (number of employees) of the respondent. The limitations are stated as follows:

15 to 100 employees:	$50,000
101 to 200 employees:	$100,000
201 to 500 employees:	$200,000
501 employees or more:	$300,000

EEOC Review Procedures

The EEOC acknowledged receipt of the June 2 letter of complaint on June 3, 2001. The typical procedure is for the EEOC to conduct an informal investigation at this point, sending an investigator to meet with the employer and its representative(s) and the employee.

The EEOC has a tremendous caseload: 77,444 charges were filed in fiscal year 1999 (October 1, 1998–September 30, 1999). This places a tremendous burden on its investigatory and litigation staff. To mitigate this burden and assist the parties in resolving disputes, the EEOC has instituted a Mediation Program.

In this particular instance, the EEOC has recommended that the parties (Ms. Wilcox and Telit) avail themselves of the Mediation Program.

Both have consented voluntarily to do so. Accordingly, a mediator has been assigned to the case, who has contacted the parties and their respective counsels (where appropriate). A mediation session of one hour was scheduled for June 6. The mediator's objective is to help the parties reach a mutually satisfactory objective. If this does not occur, the complainant may file a formal charge.

ADDITIONAL BACKGROUND INFORMATION ON THE PARTIES

The parties attending the mediation session are:

Mr. Webb
Ms. Wilcox
Mediator
Counsel for Mr. Webb
Counsel for Ms. Wilcox

The following sections give additional background information and instructions that can be used in portraying these participants in a role-playing session.

Ms. Wilcox, Vice President, Research, and Her Counsel

- You are an ambitious, proud, hard-driving, no-nonsense person.
- You enjoy the type of work you do at Telit. It is intrinsically rewarding.
- You also believe that Telit reflects a general problem of sexism in your industry.
- On the whole, you like your colleagues at Telit. You find them just a bit socially immature and rough around the edges at times.
- Sometimes, you feel that you are not taken as seriously as you should be because you are a woman.
- Given your single-parent status (you have a six-year-old daughter in first grade), you do not have the time or inclination to partake in

the social amenities at work. You struggle to balance work and family, and work is work, not play.

- You are genuinely miffed at Mr. Webb, whom you generally like, for passing you over. He didn't even offer an explanation. This incident caused you to reflect more deeply about more systemic patterns of sex discrimination and harassment at Telit.

- You do not want to leave Telit, nor do you want to sour relationships beyond repair. You want justice and dignity, and an opportunity for advancement. You also want to give Telit a wake-up call.

- At the mediation session, you are prepared to recount some more specific incidents of discrimination/harassment, of which Webb may be unaware. You have discussed these with your attorney. Included among the list are:

1. Repeated requests for dates by two other VP's, who are single
2. Sexually explicit material left mysteriously on your desk several times over the past few months
3. Derogatory comments made at meetings about your aloofness, antisocial qualities, and assertiveness

Mr. Webb, Jr., CEO, and His Counsel

- You are the founder of Telit. As a 1989 graduate of the Harvard Business School, you are realizing a dream.

- Married with two children, you are a devoted family person.

- You are an avid sports fan and athlete.

- You are hardworking (Type A personality) and ambitious. You want Telit to be the biggest and best.

- Keeping and recruiting talented people is critical. You rely on your instincts and colleagues for help in recruiting.

- You have very limited formal training in or interest in human resource management. HRM seems a necessary evil, and an unavoidable overhead expense.

- You manage quickly (you think, as well, intelligently). You see yourself as a person of action.

- You were genuinely shocked at receiving notice of Ms. Wilcox's complaint. You always have regarded her highly as a colleague and as a friend.
- In your mind, you did consider her seriously for the COO position. But you felt that she lacked the experience.
- You considered each of the VP's record of performance, as shown in the following chart.

Position	Education	Performance Rating	Interpersonal Skills
VP, HR	M.B.A., Syracuse	H	M
VP, Research	M.B.A., Pittsburgh	H	H
VP, IT	M.B.A., Harvard	H	M
VP, Customer Service	M.B.A., Stanford	H	H
VP, Marketing	M.B.A., Wharton	H	H

- After receiving notice of the complaint, you talked to your VP of HR. During this conversation, you realized that Telit had no formal HR planning process, that Telit had no formal affirmative action plan, and that Telit had not done any training in the HR area among its general ranks, including executives and managers, as well as professionals. Everyone was too busy meeting immediate goals, hustling the business, and, simply, hiring.

Sources

The following listing identifies some of the most useful sources we have found on the topic of conflict resolution, especially as it pertains to the workplace. The list—which contains general references, government publications, journals, and Web sites—is not an exhaustive list, but it provides more than enough to get you started in any aspect of this field you want to explore.

GENERAL REFERENCES

American Arbitration Association. *1999 American Arbitration Association Annual Report*. New York: American Arbitration Association, 2000.

American Federation of Labor–Congress of Industrial Organizations. *A Labor Perspective on the New American Workplace—A Call for Partnership*. Washington, D.C.: AFL-CIO, 1994.

American Federation of Labor–Congress of Industrial Organizations. *Americans' Attitudes Toward Unions. www.aflcio.org*, 2001.

Ancona, Deborah, Thomas A. Kochan, Maureen Scully, John Van Maaen, D. Eleanor Westney, Deborah M. Kolb, John E. Dutton, and Susan J. Ashford, eds. *Organizational Behavior and Processes: Managing for the Future*. Cincinnati, Ohio: South-Western College Publishing, 1999.

Andersson, Lynne. "Tit for Tat? The Spiraling Effect of Incivility in the Workplace." *Academy of Management Review*, July 1999, pp. 452–470.

Beer, Jennifer E., with Eileen Stief. *The Mediator's Handbook*. Gabriola Island, B.C., Canada: New Society Publishers, 1997.

Bennett, Mark D. *The Art of Mediation*. Notre Dame, Ind: National Institute for Trial Advocacy, 1995.

Bingham, Lisa B. "Mediating Employment Disputes: Perceptions of Redress at the United States Postal Service." *Review of Public Personnel Administration*. Spring 1997, pp. 20–30.

Bluestone, Barry and Irving Bluestone. *Negotiating the Future: A Labor Perspective*. New York: Basic Books, 1992.

Brooks, Rick. "Blizzard of Grievances Joins a Sack of Woes at U.S. Postal Service." *The Wall Street Journal*. June 22, 2001, pp. A1, A4.

The Burke Group. "Staying Union Free." *www.djburke.com*, 2001.

Burley-Allen, Madelyn. *Listening: The Forgotten Skill, 2nd edition*. New York: John Wiley & Sons, 1995.

Bush, Robert A. Baruch and Joseph P. Folger. *The Promise of Mediation: Responding to Conflict Through Empowerment and Recognition*. San Francisco: Jossey-Bass, 1994.

Chorda Conflict Management. "The Halliburton Dispute Resolution Program." *www.chorda.com*, 2001.

Clarke, R. Oliver. "Dispute Resolution in Western Europe." In Gleason, Sandra E., ed. *Workplace Dispute Resolution: Directions for the 21st Century*. East Lansing, Mich: Michigan State University Press, 1997, pp. 157–186.

Cloke, Kenneth and Joan Goldsmith. *Resolving Conflicts at Work: A Complete Guide for Everyone on the Job*. San Francisco: Jossey-Bass, 2000.

Commerce Clearing House, Inc. *Labor Law Course*. Chicago, Ill: Commerce Clearing House, 1987.

Commission on the Future of Worker-Management Relations. *Report and Recommendations*. Washington, D.C.: Government Printing Office, December 1994.

Costantino, Cathy A. and Christina Sickles Merchant. *Designing Conflict Management Systems: A Guide to Creating Productive and Healthy Organizations*. San Francisco: Jossey-Bass, 1996.

Curtin, Leah L. "Why Good People Do Bad Things." *Nursing Management*. July 1996, pp. 63–72.

Dana, Daniel. *Conflict Resolution*. New York: McGraw-Hill, 2001.

Dunlop, John T. and Arnold M. Zack. *Mediation and Arbitration of Employment Disputes*. San Francisco: Jossey-Bass, 1997.

Eaton, Adrienne E. and Jeffrey H. Keefe, eds. *Employment Dispute Resolution and Worker Rights in the Changing Workplace.* Champaign, Ill: Industrial Relations Research Association, 1999.

Ertel, Danny. "Turning Negotiation into a Corporate Capability." *Harvard Business Review*, May/June 1999.

Ewing, David W. *Justice on the Job: Resolving Grievances in the Nonunion Workplace.* Boston: Harvard Business School Press, 1989.

Feuille, Peter. "Grievance Mediation." In Eaton and Keefe, eds., op. cit., pp. 187–218.

Fisher, Roger and Danny Ertel. *Getting Ready to Negotiate: A Step-by-Step Guide to Preparing for Any Negotiation.* New York: Penguin Books, 1995.

Fisher, Roger and William Ury. *Getting to Yes: Negotiating Agreement Without Giving In.* New York: Penguin Books, 1981.

Ford, John. "Workplace Conflict: Facts and Figures." *www.mediate.com/workplace/Ford,* 2001.

Gesteland, Richard R. *Cross-Cultural Business Behavior: Marketing, Negotiating and Managing Across Cultures.* Copenhagen: Handelshojskolens Forlag (Business School Press), 1999.

Gleason, Sandra E., ed. *Workplace Dispute Resolution: Directions for the 21st Century.* East Lansing, Mich: Michigan State University Press, 1997.

Goodman, Alan H. *Basic Skills for the New Arbitrator.* Rockville, Md: Solomon Publications, 1993.

Goodman, Alan H. *Basic Skills for the New Mediator.* Rockville, Md: Solomon Publications, 1999.

Gray, George R., Donald W. Myers, and Phyllis S. Myers. "Cooperative Provisions in Labor Agreements: A New Paradigm." *Monthly Labor Review,* January 1999, pp. 29–45.

Hallberlin, Cynthia J. "On the REDRESS™ Mediation Program." Statement before the House Government Reform Subcommittee on Civil Service. U.S. House of Representatives. *www.house.gov,* March 19, 2000.

Heller, Robert and Tim Hindle. *Essential Manager's Manual.* New York: DK Publishing, 1998.

Henry, James F. "Mediation Without Administration." Article adapted from Spring 1997 issue of *NIDR News.* Available at CPR Institute for Dispute Resolution Web site: *http://www.cpradr.org,* 1997.

Holley, William H., Jr., Kenneth M. Jennings, and Roger S. Wolters. *The Labor Relations Process*. Fort Worth, Tex: Harcourt College Publishers, 2001.

Illinois State Police. "Combating Workplace Violence." *www.state.il.us/isp*, 2001.

International Association of Machinists. *High Performance Work Organization Field Manual*. Washington, D.C.: IAM, undated.

International Association of Machinists. "Ten Steps to Achieving a High Performance Work Organization Partnership." *www.iamaw.org*, 1996.

International Association of Machinists. "The Challenge of the Global Workplace." Washington, D.C.: IAM, 1996.

Jehn, Karen A. "Benefits and Detriments of Workplace Conflict." *The Public Manager*, Summer 2000, pp. 24–27.

Karrass, Chester L. *In Business as In Life—You Don't Get What You Deserve, You Get What You Negotiate*. Los Angeles: Stanford Street Press, 1996.

Kaufman, Bruce, ed. *Government Regulation of the Employment Relationship*. Madison, Wis: Industrial Relations Research Association, 1997.

Kheel, Theodore W. *The Keys to Conflict Resolution: Proven Methods of Settling Disputes Voluntarily*. New York: Four Walls Eight Windows, 1999.

Kinlaw, Dennis. *The ASTD Trainer's Sourcebook: Facilitation Skills*. New York: McGraw-Hill, 1996.

Kinney, Joseph A. *Violence at Work*. Englewood Cliffs, NJ: Prentice Hall, 1995.

Laabs, Jennifer J. "Remedies for HR's Legal Headache." *Personnel Journal*, December 1994, pp. 66–76.

Lang, Michael D. and Alison Taylor. *The Making of a Mediator: Developing Artistry in Practice*. San Francisco: Jossey-Bass, 2000.

Levine, Gene. "How to Remain Union Free." *www.genelevine.com*, 2001.

Levine, Stewart. 1998. "The Many Costs of Conflict." *http://www.mediate.com/articles/levine1.cfm*. Excerpted from *Getting to Resolution*. San Francisco: Berrett-Koehler, 1998.

Lipsky, David B. and Ronald L. Seeber. *The Appropriate Resolution of Corporate Disputes: A Report on the Growing Use of ADR by U.S. Corporations*. Ithaca, NY: Cornell/PERC Institute on Conflict Resolution, 1998.

Litras, Marika F.X. "Civil Rights Complaints in U.S. District Courts,

1990–98." Washington, D.C.: U.S. Department of Justice, February 2000.

Locke, Richard. "The Transformation of Industrial Relations? A Cross-National Review." In Kirsten S. Wever and Lowell Turner, eds. *The Comparative Political Economy of Industrial Relations*. Madison, Wis: Industrial Relations Research Association, 1995, pp. 9–32.

Mantell, Michael and Steve Albrecht. *Ticking Bombs: Defusing Violence in the Workplace*. Burr Ridge, Ill: Irwin Professional Publishing, 1994.

Masters, Marick F. *Unions at the Crossroads: Strategic Membership, Financial, and Political Perspectives*. Westport, Conn: Quorum Books, 1997.

Mayer, Bernard. *The Dynamics of Conflict Resolution: A Practitioner's Guide*. San Francisco: Jossey-Bass, 2000.

McDermott, E. Patrick, Ruth Obar, Anita Jose, and Mollie Bowers. "An Evaluation of the Equal Employment Opportunity Commission." Washington, D.C.: EEOC, September 2000.

National Partnership Council. *A Report to the President on Progress in Labor-Management Partnerships*. October 1996.

Onaitis, Susan. *Negotiate Like the Big Guys*. Los Angeles: Silver Lake Publishing, 1999.

Roberts, Barry S. and Richard A. Mann. "Sexual Harassment in the Workplace." *Akron Law Review*, 9, Winter 1996.

Rowe, Mary. "Dispute Resolution in the Non-Union Environment: An Evolution Toward Integrated Systems for Conflict Management." In Gleason, ed., op. cit., pp. 79–106.

Sandler, Susan F., ed. "The New Rules of Termination," *HR Focus*, May 2001, pp. 1, 11–15.

Senger, Jeffrey M. "Turning the Ship of State." *Journal of Dispute Resolution* (79), 2000.

Slaikeu, Karl A. and Ralph H. Hasson. *Controlling the Costs of Conflict: How to Design a System for Your Organization*. San Francisco: Jossey-Bass, 1998.

Stallworth, Lamont E. "Government Regulation of Workplace Disputes and Alternative Dispute Resolution." In Kaufman, ed., op. cit., pp. 368–402.

Stone, Katherine. *Private Justice: Alternative Dispute Resolution and the Law.* New York: Foundation Press, 1999.

Sygnatur, Eric F. and Guy A. Toscano. "Work-related Homicides: The Facts." *Compensation and Working Conditions.* Spring 2000, pp. 3–8.

Ury, William. *Getting Past No: Negotiating Your Way from Confrontation to Cooperation.* New York: Bantam Books, 1993.

Van Slyke, Erik J. *Listening to Conflict: Finding Constructive Solutions to Workplace Disputes.* New York: AMACOM, 1999.

Volkema, Roger J. *The Negotiation Tool Kit: How to Get Exactly What You Want in Any Business or Personal Situation.* New York: AMACOM, 1999.

Warchol, Greg. U.S. "Workplace Violence, 1992–96." Washington, D.C.: U.S. Department of Justice, July 1998.

Zumeta. Zena D. "Styles of Mediation: Facilitative, Evaluative, and Transformative Mediation." Mediation Training and Consultation Institute. *www.learn2mediate.com,* 2000–2001.

GOVERNMENT PUBLICATIONS

U.S. Equal Employment Opportunity Commission. "Enforcement Statistics and Litigation." *www.eeoc.gov,* 2001.

U.S. Equal Employment Opportunity Commission. "Federal Laws Prohibiting Job Discrimination: Questions and Answers." www.eeoc.gov, 2001.

U.S. General Accounting Office. *Alternative Dispute Resolution: Employers' Experiences with ADR in the Workplace.* Washington, D.C.: GAO, August 1997.

U.S. General Accounting Office. *Employment Discrimination.* Washington, D.C.: GAO, July 1995.

U.S. General Accounting Office. *Little Progress Made in Addressing Persistent Labor-Management Problems.* Washington, D.C.: GAO, October 1997.

U.S. General Accounting Office. *U.S. Postal Service: Labor-Management Problems Persist on the Workroom Floor,* Volume II. Washington, D.C.: GAO, September 1994.

U.S. Interagency Alternative Dispute Resolution Working Group. *Federal*

ADR Program Manager's Resource Manual. Washington, D.C.: Department of Justice, 2000.

U.S. Interagency ADR Working Group. *Report of the Interagency ADR Working Group to the President.* Washington, D.C.: Interagency ADR Working Group, January 2001.

U.S. National Institute for Occupational Safety and Health. *Violence in the Workplace.* Washington, D.C.: NIOSH, June 1997.

U.S. Occupational Safety and Health Administration. *Guidelines for Preventing Workplace Violence for Health Care and Social Service Workers.* Washington, D.C.: OSHA, 1998.

U.S. Occupational Safety and Health Administration. *Workplace Violence.* Washington, D.C.: OSHA, 1999.

U.S. Office of Personnel Management, Office of Workforce Relations. *Alternative Dispute Resolution: A Resource Guide.* Washington, D.C.: OPM, July 1999.

U.S. Office of Personnel Management. *Dealing with Workplace Violence: A Guide for Agency Planners.* Washington, D.C.: OPM, 1998.

U.S. Office of Personnel Management. "Memorandum for Heads of Departments and Agencies." Washington, D.C.: OPM, March 1, 2001.

JOURNALS

Academy of Management Journal

ADR Alert

ADR Currents

Canadian Arbitration and Mediation Journal

Conflict Resolution Notes

Dispute Resolution Journal

Dispute Resolution Times

Employee Relations Law Journal

Employee Responsibilities and Rights Journal

Harvard Business Review

Harvard Negotiation Law Journal

HR Focus

HR Magazine
Industrial and Labor Relations Review
Industrial Relations
International Journal of Conflict Management
Journal of Conflict Resolution
Journal of Dispute Resolution
Journal of Management
Labor Law Journal
Labor Studies Journal
Mediation Quarterly
Ohio State Journal on Dispute Resolution

WEB SITES

ADR and Mediation Resources
   www.adrr.com
ADR World.com
   Covers ADR developments. Bought by AAA.
   www.adrworld.org
AFL-CIO
   Union federation
   www.aflcio.org
American Arbitration Association
   Provider of dispute resolution services
   www.adr.org
American Bar Association (Section on Dispute Resolution)
   Provides information about ADR
   www.abanet.org/dispute/home.html
Association for Conflict Resolution (ACRE)
   Professional organization of dispute resolution specialists. Recently
      formed provider of information about conflict resolution. Result of
      merger between the Academy of Family Mediators, Conflict Reso-

lution Education Network, and the Society of Professionals in Dispute Resolution.

www.acresolution.org

Conflict Resolution Education Network (CRENet)

www.crenet.org

Cornell/PERC-Institute on Conflict Resolution

www.ilr.cornell.edu/depts/ICR

CPR-Institute for Dispute Resolution

Provider of dispute-resolution services

www.cpradr.org

Dispute Resolution Specialists

Provider of ADR Services

www.mediates.com

GAMA: Global Arbitration Mediation Association

Provider of ADR services

www.gama.com

Interagency Alternative Dispute Resolution Working Group

Interagency group in federal government promoting ADR

www.financenet.gov/financenet/fed/iadrwg

International ADR: International Arbitration Resources

www.internationaladr.com

International Labour Organization

UN-sponsored specialized agency

www.ilo.org

JAMS

Provider of ADR services

www.jamsadr.com

Laborlink

Information about unions

www.laborlink.org

Mediation Essays, Mediation Forms and Mediation Materials

Provides on-line ADR information

www.adrr.com

Mediation Information and Resource Center

Provides information about mediation

www.mediate.com

Mediation Works
  Provider of ADR services
  www.mwi.org
National Arbitration Forum
  Provider of ADR informational services
  www.arb-forum.com
Negotiation Skills Company
  www.negotiationskill.com
The Ombudsman Association (TOA)
  Professional organization devoted to ombuds
  www.ombuds-toa.org
Online Ombuds Office
  www.ombuds.org
Program on Negotiation
  Harvard Program
  www.pon.harvard.edu
SPIDR: Society of Professionals in Dispute Resolution
  Professional organization provider of information. Merged recently
    into ACRE (above).
  www.spidr.org
United States Arbitration and Mediation
  Provider of ADR services
  www.usam.com
U.S. Department of Justice, Bureau of Justice Statistics
  Sources of information about EEO litigation and workplace violence
  www.ojp.usdoj.gov/bjs
U.S. Department of Labor, Bureau of Labor Statistics.
  Source of information about union membership, work stoppages, and
    employment trends
  www.bls.gov
U.S. Equal Employment Opportunity Commission
  Independent federal agency that administers antidiscrimination laws
  www.eeoc.gov
U.S. Federal Mediation and Conciliation Service
  Government provider of dispute resolution services and information
  www.fmcs.gov

U.S. Occupational Safety and Health Administration
Source of information on workplace violence
www.osha.gov

U.S. Office of Personnel Management
Federal government's personnel office
www.opm.gov

Workplace Solutions: Conflict and Crisis Prevention
Management consulting group
www.wps.org

Workplace Violence Research Institute
Provider of information about workplace violence
www.workviolence.com

World Intellectual Property Organization Arbitration and Mediation Center
www.arbiter.wipo.int

Zero Tolerance
Management consulting firm specializing in employment discrimination and sexual harassment claims
www.zt-inc.com

Index

accommodation, as conflict
management option, 76, 77
administered ADR arrangements,
282–283
administered arbitration, 171
ADR, *see also* arbitration; facilitation;
mediation; negotiation
administered *vs.* self-administered
arrangements, 282–283
defined, 98
international acceptability of, 252
international availability of, 261,
262–263
preventive, 191
program managers, 290–291
used to prevent workplace violence,
214
adversarial bargaining
defined, 107
tactics used in, 108–109
vs. collaborative negotiation,
107–109
advisory arbitration, defined, 26
advisory intervention, 88
in interest-based conflicts, 89
Age Discrimination in Employment
Act, 223
alcohol and drug abuse, as source of
conflict, 50
alternative dispute resolution (ADR),
see ADR
American Airlines
ADA violation suit, 11
use of binding arbitration, 163

American Arbitration Association
(AAA)
on advantages of administered
ADR, 283
code of conduct, 179
National Rules of Arbitration, 173
pre-dispute agreement of, 153–154
as source of arbitrators, 171, 172,
173
as source of mediators, 150, 151
American Bar Association
as source of arbitrators, 172, 173
as source of mediators, 151
Americans with Disabilities Act
(ADA), 223
arbitration
administered *vs.* self-administered,
171
advantages of, 167–168
binding *vs.* advisory, 165–166, 180
by-issue, 180, 181
by-package, 180, 181
conventional, 180–181
final offer, 180–181
five-step process of, 174–177
Halliburton dispute resolution
program, 241–242
ILO recommendations for, 257
measuring effectiveness of,
181–182
"peek-a-boo," 199
position in ADR spectrum,
166–167

arbitration (*continued*)
   vs. facilitation, 126
   vs. litigation, 167–168
   vs. mediation, 126, 167–168
   vs. negotiation, 126
   when to use it, 169–170
arbitration calculator, 182, 183
arbitration hearing
   for employment disputes, 177–179
   location of, 177
arbitration management conference,
   176
arbitrators
   AAA code of conduct for, 179
   panel *vs.* single, 171, 180
   qualification of, 173–174
   selection of, 170–171
   sources of, 172
Arthur Andersen, arbitrated split of,
   249, 250
audits
   conflict, 273, 274
   organizational, 272
avoidance, as conflict management
   option, 76, 77

Belgium
   availability of ADR in, 261
   disputes covered by labor courts,
   258, 259
binding arbitration, defined, 26,
   165–166
binding intervention, 88
   in power-based conflicts, 89
   in rights-based conflicts, 89
brainstorming, as facilitation
   technique, 134
Bush, Robert A. Baruch, 157
by-issue arbitration, 180, 181
by-package arbitration, 180, 181

Civil Rights Act of 1964, 223
Civil Rights Act of 1991, 223
collaboration
   appropriateness of, 79, 84
   as conflict management option, 76,
   77
   "failure" of, 85, 86
   as first step in conflict resolution,
   86
   nine-step process, 79–84
   workplace application of, 84–85
collaborative negotiation
   defined, 107
   tactics used in, 109
   vs. adversarial bargaining, 107–109
competition, as conflict management
   option, 76, 77
compromise, as conflict management
   option, 76, 77
conciliation
   defined, 186, 187
   ILO recommendations for, 257
   when to use, 192
conflict, *see* workplace conflict; *see also*
   conflict resolution
conflict audit, 273, 274
conflict management, goals of, 72–74,
   75
conflict resolution
   audit, 273
   available options for, 25–26
   building blocks of, 88–89
   core competencies for, 91–92,
   291–292
   cross-national methodologies,
   251–252
   "dual-concerns" model, 78
   education and training (*see* conflict
   resolution education)
   five-phase methodology, 269–271

ILO policies on, 253–254
impact of globalization on, 249–250
map, 300
methodologies, 101–102
specialists, 277
stakeholder community, 290–291
system (*see* integrated conflict
   resolution system)
venues for, 252
Conflict Resolution Center
   International, as source of
   arbitrators, 172
conflict resolution education
   of general audience, 292–293
   of outside neutrals, 295
   of program managers, 294
   of users, 293–294
Construction Mediation Inc., as
   source of mediators, 151
conventional arbitration, 180–181
core competencies, for conflict
   resolution, 91–92
Costantino, Cathy A., 271
CPR Institute for Dispute Resolution
   and self-administered ADR, 282
   as source of arbitrators, 171, 173
   as source of mediators, 150, 151

decisional ADR procedures, 191
demographics, and impact on conflict,
   36
Denmark
   availability of ADR in, 261, 262
   disputes covered by labor courts,
   259
Design Task Force, 272
   audits by, 274
   goals of, 274
   policy issues of, 275
   programmatic considerations for,
   275–276

dispute panels, defined, 187, 188
Dispute Prevention/Resolution
   Services
   as source of arbitrators, 172
   as source of mediators, 151
dispute resolution, *see* conflict
   resolution
Dunlop, John T., 271

early neutral evaluation
   defined, 187, 188
   procedure, 198–199
   when to use, 192
education, *see* conflict resolution
   education
Equal Employment Opportunity
   Commission (EEOC)
   as source of mediators, 151
   voluntary mediation program, 141
Equal Pay Act of 1963, 223
Ertel, Danny, 104
European Council, 253
European Social Charter, 256
evaluative intervention, 87–88
Ewing, David W., 240, 271

facilitated intervention, 87
facilitation
   defined, 25, 124
   importance of brainstorming in,
   134
   measuring results of, 135
   seven-step guide to, 130–132
   tools for, 133–134
   use of technology in, 136–137
   vs. arbitration, 126
   vs. mediation, 126
   vs. negotiation, 126
   when to use, 128–129
facilitation calculator, 136

facilitator, competencies of, 132–133
factfinding
    defined, 187, 189
    procedure, 194–195
    when to use, 192, 193
factual intervention, 87
FBI, antidiscrimination suit, 221
Federal Mediation and Conciliation
    Service (FMCS), 137, 141
    as source of arbitrators, 172, 173
    as source of mediators, 151
final offer arbitration, 180–181
Finland, availability of ADR in, 261,
    262
Fisher, Roger, 104, 110
Folger, Joseph P., 157
Ford Motor Company
    discrimination suits against, 29
    and Firestone tire recall, 38
    sexual harassment suit, 221
Ford, William Clay, Jr., 29

Galvin, Christopher, 29
General Motors, cost of United
    AutoWorkers strike, 70
Germany
    availability of ADR in, 261, 262
    conflict resolution venues in, 252
    disputes covered by labor courts in,
        258, 259
Global Arbitration Mediation
    Association
    as source of arbitrators, 172
    as source of mediators, 151
globalization, impact on conflict
    resolution, 249–250
grievance procedures
    Halliburton dispute resolution
        program, 241–242
    nonunion, 241
    union, 240–241

grievances
    labor, 54–55
    nonlabor, 56

Halliburton dispute resolution
    program (DRP), 241–242
health care, as cost of workplace
    conflict, 62
health risks, as source of conflict,
    44–45
Henry, James F., 281

IBN, *see* interest-based negotiation
integrated conflict resolution system,
    269–271
    creation of process, 270, 271–273
    data collection for, 278, 279
    design of system, 270, 273–274,
        281
    Design Task Force for (*see* Design
        Task Force)
    evaluation of system, 270, 278
    evaluative metrics for, 278, 279
    guideposts for, 301–302
    implementation of system, 270,
        277–278
    key features of, 280
    modification of system, 270,
        278–279
    program analysis for, 278, 279
    prototype of, 279–282
    real world example of, 284
    triggers for, 276
interest-based conflicts, 89–90
interest-based negotiation (IBN)
    benefits of, 121
    defined, 110
    key principles of, 110
interests, conflicts over, 17

International Academy of Mediators, as source of mediators, 151
International Center for Dispute Resolution, 249–250
International Court of Arbitration, as source of arbitrators, 172
international labor standards, 252–257
International Labour Organization (ILO)
  on collective bargaining, 254
  objectives of, 253
  on right to organize, 254
  on termination of employment, 255
  UN mandate of, 253
intervention, types of, 86–88
investigative ADR procedures, 191
Israel
  availability of ADR in, 261, 262
  disputes covered by labor courts, 258, 259
Italy
  availability of ADR in, 261, 262
  disputes covered by labor courts, 259

Jacques Nasser, ouster of, 29
Judicial Arbitration and Mediation Services (JAMS)
  as source of arbitrators, 172, 173
  as source of mediators, 151

Karrass, Chester L., 100, 114
Kheel, Theodore, 143–144, 145
  on arbitrator panels, 171

labor courts, roles of, 258–259
labor market, and impact on conflict, 35

leased employees, as source of conflict, 45–46
Lipsky, David B., 141, 146
litigation
  as cost of workplace conflict, 62, 299
  and impact on conflict, 35–36
  vs. arbitration, 167–168

management change, as source of workplace conflict, 41
management style, as source of workplace conflict, 37, 40–41
manager's checklists
  conflict assessment, 26–27
  conflict cost calculator, 67–68
  conflict indicators, 66–67
  conflict stressors, 65–66
  criteria for decision making, 201
  dealing with conflict, 93–94
  education and training programs, 295–296
  employee interest in unionization, 246–247
  integrated conflict resolution system, 285–287
  international dispute resolution options, 263–264
  organization's negotiation ability, 117
  use of ADR for EEO claims, 232–233
  using arbitration, 182–184
  using facilitation, 137–138
  using mediation, 161
  workplace security hazards, 218–219
Mann, Richard A., 230
Mason-Draffen, Carrie, 205
Mayer, Bernard, 271

McDermott, Michael, 1
mediated intervention, 87
mediation
   advantages of, 146–148
   defined, 25–26, 144
   increasing popularity of, 141
   measuring effectiveness of, 159
   position in ADR spectrum, 146
   process of, 153–155
   session, 155–156
   transformative (*see* transformative
     mediation)
   vs. arbitration, 126, 168
   vs. facilitation, 126
   vs. negotiation, 126
   vs. transformative mediation, 158
   when to use, 148–149
mediation calculator, 160
mediator
   qualifications of, 151
   roles of, 145
   selection of, 150
medical problems, as source of
   workplace conflict, 49–50
Merchant, Christina Sickles, 271
mergers and acquisitions, and impact
   on workplace conflict, 39
minitrials
   defined, 187, 189
   procedure, 189
Myers-Briggs Type Indicators (MBTI),
   47

National Academy of Arbitrators, as
   source of arbitrators, 172, 173
National Arbitration Forum, as
   source of arbitrators, 172
National Mediation Board, 141
National Mediation Program
   key features of, 227
   pilot program, 226

negotiation
   collaborative (*see* collaborative
     negotiation)
   core elements of, 104–106
   defined, 25, 101
   four-step preparation for, 113
   guidelines for, 116–117
   importance of communication in,
     105
   importance of relationships in, 105
   interest-based (*see* interest-based
     negotiation (IBN))
   reasons for, 102–103
   reasons for breakdown in, 122
   vs. arbitration, 126
   vs. facilitation, 126
   vs. mediation, 126
   when to use, 104
negotiator, characteristics of, 115
nonadministered ADR arrangements,
   282–283
nonadministered arbitration, 171
nonbinding arbitration, defined, 166
North American Free Trade
   Agreement, 250
Norway
   availability of ADR in, 261, 262
   disputes covered by labor courts,
     259

ombuds
   defined, 26, 187, 189
   function of, 195–196
   origin of, 195
   procedure, 196–198
   when to use, 192, 193
organizational audit, 274
organizational effects of conflict, 21,
   22, 24
overhead, as added cost of workplace
   conflict, 61

partnering, 187–188, 190
pay-reward policy change, and impact on workplace conflict, 41–42
"peek-a-boo" arbitration, 199
peer review
    defined, 188, 190
    procedure, 199–200
    when to use, 192, 193
personal effects of conflict, 21, 22–23
personalities, as source of conflict, 48
personality factors ("Big Five"), 47
post-incident counseling, 216
power-based conflicts, 17, 89
    defined, 91
pre-employment screening, to prevent workplace violence, 213, 214
preventive ADR procedures, 191
productivity, effect of conflict on, 24
product obsolescence, and effect on conflict, 35
professional effects of conflict, 21, 22, 23
psychological disorders, as source of workplace conflict, 49

quality of work life (QWL), effect of conflict on, 59–60

REDRESS program, of U.S. Postal Service, 159
restructuring, and effect on conflict, 38
Retsky, Maxine Lans, 185
rights
    conflicts over, 17
    governed by federal statutes, 17–18
rights-based conflicts, 89, 90
Roberts, Barry S., 230
Rowe, Mary, 241

security, added cost created by workplace conflict, 62
Seeber, Ronald L., 141, 146
self-administered ADR arrangements, 282–283
self-administered arbitration, 171
sex discrimination litigation, 299
sexual harassment
    antiharassment policy, 230–231
    complaint procedure for, 231–232
    dispute resolution procedure, 228–229
    EEOC guidelines on, 229
    employer liability for, 230
    indemnification against, 232
    rise in complaints of, 228
    types of, 229–230
Society of Professionals in Dispute Resolution
    as source of arbitrators, 172, 173
    as source of mediators, 151
SOLUTION conflict resolution system, 283–285
Spain, disputes covered by labor courts, 260
strategic change, and effect on conflict, 39–40
substance abuse, as risk factor for workplace violence, 214
summary jury trial, defined, 188, 190
supervision
    nature of, 47
    as source of conflict, 47

Task Force on ADR in Employment, 295
Technology Assisted Group Solutions (TAGS), 137
termination, precautionary steps in, 216–217

third-party intervention, *see*
     intervention
training, *see* conflict resolution
     education
transformative mediation
     defined, 157
     use by U.S. Postal Service, 159
     vs. traditional mediation, 158
turnover, as cost of workplace
     conflict, 62

unionization
     employee interest in, 246–247
     as evidence of conflict, 55
     international rates of, 257–258
union prevention strategy
     avoidance as, 237–238
     dispute resolution as, 239–242
     resistance as, 239
     substitution as, 238
unions
     declining influence of, 236–237,
          258
     grievance procedures of, 239
     membership statistics, 236, 237
     negotiating with, 242–245
     prevention of (*see* union prevention
          strategy)
United Kingdom
     availability of ADR in, 261, 263
     disputes covered by labor courts,
          260
United Parcel Service (UPS),
     Teamsters strike againsts,
     245–246
United States, conflict resolution
     venues in, 252
University and College Ombuds
     Association, 195
Ury, William, 110

U.S. Equal Employment Opportunity
     Commission (EEOC)
     complaint procedure, 225
     enforcement of legislation, 222
     National Mediation Program,
          226–227
     sexual harassment guidelines, 229
U.S. Navy, use of mediation by, 141
U.S. Office of Personnel Management
     (OPM)
     on arbitration, 165–166
     on facilitation, 124–125, 128
     on mediation, 144
     on workplace violence, 212
U.S. Postal Service
     grievances at, 11, 70
     REDRESS program of, 159
U.S. Supreme Court, Circuit City
     decision, 164

Venezuela, disputes covered by labor
     courts, 260
Verizon, employees' strike, 11
violence, *see* workplace violence

Wal-Mart, sex-bias suit, 11
workers' compensation, as cost of
     workplace conflict, 62
workforce composition, as source of
     conflict, 44
workload change, and impact on
     conflict, 43–44
workplace
     defined, 14
     ensuring security of, 215
workplace conflict
     categories of, 17
     cost assessment of, 30
     costs of, 30–31
          direct, 61–63

indirect, 63–64
opportunity, 64
types of, 61–64
defined, 14
effective responses to, 12–13
effects, 21
impact on bottom line, 24
impact on quality of work life, 59–60
model for diagnosing and measuring, 31–32
negative view of, 2
parties involved in, 19
resolution (*see* conflict resolution)
and risk of litigation, 24
sources of, 32–33
strategic approaches to, 76–77
types of, 89
workplace conflict indicators
absenteeism and turnover, 52–53
grievances, 54–55
increased sabotage, 57
increased violence, 57
poor decision making, 58–59
productivity rate, 53–54
during recruitment, 52

security threats, 55
unionization, 55
work stoppages, 55–56
workplace violence
community response to, 208
company response to, 208
at Edgewater Technology, Inc., 1
establishing a policy statement on, 211–212, 218
forms of, 207
at IKEA, 1
incidence statistics, 205
indemnifying against, 217
monetary awards to victims of, 217
post-incident counseling, 216
preventability of, 207–208
protection against, 211–212
reasons for, 207
seriousness of, 206–207
warning signs, 208–210
World Intellectual Property Organization Arbitration and Mediation Center, 151, 172

Zack, Arnold M., 271
Zumeta, Zena D., 159

About the Authors

Marick F. Masters, Ph.D., is the Executive Director of the Center on Conflict Resolution and Negotiation at the University of Pittsburgh, where he is also a Professor of Business Administration at the Katz Graduate School of Business. His articles have appeared in *The Academy of Management Journal*, the *American Political Science Review, Harvard Business Review*, the *Social Science Review*, and many other publications. He is the author of *Unions at the Crossroads* and the forthcoming *The Business of Negotiating*. His consulting firm specializes in strategic business planning, conflict management, negotiation, and designing executive education programs. Dr. Masters lives in Pittsburgh, Pennsylvania.

Robert R. Albright, Ph.D., is currently an Associate Professor at Rensselaer at Hartford's Lally School of Management. He received his Ph.D. in Human Resource Management and Labor Relations from the University of Pittsburgh's Graduate School of Business in 1994. Before entering academe, Bob, a 1981 graduate of the U.S. Coast Guard Academy, served as the skipper of a Coast Guard patrol boat engaged in narcotics interdiction in south Florida. Bob has published in a wide array of scholarly journals on such topics as conflict resolution, strategic labor relations, and organizational change. He has also received fellowships from the American Council of Education and Yale University. Current consulting clients include Pfizer Chemical, Swarovski, Gateway Healthcare, and People's Bank. An avid boater, skier, and racquetball player, Bob, his wife Nancy, and their three daughters live in East Lyme, Connecticut.